THE COUNCIL IN ACTION

THE COUNCIL
IN ACTION

Theological Reflections on the Second
Vatican Council

HANS KÜNG

**PROFESSOR IN THE CATHOLIC THEOLOGY
FACULTY OF THE UNIVERSITY OF TÜBINGEN**

Translated by Cecily Hastings

SHEED AND WARD — NEW YORK

Nihil obstat:

RUSSELL J. COLLINS
DIOCESAN CENSOR

Imprimatur:

✠ RICHARD CARDINAL CUSHING
ARCHBISHOP OF BOSTON

MAY 1ST, 1963

Preface

So MUCH THAT was decisive in the first session of the Second Vatican Council did not happen in the *aula*. Outside the individual sessions, too, bishops and theologians set themselves energetically to clarifying and discussing the problems that arose. The point of the papers collected here, whose publication was urged on me by my Dutch publisher, is a glance both forwards and backwards.

Backwards: They are meant to give an impression of the work bound up with this first session of Vatican II. They consist of lectures and statements made at Rome during that time, to numerous meetings of bishops from various countries and continents, in pontifical colleges and houses of orders, in press conferences and broadcasts. From the nature of the case, much that is in them (repetition being sometimes unavoidable) harks back to things I had published earlier, especially *The Council, Reform and Reunion* and *Strukturen der Kirche,** conceived as a preparation for the Council and for what would come after it. There are also a few inevitable repetitions within the text itself, as the same material is approached from slightly different angles.

These papers are a reflection both of the freedom and of the sanity of the Council's discussions, which always called a spade a spade and thus made it possible for even this first session to make an essential contribution to the renewal of the Church in preparation for the reunion of separated Christians.

Forwards: Vatican II is not an end but a beginning. Everything discussed and decided at it needs to be explained and, above all, put

* A translation of this, to be called *Structures of the Church*, is in preparation and will be published by Thomas Nelson and Sons, New York.

into practice. The real work has to be done after the Council; in the Churches of each continent and country, each town and village, by believing Christians in all their different ministries and offices. These lectures are meant to help towards an understanding of the Council, its aims and its decisions, and to seek out a way from the Council into the life of the Church, from theory into practice.

The Council is our Council, all of ours. It represents our worries and problems, our expectations and hopes. It desires, too, to represent, vicariously, the worries and problems, the expectations and hopes of the whole of Christendom, and to represent them credibly.

Tübingen, December 1962

Contents

THE COUNCIL IN ACTION

Part I

THE COUNCIL'S PROGRAM

I

Could the Council Be
a Failure?

Conditions for success

ANYONE WHO DOES any public speaking in connection with the
Second Vatican Council is continually made aware on the one hand
of the great *expectations* which have been awakened by the announcement of the Council, and on the other of how little *certainty*
there is that these great expectations will be fulfilled. It is easy to as-
certain the great extent to which many Christians, Catholic and
Protestant, have been losing their original interest in the Council,
and to which scepticism has been spreading, particularly amongst
theologians and educated people. This is not simply a question of
the initial misunderstanding of the term "ecumenical" council, by
which is in fact meant not an inter-Church meeting but an assembly of the Roman Catholic Church. Nor is it simply that all too
little attention has been paid, outside our Church, to that ecumenical orientation of the Council which has made it anything but a
purely internal concern of Catholics. What is at work is rather a
doubt whether, amid the confusions and bewilderments of our
times, the Council will achieve that *decisive* action which the
Church's predicament at this point of history demands. In other
words, it is not that anyone, inside or outside the Church, doubts
the good intentions of the Pope (his epoch-making action, with all
its wealth of consequences, is sure of its place in Church history at

all events).* Nor does anyone doubt the good will of those who have prepared for the Council, some of them outstanding men, who have unquestionably taken the utmost pains in doing their part, strenuously and selflessly, in preparation for this assembly. It is rather that, on account of various facts, there is a doubt whether, for all its good intentions, good will and hard work, the Council is going to have that *interior success* for which we long.

Two courses

Even during the preparatory period there were ominous events being spoken of in this connection: the disappointment of the Roman Synod; the persistent anti-modernist pressure against the Pontifical Biblical Institute in Rome; measures taken from Rome—sometimes without reason given—against reputable Catholic theologians, and that even against the will of their bishops; prejudicial actions on the part of the Curia in connection with Latin and the liturgy; suppression of the Italian translation of the Dutch hierarchy's pastoral on the Council; the pointed ignoring of the Catholic theological faculties of the German universities when the advisory body for the Council was being formed; the onesided composition and work of some of the preparatory commissions etc. Not only did one hear all this in private conversation and in discussion groups; one read it in the press.

What is a believing Christian to do in face of this scepticism? What, in particular, is a priest or professor to do, or a journalist or lecturer, who has to give responsible answers to questions about the Council (and it would be a good thing if more of this were being done)? There are two possible courses.

The first is that of superficial apologetics. You take up each point in turn, giving it the "Yes-granted-but" treatment, reciting in this connection something or other which, while unquestionably true, is not to the point, and come finally to the consoling conclusion that

* Since this book was completed in December, 1962, all references to the reigning pontiff are, of course, to Pope John XXIII.

it isn't all that bad really. Or rather, that the really bad types are
the ones who make out that it is bad. What is achieved by taking
this course? People who read only conformist writing, and even that
not thoroughly, are reassured and reinforced in their opinion that
it is right and proper for everything in the Church of God to go
quietly on as before. But for people who think, and whose eyes are
open to the needs of the times and of the Church, it can be at best a
well-meant but inappropriate whitewash-apologetics. They find the
answer disappointing, lose all hope that the leaders of our Church
see the problems for what they really are, and mentally write off the
Council. If a theologian, especially, takes this course, such Christians get the impression that he has not, basically, learnt much
either theologically or practically since the First Vatican Council,
despite the fearful state of the world and of Christendom, and that
in these circumstances the Council is not going to do much for reunion beyond fine words and appeals. Hence superficial apologetics
of this sort makes for passivity, whether complacent or defeatist.

The other course is that of *honest appraisal*. For the Church's sake,
for the Council's sake, you call black black, grey grey and white
white, without trying to draw a neat little veil over each difficulty
that arises—a veil that usually fails to cover it anyway. Difficulties
are honestly stated, but the accent is laid on the positive aspects of
the Council:

(1) The comfort and encouragement given to so many Christians
by the ecumenical attitude of our present Pope, with his magnificent programme for the Council: "Through renewal of the Catholic
Church to re-union of separated Christians."

(2) The positive factors in the preparation for the Council: the
change, due to the Pope's initiative, in the ecumenical climate
throughout the Church, the erection of the Secretariat for Christian
Unity in Rome under the outstanding leadership of Cardinal Bea,
the radical stress on the link between reunion and the self-reform of
our own Church, etc.

(3) The positive possibilities of carrying out the Council's programme, both basically and in concrete practical terms.

This is the way to fight scepticism and defeatism, and to combine a necessary realism with hope and encouragement. An honest appraisal of this sort is a summons to work for the fulfilment of the Council's goal.

What the Church needs above all today is honesty; the honesty to make a just assessment, without illusions, of the situation of our own Church and of others. And secondly courage; the courage to say, in season, out of season, what the situation demands in the light of the Gospel of Jesus Christ, even at the grave risk of making oneself unpopular; and finally readiness, readiness to work tirelessly, in whatever place God our Lord has set us, at the realization of the Council's goal.

Divine and human convocation

The basic theological question here is: Can an ecumenical council be interiorly a failure? One hears it said: "It is true that the *convocation* of an ecumenical council does not necessarily ensure its success, and hence, of course, its interior success." But the only ground for this is supposed to be that "a council may be *convoked* and then not take place or not be concluded. The Pope may, for instance, cancel his convocation of it, or fail to confirm it once it is convoked."* But is it not necessary to go deeper than this?

It must be said, as a fundamental principle, that the human element and its failings provide many causes which may rob an ecumenical council of interior success. It is true that no ecumenical council will ever have taken place without producing some sort of beneficial effect, whether hidden or obvious, direct or indirect; for them that love God, *all* things work ultimately for the best. But we could say as much as this (or as little) for many other kinds of assembly. Even a council that does have various sorts of beneficial effect may, looked at as a whole, i.e., with reference to the purpose for which it was convoked, be a failure. We firmly believe in the assist-

---

* References by name are not given in this chapter, since they are irrelevant and the intention here is not polemical.

ance of the Holy Spirit, promised to the Church and hence to the Ecumenical Council. But the assistance of the Spirit does not protect a council against failure. There is a distinction between that ecumenical council which is convoked *by God,* which is the Church herself, and that ecumenical council which is convoked *by men,* which is only one representation of the Church (though the most comprehensive one).* Divine convocation provides in advance, by grace, that that ecumenical council which is the Church can never, regarded as a whole (that is, eschatologically), become a failure. But *human* convocation does not have the power to provide in advance that the human council shall not be a failure.

The Church is not wrecked even when a council is. A council, as one individual event within Church history, can fail in its historical task. The *special* assistance given to it by the Spirit is essentially negative (protection against error), not positive (as giving it a quasimiraculous success in spite of the inadequacy and resistance of human beings). Hence, because of the essentially *human* character of the ecumenical council (which works quite differently in the council as convoked by men from the way it does in the council as convoked by God), the fact that a council has been convoked does not guarantee in advance that it will be an interior success. An ecumenical council may be held and yet, despite all its imposing external solemnity and all its proclamations and excommunications, fail to meet the really pressing demands of the Church and of the age.

The fact that this is not a merely theoretical possibility is shown by the Fifth Council of the Lateran (1512–17): "Instead of any hesitations and misgivings with which such a Council might have been regarded—not without good reason—its announcement was hailed with enthusiasm as the dawn of a new and better age, as the beginning of the reform of the Church."[1] Reform of the Church was set before the assembly as its principal task in the opening speech by the General of the Augustinians, Egidius of Viterbo (Martin Luther's superior general). The two Venetians, Tommaso Giustiniani and Vincenzo Quirini, who had recently entered the Camaldolese Or-

* For the meaning of this distinction, cf. Part 2, 1 of this book.

der, presented a scheme of far-reaching reforms, "both the widest and the boldest of all the many reform programmes drawn up since the conciliar era."[2] The ecumenical council was convoked, its great purpose proclaimed; it met, made some definitions against Averroism, talked a great deal about reform—and was nevertheless an appalling failure:

> It is no exaggeration to say that the reform programme of the two Camaldolese monks preoccupied the Church for more than a century. The Council of Trent, the liturgical reforms of Pius V, the Bible of Sixtus V, the foundation of Propaganda, are all in line with these plans. But the vision which the the trained and prophetic eye of the high-minded Venetians beheld was too lofty both for the Pope to whom they addressed themselves and for the Council assembled before their eyes. Pope and Council disappointed the hopes that had been set on them.[3]

The failure of this ecumenical council, after being several years in session, was a catastrophic one for the Church; six months after its conclusion the Lutheran Reformation broke out.

Unsuccessful definitions?

Dogmatic definitions can be successful achievements. But the example of the Fifth Council of the Lateran is enough to show that even conciliar definitions infallibly declared by the Catholic Church are not enough by themselves to make a council as a whole a success in respect of the goal set before it. For some theologians, dogmatic definitions are only subject to failure in so far as men "shut themselves against the truth solemnly proclaimed by the Church in council. Failure in this sense is possible." One may finish this off with the lapidary statement that "Truth cannot be a failure."

But what we have to ask ourselves here is another question: Is the fact that a council makes a definition, without error, enough to make it interiorly a success? Here again it is not in dispute that one could scarcely find a dogmatic definition that has had no beneficial effect, obvious or hidden, direct or indirect. But not even a definition, correct in itself and pronounced by a council, is enough in every case to make that council a success as a whole. It is standard textbook teaching that the fact that a truth is defined does not in the least define that the definition was opportune. A definition may be true and yet not in the good sense opportune, appropriate to the times. It may be defined without reference to the true requirements of the Church and of the age. The fact that the Fifth Lateran Council defined that the spiritual soul, the *forma substantialis* of the body, is immortal and distinct for each individual was not enough to make the Council a success. It was a failure all the same.

Some theologians are openly in favour of a large number of definitions and declarations to be made by the Council; there have been hints in this direction already. But it is to be hoped that the theological preparatory commission was more clear-sighted. The history of the First Vatican Council could have provided a valuable lesson here, when the theological commission aimed at the greatest possible number of definitions and only managed (not only because of the time-factor) to get very few of them (and those radically altered) accepted by the Council itself. Pope John, at all events, is, to judge by all his pronouncements to date, a great deal less interested than most in conciliar declarations, condemnations, excommunications, anathemas and new dogmas.

If a theologian says that it would be a deplorable failure "for the Church to keep silent in a case where the present situation and the truth demand that she should speak, and speak clearly" yet it is also possible to say the opposite; it would be a deplorable failure for the Church, or the Council, to speak in a case where the present situation, and the truth, demand that they should keep silent and not define anything. This applies particularly to decisions on questions of doctrine which are disputed within Catholic theology. What Pius IV laid down for the Council of Trent is still to the point today; when important dogmatic questions were being dealt with, definitions were only to be made where there was *unanimous agreement*

among the Fathers! Which, as one knows, is not an easy thing to
establish. This puts one on one's guard against making the maximum number of definitions. "Art for art's sake" has no place here.
One will rather be ready to follow the good Catholic tradition of deciding, for the sake of the Church, only what has to be decided because of incursions of heresy. It is not for nothing that John XXIII
has refurbished and applied to doctrinal disputes between Catholics the ancient maxim: *"In necessariis unitas, in dubiis libertas, in omni-
bus autem caritas"*—"Unity in what is *necessary*, liberty in what is
doubtful, but love in all things."

A council does, in certain circumstances, have to pronounce
against the errors of the age (though it would be harder now than
ever before, at a time when the magisterium has taken its stand in
innumerable declarations against all the errors of our age, to establish dogmatically that this is necessarily a task for a council); but it
cannot and must not take over the work of theology. Furthermore,
to decide on questions which are disputed amongst Catholics would
be a far too difficult business for an assembly of two thousand bishops, unable to remain for an indefinite period away from their dioceses. The work would fail to go through, as at the First Vatican
Council. Is it not an over-simplification when a theologian who
bases himself chiefly on nineteenth-century neo-scholasticism finds,
for instance, that the whole doctrine of the episcopal office has been
made so explicit already "that it is only necessary to assemble it together in order to have the clear Catholic doctrine displayed before
one's eyes"? Is what was good enough for the First Vatican Council
still good enough for the Second? Compare some neo-scholastic
treatments of the primacy and episcopacy—over-simplified, based
chiefly on canon law, and to some extent quite unhistorical—with
the genuine theology (and *therefore* good canon law) expounded by
Karl Rahner and Joseph Ratzinger;[4] theologians who make a penetrating examination of a highly complex problem and all the difficulties immanent in it and then, by a deepening of exegetical,
historical, dogmatic and canonical insight, do not simply repeat

textbook propositions (which, while universally acknowledged, are to a large extent unclear) but produce solutions, both theoretical and practical, making for greater depth and further advance.

In this question, as in others also discussed before the Council, what is called for is not only the canon lawyer's approach but that of an authentic theology, making use of all the progress made in theology in this century, and not only in the nineteenth (and especially of advances in exegesis and Church history, and the history of dogma, law and ideas).

But what needs particular consideration in any definition is its *ecumenical effect*. The Pope's intention is that the Council should further reunion through renewal of the Church. Hence nothing must be done to endanger the Council's goal. A council with such a goal as this could be robbed of interior success precisely by unnecessary definitions tending to deepen or harden schism. Thus, for instance, there are few things the Council could do which would damage reunion as much as defining another Marian dogma would. On this it needs to be clearly stated that it is not only a question of being opportune but one of moral responsibility for every Christian body to refrain from building up its own confessional peculiarities without need, forgetful of its own share of guilt in the schism, forgetful of its duty to make reparation and diminish hindrances, forgetful of St. Paul's demand that we avoid, for Christ's sake, giving scandal to those who are weak in faith, forgetful, finally, of that love of the brethren which is a command implicit in these very questions themselves.[5]

Unsuccessful reforms?

It is possible for a council to fail in its historical task. Even a theologian who does not care to hear this necessary but uncomfortable truth in connection with dogmatic definitions cannot fail to admit it elsewhere; that is, in connection with ecclesiastical reforms. "But when the word failure is used of the Council, what one has in

mind, primarily, are ... reforms which may be left undone or done
to an inadequate extent. The disciplinary measures, new laws and
reforms of a council will indeed never contradict the teaching of revelation, but this is not in fact to say that they are absolutely bound
to do justice to the requirements of the age and the true needs of the
Church." Thus it is perfectly clear that a council can, precisely as a
reforming council (and that is what, according to the mind of the
Pope, Vatican II is meant to be), be a radical failure.

What a joy it will be for everyone if the Council's reforms are
crowned with success and things go better in the Second Vatican
Council than they did in the first! Innumerable proposals for reform were brought forward then (300 columns in folio of them).
Yet not one single expectation of reform was fulfilled by the Council.
Forty-six schemata had been prepared on ecclesiastical discipline
and the religious life. Only four were discussed at all, and not one
was adopted. This despite the fact that the subject was discussed
from 8 January to 22 February, and that the decrees were revised
and discussed again in May. The far-reaching proposals prepared
by the third and fourth commissions on the religious life, the Eastern Churches and the missions were never debated at all.

The failure of the Council to achieve reforms was obviously not
due merely to lack of time. Among other things, there were two
reasons for it:

(1) The preparatory work had been done zealously but one-
sidedly. It was not as representative as the bishops were of all parts
of the Church and all the tendencies within her.

(2) Attention was concentrated not on essential needs viewed in
the light of the Gospel but on secondary questions, so that it got
lost in a maze of detail. As Darboy, the Archbishop of Paris, declared in discussion within the Council:

But we are confusedly walking through a thicket of particu-
lars and the vain and uncertain "placita" of the schools. We
are gravely discussing questions of canonists, and are being
set to labour over all kinds of trivialities [*puerilia*]. Many had

been fearing that the Vatican Council was going to attempt greater things than a sick society could bear. My fear is, lest having arrested the attention and the expectation of all, the Council be found unequal to the task it took in hand, in the judgement of those who make up that queen of the world, public opinion.[6]

The success of the Council

When is a council a success? What, in particular, will make this council a success? It is a platitude, these days, to say that we are living in an age of upheaval. Extraordinary times call for extraordinary measures. It is not enough to "maintain contact with tradition" and lay stress on "the harsh demands of truth"; it is not enough to "campaign against error" and defend "penal exclusion from the communion of the faithful with the consequences laid down by law"; it is not enough simply to call on the other side to "recognize the continuity of the Petrine office in the Church," to summon them to "return to their father's house," to take "the path to Rome." Can this kind of thing ever lead to that radical renewal of the Church which is the immediate aim of the Council and to the reunion which is its ultimate goal?

In every quarter of the Church there must be an absolutely clear realization today that, if the idea of renewal and preparation for reunion is to be taken seriously, the Council cannot achieve success through petty measures. What then must happen for a council, and this Council in particular, to be a success? There can be no room for doubt in the minds of any of those who (in however many different ways) are working for the Council's interior success. Only one thing can give real success to any council, and in a very special way to this Council; neither some sort of opportunistic "modernization" nor some sort of traditionalistic "restoration," but only a radical theological and practical concentration—proceeding *from* our own times and *for* our own times, in the Holy Spirit—on the Gospel of our Lord Jesus Christ.

NOTES:

¹ Hubert Jedin, *A History of the Council of Trent.* Saint Louis, Herder, vol. 1 (1957), p. 114.

² Jedin, p. 128.

³ Jedin, p. 130.

⁴ K. Rahner and J. Ratzinger, *The Episcopate and the Primacy,* New York, Nelson (1962) (*Quaestiones Disputatae, 4*); and cf. the symposium edited by Y. Congar and B.-D. Dupuy, *L'Épiscopat et l'église universelle,* Paris (1962).

⁵ On this difficult question of the conditions for a solemn decision on a matter of faith, which obviously cannot be dealt with thoroughly here, see O. Karrer, "Spiritualität und Dogma in ökumenischer Fragestellung," in *Kirche und Überlieferung. Festschrift für J. R. Geiselmann,* Freiburg, Bâle and Vienna (1960), pp. 311–329.

⁶ C. Butler, *The Vatican Council 1869–1870,* Fontana edition, London (1962), p. 190. (Westminster, Newman, 1963.)

2

What Do Christians Expect of the Council?

WHAT DO CHRISTIANS expect of the Council? An often-heard answer to this question has been a terse "Nothing." At all events, nothing of decisive importance for our age. All this gorgeous pageantry of assembled prelates, one has heard people say, this thoroughly unevangelical, worldly spectacle of boasted Catholic unity for the benefit of the press, the picture magazines and the television cameras—can one imagine Christ, the Lord of the Church, and his apostles, ever taking part in an event of that sort? Or again: How can one expect anything to come of a monolithic ecclesiastical party conference, where only one opinion is allowed to be expressed, where there has to be complete deference to the boss over every question, and where the only thing the assembly can do is proclaim how great and organized and virtuous and truthful it itself is, while condemning and excommunicating all other ideas? What is there to be expected of it in an age when almost one half of humanity is being welded into an even more rigid unity by the Communist *oikoumene,* and at the same time sealed off from the outside world; an age when new continents are competing for world leadership while Christianity, divided within itself, is seen to be only one world religion amongst others; an age in which the mastery not only of this earth but of the moon and the whole of space is at stake; an age, finally, in which we are threatened, after two world wars, with an atomic war that is liable to make a definitive end of all our idiotic sectarianism by blowing it to bits? What can we expect of an ecclesiastical assembly from which, along with its proclamations and condemnations, we may possibly get a few more ploddingly elaborated reforms of the rubrics of the Roman Mass, a dozen or so new enactments of canon law, and maybe even a new dogma or two? Are we not stimulating illusions, sure to be followed by appalling disappointment, if we expect anything more from the Council than this? The people who have talked, and to a certain extent still talk, like this are not by any means all men of ill will anxious to foster defeatism in the Church; some of them are Christians, both Protestant and Catholic, who very much deserve to be taken seriously —more especially, Protestant and Catholic theologians. We shall not at this point go once again through the reasons for their scepticism about the Council; it has to be acknowledged that they are not insubstantial fancies. Nor would there be any sense in refuting them with skilful apologetics. Why not? Because the notion that nothing is to be expected of the Second Vatican Council cannot be refuted with words. It can only be refuted with deeds done by the Council itself.

What the Pope expects

One thing at least is sure: the man who summoned the Second Vatican Council is not expecting nothing, or nothing important, from it. And this may well be enough for us; this may well give us cause to hope, despite all the gloomy and by no means groundless prognoses. What does Pope John XXIII expect of the Council?

In the programme outlined in his inaugural encyclical *Ad Petri Cathedram* of 29 June 1959, Pope John formulated his expectations in this way:

> . . . "There will be one fold and one shepherd." This irresistible assurance was the compelling motive which led Us to announce publicly Our resolve to call an Ecumenical Council.

Bishops will come together there from every corner of the world to discuss important matters of religion. But the most pressing topics will be those which concern the spread of the Catholic faith, the revival of Christian standards of morality, and the bringing of ecclesiastical discipline into closer accord with the needs and conditions of our times. This in itself will provide an outstanding example of truth, unity and love. May those who are separated from this Apostolic See, beholding this manifestation of unity, derive from it the inspiration to seek out that unity which Jesus Christ prayed for so ardently from His heavenly Father.

What does this mean? That according to the mind of John XXIII *the reunion of separated Christians is bound up with renewal within the Catholic Church, to which the Council is intended to make an essential contribution.*

In many addresses during the preparatory period the Pope has given a more precise description of his expectations. Let us quote one particularly explicit talk to the diocesan presidents of Italian Catholic Action:

The Ecumenical Council will be a demonstration, uniquely far-reaching in its significance, of truly world-wide catholicity. What is happening is proof that the Lord is assisting this salutary plan with his holy grace. The idea of the Council did not come as the slowly ripening fruit of long deliberation but was like the sudden flowering of an unexpected spring . . . By God's grace, then, we shall hold this council; we shall prepare for it by working hard at whatever on the Catholic side most needs to be healed and strengthened according to the teaching of our Lord. When we have carried out this strenuous task, eliminated everything which could at the human level hinder our rapid progress, then we shall point to the Church in all her splendour, *sine macula et ruga,* and say to all those who are separated from us, Orthodox, Protestants, and the rest: Look, brothers, this is the Church of Christ. We have

striven to be true to her, to ask the Lord for grace that she
may remain forever what he willed. Come; here the way lies
open for meeting and for homecoming; come; take, or resume,
that place which is yours, which for many of you was your
fathers' place. O what joy, what a flowering even in civil and
social life, may be looked for by the whole world if we once
have religious peace and the re-establishment of the family of
Christendom!

What do the Pope's words lead us *not* to expect? That the Second
Vatican Council should be a council of union. The eastern schism
has been going on for over nine hundred years, the northern one for
over four hundred. Nine hundred years and four hundred years of
schism cannot be simply uprooted by a conference. Differences in
cult, in law, in doctrine, in prayer, in life are involved. It is true that
reunion need only be restricted to essentials. But to achieve even a
reunion restricted to essentials at all these levels needs time, patience, perseverance and a great deal of prayer and theological and
practical work. A tremendous effort is needed on the part of all the
Christian bodies if reunion is to be achieved. The kind of exaggerated enthusiasm which expects everything to be done by a summit
conference can only cause delay. Hence, to have non-Catholic
Christians taking part in the Council only as observers is according
to the dictates of sober prudence. None of us is ready for more than
this as yet. The problems certainly lie at a deeper level than that of
organizational negotiations. So we rule out the possibility of expecting negotiations for reunion.

What *do* the Pope's words lead us to expect? We can expect the
Second Vatican Council to make an essential contribution to renewal of the Church and *thus* to the preparation for reunion. The
epoch-making thing about the Pope's initiative in calling the Council is that the reunion of separated Christians has been essentially
linked up with the Catholic Church's taking stock of herself, examining herself, reforming and renewing herself. What, more precisely,
does this mean?

Wrong ways towards reunion

There are good ways and wrong ways towards reunion. The way that has been undertaken in connection with the Second Vatican Council is sharply differentiated from others. There are three ways which cannot reach the goal.

(1) The reunion of separated Christians will not be attained by refraining from action and summoning them back to the Catholic Church: "Come to us! We have everything! We are the one, holy, catholic and apostolic Church!" We have been calling to the Protestants in vain for four hundred years and to the Orthodox of the East for nine hundred. These appeals to "return" seem to suggest that it is only the others who bear the guilt of schism, only the others who have anything to make good. It is true that the Pope, too, still uses words like "return," which to a Protestant are open to misunderstanding. But at the same time he speaks of "meeting." And what is more important, the meaning of these words has changed. What lies behind them is not a spirit of unrepentant self-satisfaction, simply demanding repentance from the other side. The Pope, too, recognizes the guilt that Catholics share for the schism: "Responsibility is divided." The Pope, too, recognizes that the Catholic Church also needs to do her part in examining and reforming herself according to the will of the Lord: ". . . by working hard at whatever on the Catholic side most needs to be healed and strengthened according to the teaching of our Lord." According to him, it is only when this "strenuous task" has been carried out that reunion will be possible. Christians can expect that the Council will correspond to the intentions of the Pope; that it will not expend itself in programmes and proclamations about "return" but rather make a solid contribution to a self-appraisal, self-examination, self-renewal and reform of the Catholic Church, and thus seriously prepare, on the Catholic side, for reunion.

(2) Reunion will not be attained simply through *individual conversions*. This is undoubtedly how many Catholics have imagined reunion; conversions to the Catholic Church, more and more and more of them, until at last all, or at least the majority, of Orthodox,

Lutheran, Anglican and Free-Church Christians have rediscovered their home in the Catholic Church. But individual conversions of Protestants have been going on for four hundred years; individual conversions of Orthodox for nine hundred; and they have not brought the reunion of separated confessions as such any nearer. Let nothing, indeed, be said against conversions that really are conversions; real conversions, not for any external convenience but for serious reasons of faith, conversions in which the convert does not remain in a state of reaction and protest against his own past but integrates his past and makes it fruitful in the Catholic Church. When a non-Catholic Christian clearly sees the light of Christ's truth shining in a new way within the Catholic Church, he will not hesitate to follow his conscience. Nor is it possible to overlook the way in which Catholic theology and the Church have been greatly enriched by a number of important conversions, especially of theologians and writers, and that this has made her voice more clearly audible to other Christians. But, once again, reunion is not attainable along this road. All too often Catholics have counted only conversions to the Catholic Church and not the numerous conversions from the Catholic Church to others. Above all, they have not counted the large number of people who, because of difficulties arising out of the schism—in a mixed marriage, perhaps—give up all connection with any religious body. There is no overlooking the fact that the number of converts is simply laughable in comparison with the number of non-Catholic Christians. And when a Catholic exaggerates the value of individual conversions in connection with reunion, is he not in danger of overlooking the truth that we Catholics, too, need to be converted, to be constantly converted afresh to Christ and his Gospel, to which neither we nor our Church are anything like adequately conformed? In this Second Vatican Council, Pope John is not thinking of individual conversions but of the reunion of separated Christian bodies as such. Christians can expect that the Council will correspond to the Pope's intentions: that it will not see "conversions" from the other side as the way to reunion, but that it will serve reunion by giving the whole Church, from top to bottom and in all her local Churches, a strong thrust towards that conversion which never ceases to be required of every Christian, conversion to Christ in accordance with his Gospel.

(3) Reunion of separated Christians will not be attained simply by *general moral reform*. One hears Catholics saying that reunion could be achieved if only we Catholics were better Catholics; we Catholics should become more Catholic. It is well said, but liable to be misunderstood. Is all that is wanted in connection with the reunion of separated Christians that we do a better job at keeping the ten commandments of God and the commandments of the Church on top of them? There is no doubt that keeping the Commandments is a task the Church always has to fulfil; but that is just it—a task she *always* has to fulfil, "eternally," as it were, in so far as men have always been sinners and always will be. But schism in the Church is not a matter of the "eternal" sins of humanity. However large a part they may have played in the schism, it remains true that the schism is not part of humanity's "eternal" sinfulness, but is something that came about *historically* and can, by the grace of God, be removed. But this calls not merely for general moral effort, but for efforts with this special aim in view. So let us be better Catholics, but in what sense? Better Catholics in relation to Christians separated from us! The Pope, too, is not concerned simply with moral reform in general, but with a renewal of the Church *in relation to the reunion of our separated brethren*. Christians can expect the Council to correspond to the intentions of the Pope; not (as tended to be suggested by some of the Roman commentaries on some of the work of the preparatory commissions) address itself to evil humanity with unhelpful moralizations and condemnatory exhortations, but find positive solutions in the light of the Good News, and serve the world by renewing the Church while directing all its work of renewal towards the reunion of separated Christians. And this brings us to our positive point.

The right way to reunion

The only way for the Ecumenical Council to make an essential contribution towards preparing for reunion is through a renewal of the Catholic Church by carrying out the justified demands of the other side in the light of the Gospel of Jesus Christ; a renewal of the Catholic Church springing, indeed, from her own essential nature as it has always been but at the same time—this is the decisive thing —*fulfilling the justified demands of Lutherans, Calvinists, Orthodox, Anglicans and Free Churchmen in the light of the Gospel of Jesus Christ.* Let it be the Gospel of Christ which decides, as between other Christians and ourselves, which of their demands are justified and which are not.

Even the Catholic Church has to apply to herself the description of *ecclesia semper reformanda,* the Church that has always to be reformed. I have enlarged on this elsewhere, from the point of view of theology, Church history and practical application.[1] The form this takes today is a reform with a special object in view, namely (as far as concerns our part of the world) a reform aimed at the demands made *by the Reformation.* In other words, the protest made by protesting Protestants against the Catholic Church must, in so far as it contains an element of justice, be deprived of its object by the Catholic Church itself. It is true that the Catholic Church, being made of human beings, and sinners at that, is always going to be *ecclesia semper reformanda,* always going to need renewal. But is it not possible to think of a Catholic Church, now that the age of polemic is to a large extent happily over, who would have positively fulfilled whatever valid demands were made at the Reformation so that she would be, not indeed finally and in every respect, but nevertheless *in regard to the demands of the Reformation,* a reformed and renewed Catholic Church, *ecclesia catholica reformata?*

Such a program is not something that has to be begun as from today. Without resorting to boastfulness, we can affirm that as far back as the so-called Counter-Reformation, which was by no means exclusively a counter-reformation, the Catholic Church accomplished and manifested a vast work of reform; reform of the Church was not a preserve of the Reformers. Furthermore, especially since the time of Leo XIII at the end of the last century, the Church has gone beyond the sixteenth- to nineteenth-century type of reform (which was, in the last analysis, somewhat restorational in charac-

ter) and on into positive, creative reform, a genuine Catholic renewal, in fact, midway between restoration on conservative and reactionary lines to the Right and revolution regardless of the
continuity in the Church and her leadership to the Left. A whole
book could be written about how the Church since Leo XIII, in the
decades leading up to this Council, has set about fulfilling, from the
sources within her own essential being, a whole series of valid Protestant demands for reform, though without having this aim directly
in view. To give a few headline summaries:

(1) The revaluation of the Scriptures in Catholic dogma, exegesis,
preaching and private reading.

(2) Development of Catholic liturgy into a genuine people's liturgy, at the level both of theoretical foundations and of practical
measures; widespread introduction of the vernacular in the administration of the sacraments and in liturgical singing; introduction of
an intelligible community mass.

(3) Sense of the universal priesthood, both in theology and in lay
action.

(4) Increased adaptation of the Church to the nations of the
world, and a reduction of Latinism in mission countries.

(5) Far-reaching de-politicizing of the Papacy, in connection both
with the fortunate loss of the papal states and the beginnings of curial reform under Pius X.

(6) Growing appreciation of tolerance and the individual conscience (cf. Pius XII's address on the subject and John XXIII's encyclical, *Pacem in Terris*).

(7) The admission of several married Lutheran pastors to the
Catholic priesthood, implying practical recognition of the possibility
that there may be a valid vocation to the Roman ministry even outside the organization of the Catholic Church.

(8) Despite all only too obvious shortcomings, a strong increase,
in comparison with the Middle Ages, the Baroque period and the
nineteenth century, in the interiority and concentration of popular
piety, at least amongst the Catholic elite.

And despite all our differences in doctrine, there is undoubtedly

a whole series of matters, even in theology, in which we have manifestly and sometimes astonishingly come closer to each other, such
as the concept of dogma as essentially historical and conditioned by
time, and hence susceptible of improvement; and the teaching on
Scripture and tradition, grace and justification, and the Church and
the sacraments.

Obviously the point is not to falsify the actual situation of the
Church and Catholic theology by painting them in rosy colours.
Catholics too are well aware of their weaknesses and shortcomings
(though it is equally unjustified on the Protestant side to compare
run-of-the-mill Catholicism with some sort of imaginary ideal Protestantism). It is precisely because the Catholic Church is aware of
her own weaknesses and shortcomings that this Council has been
summoned for the renewal of the Church. But it is necessary to point
explicitly to the reforms accomplished already in the Catholic
Church so as to make three points clear:

(1) The Catholic Church of today is not simply the unreformed
Church of the Reformation period.

(2) The protests of the Protestants of that time cannot continue to
be, unexamined, the protests of the Protestants of today.

(3) It is not simply a matter of the Church of today having
to catch up with the Reformation four hundred years later, or
four hundred years too late. This last point calls for further treatment.

Expectations on both sides

The theme of this chapter is what *Christians* expect of the Council. It seems to me that it would be a grave misunderstanding of it
if the plan of the Council were made a reason for us Catholics to
be the only ones from whom anything is expected. Let us say quite
explicitly that there are expectations on both sides. Both Catholics
and Protestants are at fault, gravely at fault, over the schism. They
both have the obligation, the grave obligation, to restore Church

unity, this restoration being demanded not for some current opportunistic reason (e.g., fear of Communism) but by the Lord of the
Church himself, who prayed for this unity. Protestant Christians
have a brotherly right to expect a great deal from us Catholics for
the sake of reunion. But Catholic Christians have a brotherly right
to expect as much from Protestants; stocktaking and self-examination and self-renewal in their Churches too. We have described the
task set for us Catholics as reunion through carrying out the justified
demands of Protestants in the light of the Gospel of Jesus Christ.
The corresponding programme for Protestants needs to be stated as
clearly; reunion through carrying out the justified demands of *Catholics* in the light of that same Gospel of Jesus Christ. We Catholics,
too, have demands, and big demands, to make of the Protestant
Churches. A reformation that stops is not a reformation. The adjec-
tive "reformed" as applied to a Church (whether in a Lutheran or
Calvinist sense) must not be a pretext for a timid rejection of new
reforms. As Schleiermacher said, "The Reformation is still going
on." It does not absolutely have to go on in the direction of Schleiermacher. Why should it be impossible for such reforms sometimes to
turn in the direction of the Catholic Church?—not in the sense of
cheap external catholicizing and imitation, but in the sense of a re-
examination of one's own position and one's own protests in the light
of the Gospel of Jesus Christ; in the sense of honest self-examination
and courageous, energetic measures of self-improvement. There is
in the Scriptures—or so it seems to us Catholics, and many Protestant theologians, not catholicizers, agree with us—so much that is
not attended to enough or understood enough or taken seriously
enough in the Protestant Churches. We rejoice over everything that
has happened during the last few decades in the Protestant
Churches towards the fulfilment of what is valid in Catholic demands; we think particularly of the renewal of theology, of liturgy
and of the idea of the Church. We have taken innumerable steps towards each other, but there are innumerable steps still to take, from
both sides. The Ecumenical Council is a summons to both sides to

advance towards each other by one more large step—perhaps several large ones.

Expectation and fulfilment

Expectation is one thing and fulfilment another. It would be wrong not to expect much from the Council, but it would also be wrong to expect too much from the Council. The Council cannot fulfil all the expectations of Christendom. The expectations of Christendom are innumerable; it would be impossible to fulfil even a tenth of them. A council, which is merely a representation of the Church, cannot supply for the work of the Church in all her dioceses and parishes. A council which lays claim to being ecumenical can deal with problems only at world level. Even the Council needs time. The point is not to get as large a quantity of things done as possible. The point is to do something decisive on two or three points. Possibly the scope of such a decision may not be immediately plain to an outsider; it may be that it will bear visible fruit only after a certain time; think, for instance, of a restoration of the liturgy of the Word in the Mass. Prudence and restraint in judging the results of the Council will certainly be in order.

The degree to which the Council will fulfil expectations is important. But what is more important is what is going to be put into effect after the Council in the life of the Church, through unflagging day-to-day work by parishes and individuals. Here is what we can do already: we can *leave undone* so many things that widen the gulf between divided Christians; generalization, jumping to conclusions, rash judgement, unkind opinions, vague suspicions, sectarian polemics, false self-satisfaction and religious complacency. We can *do* so much that brings us nearer together: we can talk to each other; we can ask other Christians about the complaints and criticisms they have against us, the things they hope or demand that we should do, and so make ourselves informed about them; we can examine ourselves, we can begin the renewal of the Church in ourselves by a realization of the demands that others make of us, we can work as cells to prepare for reunion, we can pray for one another, and we can practise love.

NOTES:

[1] Cf. *The Council, Reform and Reunion,* London and New York, Sheed and Ward (1961).

3

Has the Council Come
Too Soon?

ONE OF THE most noteworthy of the sayings that have become
proverbial amongst the Roman Curia is the phrase *pensiamo in secoli:*
"We think in centuries!" Sudden reorientations are rare in the Curia. They are not well thought of. Hence it is no matter for surprise
that Pope John XXIII's announcement of an ecumenical council to
prepare the way for the reunion of separated Christians, while
hailed with joy throughout the world on account of its ecumenical
objective, aroused no little astonishment in Rome itself. In several
circles there, people were at pains to minimize as far as possible the
epoch-making significance of this event. If the Pope had sent the
question round his "ministerial offices" first, the verdict might well
have been more or less unanimous: "A council? Too soon!" But the
Pope, who "thinks in centuries" in another sense, made no such en-
quiry.

But there was no need to go to Rome to hear sceptical things said
of the plan for a council. On my side of the Alps, where, rightly or
wrongly, people pride themselves on being better able to read the
signs of the times, and where it is not the custom to answer questions
of extreme urgency with Rome's "Patienza! Patienza!" the reaction
in well-informed theological circles was distinctly noncommittal.
The immediate spontaneous response, heard by me, of one competent and ecumenically-minded Catholic theologian to that sensational broadcast of 25 January 1959 was: "A council? Too soon!"

But the Pope, who understood the signs of the times differently, made no enquiries about his conciliar scheme north of the Alps either.

Is it too soon for the Council? The mere fact of the summoning and assembling of the Council does not suffice to answer this question. The Pope is by no means infallible in decisions of this kind. And those who are saying "Too soon" have grounds for their scepticism. I do not mean such grounds as every central bureaucracy has for feeling that interference by "Parliament" is inconvenient, a nuisance, upsetting and really rather superfluous, because it is convinced that it itself is better able to supervise the real needs of "the people" from its superior central vantage-point, and to take whatever measures are necessary more effectively than the members of the legislature coming together from their various regions. I mean rather the grounds which are making so many serious and enlightened Catholic layfolk, pastors, theologians and bishops, all over the world, doubt whether the Catholic Church, especially at her centre, is yet ready for such a momentously daring step as a council to prepare for the reunion of separated Christians. They point to various events of the preparatory period which have greatly depressed many Christians. It is no mere sectarian tendency to paint the picture black, nor sheer defeatism, that has made many Catholic and Protestant Christians fear for the outcome of the Council.

"Is it too soon for the Council?" is no idle question. For a council that comes too soon may come to grief. It may fail to fulfil its historic task, to achieve the goal set for it. Anyone acquainted with the nature and shortcomings of a Church and council consisting of men, and sinful men, knows that it is possible for a council to miscarry. And anyone acquainted with the history of the councils of the Catholic Church knows that something of this sort is not only possible but real. Perhaps some Christians and theologians, whose thought and feeling are based on a romantic and idealistic picture of the Church rather than on a scriptural and realistic one, do not care to hear about this sombre side of the possibilities for the Council. They may feel that it is unseemly, almost indecent, to cal-

culate, in cold blood, the element of human inertia, human inadequacy and human incapacity involved in such a solemn assemblage
of bishops from all over the world. And this despite the fact that, as
we have said already, the Fifth Council of the Lateran (1512–1517),
meeting in an age of vast transition like our own, after the discovery
of America, at the beginning of the modern age, provides the classic
example of a council shipwrecked through human incapacity. It
was a demonstration that it is not always possible to "think in centuries"; that opportunities occur in the Church's history which,
once past, are gone forever, and that their passing can mean castas-
trophe for the Catholic Church. Would the Lutheran reform still
have happened, six months later, if the Fifth Lateran Council had
succeeded instead of failing in its task of reforming the Church?

Theology does a disservice to the Council if it does not face, fundamentally and soberly, the gloomy possibilities as well as the
bright ones, and thus confront the Council with its responsibilities.
Fully though we believe in the Holy Spirit, who guides both Church
and Council, it is only when we have the courage to see the possibility of a council's failing that it becomes clear what a huge
responsibility the Church takes upon herself when gathered in
council. So once again we come to the serious question: Is it too
soon for the Council summoned by John XXIII?

Four hundred years too late

Without in the least underestimating, as a theologian, the tremendous difficulties and risks facing the Second Vatican Council,
one can answer with complete conviction that it does *not* come too
soon. On the contrary. One can say that the Second Vatican Council comes four hundred years too late. Then, when the schism first
broke out, how Christendom clamoured for a council! Only a
council, it was thought, could re-establish the unity that had been
broken. For almost three decades Christians clamoured in vain for
a council; the Curia and the secular powers, the Catholics and the

Protestants, squabbled over questions of whether it was opportune and what it should be like. When at last the Council of Trent did meet, Luther was already dead and no Protestants made their appearance at it. The frontiers had hardened, and the Council gave sanction to that hardening. No one, indeed, denies that the Council of Trent did a colossal work of reform within the Church and set the Catholic Church firmly on the upward path after the decadence of the Renaissance. But it brought no reunion of separated Christians. The immediate aim of the Council was not reunion but defence, condemnation and expulsion. Nor did the First Vatican Council (1869–71) bring any change in this.

Only now, more than four hundred years after the Reformation, has a council been summoned which is to be seriously and positively concerned with reunion. The Second Vatican Council faces demands made by the Reformers which have remained unmet for four hundred years; questions to which the Council of Trent gave, in many cases, purely negative solutions, condemning errors and re-establishing the medieval *status quo ante* without pressing forward to anything bold, constructive and adapted to the new age. Think, for instance, of the demand of the Reformers for general participation in public worship, for a liturgy which would be, in its structure and language, intelligible to the people at large, for a renewal according to the Scriptures of the preaching of the word, for the giving of the cup to the laity, and so on.

So now we have before us the council which is to prepare positively and constructively for reunion. Have we the right, after waiting four hundred years for it, to complain that it comes too soon, merely because we are not yet sufficiently ready for the council either? When *shall* we be sufficiently ready? Should we not rather be grateful that at last this council is really happening? Should not we Catholics, in particular, be glad that, thanks to John XXIII's bold initiative, the supreme leadership in our Church has, for the first time since the Reformation, firmly dropped its rather passive attitude of waiting, feeling its way, delimiting, defending and summoning people back to the Church, and has addressed itself to an energetic and active encounter with our separated brethren?

No, it is not too soon for the Council. Even if this Second Council of the Vatican does not, contrary to our hopes, manage to achieve anything of its great programme of preparation for reunion, there would still remain something of incalculable importance; the programme has been formulated, the road has been signposted, the goal has been set: through renewal of the Church to reunion of separated Christians.

The change of atmosphere

Furthermore, we already have more than a mere programme. We have in fact started out. Whatever news one gets from any area of the Catholic Church, whether from Holland or Spain, from North or South America, from Asia or Africa, one thing is obvious; despite the persistence of negative factors which still have to be recognized, there is no mistaking the signs of a great stirring which have appeared throughout the Church in response to the announcement of the Council. This is further confirmation for our assertion that the Council does not come too soon.

It was heard from a well-informed source that John XXIII was asked in a private conversation what he intended by having a council. The Pope answered by opening the window and saying: "That —to let some fresh air into the Church!" And in fact, the announcement of the Council has let fresh air into the Church. Things which one scarcely dared to mention before are now being discussed with a frankness almost alarming to Catholics with an unconsciously nineteenth-century notion of the Church. There are discussions, criticisms, suggestions, new proposals and initiatives in every field; liturgy and discipline, theology and pastoral work—all of it symptomatic of new life. Before 25 January 1959, the *ecclesia catholica semper reformanda,* the Catholic Church in constant need of reformation, was not an advisable subject on which to write books offering a programme of concrete proposals for renewal. It was not until the Council was announced and had started people thinking that they woke up to the fact that we cannot let everything go quietly and slowly on, leaving it to "grow"; our age demands special and extraordinary efforts on the part of the Church. The very announcement of the Council does of course presuppose that an enormous development *has* taken place in the Church; it presupposes everything that *has been* quietly growing in the Church during these past decades, especially since the pontificate of Leo XIII. But since the announcement of the Council, this movement for renewal has become official in a way that few Catholics would have dreamed possible.

This applies particularly to the ecumenical movement within the Catholic Church. Before the announcement of the Council, working for the reunion of separated Christians was reckoned in the Catholic Church to be a matter for theological specialists or dilettante idealists. Since the announcement of the Council, reunion is no longer simply the concern of a theological *avant-garde,* to be pitied or ridiculed, opposed or admired. Against all expectation, it has suddenly become the declared concern of the Church's supreme leadership. Nor is this any merely theoretical admission of concern, a mere "Nothing against it from our side!" It is a practical, living concern: "We are in favour of it, and ready to do something about it!" And here it is possible even for Christians outside the Catholic Church to see that a central leadership of the whole Church, such as seems to us to have its foundation in the New Testament, does have some very practical advantages. The action of the chief shepherd of the Catholic Church in thus definitely, explicitly and decisively pointing out the way forward into the future for the reunion of separated Christians has automatically made reunion a matter of concern to countries, bishops, theologians and lay people who did not on their own account care much about it. The sleepers have been shaken awake by the Pope himself. Something which in other Christian communions can often not be attained even after years of discussing and conferring was in this case achieved in the

briefest possible time; namely, the concentration of the whole
Church upon one of the central issues of our time. For decades it
has been a reproach and grievance against the Catholic Church
that she stands aloof from the ecumenical movement. Today, as is
remarked by many observers, including Protestants, there are in
many areas a greater readiness and ecumenical understanding, a
stronger will to ecumenical action, amongst Catholics than amongst
Protestants. Even in Spain and South America there are very clear
signs of at least the beginnings of a change in the atmosphere. And
in our part of the world, the available experts can hardly manage
to meet all the countless demands for ecumenical lectures, sermons,
articles and so on. Ecumenical theology is now sought after. Ecumenical theology is now in demand; theologians are being positively
urged to replace "static" theology with a theology "on the march":
a theology of mutual encounter, in which truth is illuminated by
understanding love, instead of a state-of-siege theology with love
subordinated to so-called truth. A theology, in fact, which is a
preparation for reunion.

With such a change of atmosphere taking place throughout the
Church, who would care to assert that it is still too soon for the
Council?

The ecumenical secretariat

There is one event in particular which shows that the Council
does not come too soon, and which only became possible in connection with the announcement of the Council; namely, the erection of a Roman secretariat to work for the unity of Christians. The
problem of schism in the Church in the West arose at just about
the same time as that of the evangelization of the newly-discovered
continents. As early as 1622 Rome was clearly aware of how important it was to co-ordinate and strengthen the various missionary enterprises. So the Roman Department of Missions, the
congregation De Propaganda Fide, was founded. Not till nearly

three hundred and fifty years later, in connection with this Second Vatican Council, comes the foundation of the Roman Ecumenical Secretariat, a centre for co-ordinating and encouraging efforts for unity. For a long time Catholic theologians have been calling for an institution of this kind. It was the announcement of the Council that made it possible.

The Secretariat certainly does not come too soon, either. In a very short while it has shown, already, what it is capable of achieving. The Secretariat has made possible the first official contacts between the Roman Curia and the Secretariat of the World Council of Churches at Geneva. In 1961, five official Catholic observers commissioned by the Secretariat took part in the assembly of the World Council of Churches at New Delhi. And, again through the intensive work of the Secretariat, extending right into the sessions of the Central Preparatory Commission for the Council, there are now numerous observers from the World Council of Churches, from the Orthodox Churches, from the world unions of the Lutheran and Reformed Churches, from the Anglican Church, from the Methodists, etc., taking part in the Second Vatican Council. The way had been prepared by the visits of the Archbishop of Canterbury and of various Orthodox and American Church leaders to Rome. But it had also been prepared by visits on the part of the Secretariat to Geneva, to Constantinople, to various Eastern patriarchates, to England, etc. Of course these different contacts are not the start of negotiations for reunion. But nor should one be misled by the terminology of protocol into thinking of them simply as "courtesy visits." These visits have nothing to do with courtesy, any more than the participation of the non-Catholic observers at the Council has, but rather with the beginning of a new age in the relations between the Catholic Church and the Churches separated from her. What they express is that we are no longer disposed to go on living next door to each other while ignoring each other, glowering at each other and being suspicious of each other. What they express is that we want to talk together as Christians, that we want to be listened to and spoken to by other Christians, that, in short, we don't want just to exist for ourselves in splendid isolation.

Grounds for hope

No, it is not too soon for the Council. Even if it should be a failure, it is still not too soon. But we have as little cause for exaggerated pessimism as for exaggerated optimism. The things that have come into existence through this council that has now begun, in the Catholic Church and in the whole of Christendom, cannot now be undone. Too many forces for good have been awakened. The movements working now for renewal have struck their roots too deep. Support for the Pope's programme, amongst both clergy and laity, has been too strong. Even if the Second Vatican Council were to fail, such a failure would simply be a summons to the Third Vatican Council. Even if any one session of the Second Vatican Council were to fail, this would only be an added stimulus to the next session. Sessions may fail, councils may fail; the Church, thanks to her Lord's promise and his grace, does not fail when her enterprises fail.

What the Second Vatican Council may rightfully expect from all Christians inside and outside the Catholic Church is *sympathy*. It is not meant to be a purely internal Catholic affair, but an assembly of the Catholic Church with an ecumenical goal, concerned with all the others, with the whole of Christendom. What the Second Vatican Council may rightfully expect from all Christians inside and outside the Catholic Church is *patience*. It is almost a hundred years since the bishops of the whole Catholic Church throughout the world last assembled in council. So far, the Catholic Church has never had regular meetings of her top-level leaders on the lines of, say, the United Nations. Very few of the bishops meeting at the Council knew each other already. They had not yet made the experiment of working together, especially in such vast numbers, never before seen in the history of the Church. The Council has had to feel its way, not only at the technical and organizational level, but also in terms of minds and ideas. What the Second Vatican Council may rightfully expect from all Christians inside and outside the Catholic Church is *prayer;* Catholics prayed for the success of the assembly of the World Council of Churches at New Delhi. They know that their Council, too, is assured of the prayers of their brothers, Protestant, Orthodox, Anglican, of whatever Christian bodies they may be.

Has the Council come too soon? It has come *at the right time.* For all Christians that is a ground for hope and confidence.

Part II

THE COUNCIL IN THEORY
AND PRACTICE

4

What Is
an Ecumenical Council?

Is there a theology of the ecumenical council?

WE ARE HOPING with all our hearts that this council, held as it is in
an age of unprecedented transition, both secular and religious—the
end of the "modern" period, the beginning of a new age of the
world, whatever it may be called—is going to prove itself worthy
in the judgement of history and in the sight of its Lord. The condition for its doing so is honest reflection on the part of the Church,
and not least honest *theological* reflection on the nature of the ecumenical council itself.[1]

But we have to ask straight away whether there *is* such a thing as
theological reflection on the nature of the Ecumenical Council, i.e., a
theology of the Council. Has theology anything definitive to say
about ecumenical councils?

Certainly canon law has something definitive to say about them;
canons 222 to 229 of the *Codex Iuris Canonici* treat *De Concilio Oecu-
menico.* And certainly Church history has definitive things to say
about them; Hefele's history of the councils runs to nine volumes,
and Mansi's *Amplissima Collectio,* the standard source-book of conciliar history, to thirty-one or sixty volumes according to the edition. But has *theology* anything definitive to say? By theology is
meant here not that unscriptural theology which discourses at large,
*non-*definitively, on all possible and impossible subjects, and naturally on ecumenical councils as well, but that Christian theology

which recognizes itself as bound to the revelation of God in Jesus Christ, and from *that* source is called upon to make *definitive* pronouncements. Is it, then, possible to make theologically definitive, strictly dogmatic, pronouncements about the ecumenical council?

What would be all too easy, and ultimately untheological, would be simply to sketch such a "theology" from the present provisions of the Code of Canon Law or to deduce it from some one council such as Trent or Vatican I. The fact that this is the course almost invariably pursued by the textbooks does not make it any better in itself. The point of a theology of the ecumenical council cannot be to describe this or that form of it at any one particular time, but, without becoming unhistorical, to arrive at what it essentially is.

So as to focus the problem sharply, let us suppose (what is certainly not the case) that you have a canon lawyer who thinks *solely* on the basis of canon law in its present state, and a historian who thinks *solely* on the basis of Church history. It gives the theologian something to think about when he realizes that these two imaginary people would scarcely be able to agree on the outward form that an ecumenical council essentially has to take. There is scarcely a canon about the ecumenical council in the *Codex* against which the historian would not be able to affirm that at this or that ecumenical council it had just not happened like that—and yet it was nevertheless a true ecumenical council. There is no end to what has changed in the course of conciliar history; not only places and backgrounds, but the person and office of the man who convokes the council and presides over it, the range of those taking part, the matters deliberated, the mode of procedure, the necessity for explicit approbation.

Thus the canon lawyer may quote what is the first, the basic and perhaps the most far-reaching of the canons in the Codex of Canon Law which concern the Council: "Canon 222. (1) There can be no Ecumenical Council that is not convoked by the Bishop of Rome. (2) It belongs to that same Bishop of Rome to preside over the Ecumenical Council, personally or through his representative, to determine the subjects on which it will deliberate and the order in which they will be deliberated, to postpone the Council, to adjourn it, to conclude it, and to confirm its decrees." The historian will not dispute that this is correct according to the present legal position, but he will calmly add that all this simply was *not* so in the first ecumenical councils of Christian antiquity, those foundational councils which are recognized as ecumenical by all the Christian bodies of East and West. It simply was *not* the Pope who convoked these councils and determined what they should deliberate and in what order, or who postponed, adjourned or concluded them; nor, again, was it always he or his legates who presided; and finally, the fact of explicit papal approbation was disputed. As an historical comment on Canon 222, he might perhaps quote a few sentences from the article on Councils in the *Lexikon für Theologie und Kirche*,[2] which says of the early councils:

> Because of the close connection between State and Church, they were directly affairs of the State and the Empire—imperial synods. They were convoked, adjourned or postponed by the Emperor; their external organization was controlled by the Emperor or his commissioners; the Emperor's confirmation gave to their decisions the force of law, assuring that they would be carried out on the part of the State. Both the synods themselves and the popes recognized these rights.

Of course the canon lawyer can reply by distinguishing. On the matter of the functions of Pope and Emperor or in respect of the councils he may perhaps hit back with a sharp distinction into *materialiter-formaliter* or *implicite-explicite,* and thus try to sweep all the difficulties of the first thousand years under the carpet *modo dogmatico.* But it is likely that the historian will not be completely satisfied by such *a priori* distinctions: "It is my will that you assemble promptly in the said city" was the command of the Emperor, and the Emperor alone, to the bishops of the Ecumenical Council of Nicaea; there is no way of establishing historically any agreement or consent on the part of the Pope. The historian is going to answer all such *a priori* distinctions by pointing out that profound statements of this sort do nothing to shift solid, heavy lumps of historical fact, and that it almost seems to be a case of saying that what mustn't have happened just can't have happened.

This conflict of law and history causes the theologian some consternation. Ancient conciliar history and new conciliar law appear to disown one another. Where then are we to turn in our search for a possible theology of the ecumenical council?

However, the theologian is not to imagine himself as Hercules at the cross-roads, faced with a choice between vice and virtue; conciliar law and conciliar history would both have just cause for complaint. What the theologian will have to do is dig deeper so as to get down to firm ground. The conflict will have taught him something extremely important which he can lay down realistically and soberly from the start; that there are at this level of discussion practical and factual statements of law, but no definitive theological and dogmatic statements. How could there be? It is not only that the historical forms of the ecumenical councils have been extremely various. It is not only that many authors draw an essential distinction between the ecumenical councils of antiquity and of modern times on the one hand and, on the other, the Roman "general synods" of the twelfth century (1123, 1139 and 1179), which were not regarded as ecumenical councils either by their organizers or by other contemporaries, nor, along with the First Council of Lyons (1245), reckoned amongst ecumenical councils even in the later Middle Ages. It is not only that there is no official list of recognized ecumenical councils, and that it depends mostly on one's theological tendencies whether one reckons them as twenty-two, twenty-one, twenty, nineteen or even fewer in number; it is hardly necessary to point out that Denzinger's *Enchiridion* has no particular historical authority.

Over and above all this, it is the common opinion of Catholic theologians today that the Catholic Church could get along without having ecumenical councils at all, or, according to how you put it, that ecumenical councils do not belong to the essence of the Catholic Church. But if not only the concrete historical form of ecumenical councils but even their necessary *existence* in the Church can be called in question in this way, it is not going to be possible to find any definitive theology of the council at *this* level at any rate.

So if we are not simply going to stop short at a canonical or historical treatment of ecumenical councils and do without a theology for them, we shall have to find some authentic theological starting-point from which to develop a theology of the council. This starting-point, which is going to determine so much, will have to be supplied by ecclesiology. This is developed, with the necessary brevity, in the next section.

The Church herself as the ecumenical council convoked by God

While in ecclesiastical Greek the term *synodos* came to be used as a technical term (Eusebius reports it as used in the time of Dionysius of Alexandria),[3] the Latin *concilium* is already found in this sense about the year 200 in the writings of that great creator of ecclesiastical Latin, Tertullian.[4]

One cannot fail to be struck by the fact, which is not merely of surface importance, that *concilium* and *ecclesia* come from the same linguistic root. *Concilium* is from *con-cal-ium*, from the verb *concalare*.[5] *Calare* is used as a religious technical term for "summon," "call together"; thus *concilium* means "assembly." Etymological dictionaries refer explicitly from *concilium* to *synkletos* and *ekklesia*. Latin *calo* corresponds to Greek *kalo*, which in the Gospels sometimes has the ordinary sense of "call," but even in the Synoptics, and above all in St. Paul, already has the specifically theological sense of "call," i.e., of *vocation*. If we make a straightforward survey of the New Testament use of *kalo*, this is what we see; God himself is he who calls, calling in accordance with his eternal, gracious choice (Rom. 8.30:9,12,24; I Cor. 1.9:7.15,17; Gal. 1.6,15:5.8; I Thess. 2.12: 4.7:5.24; 2 Thess. 2.13; 2 Tim. 1.9; Heb. 5.4; 1 Pet. 1.15:2.9:5.10; 2 Pet. 1.3). His calling is to *salvation;* to salvation in sanctification by the Spirit and faith in the truth (2 Thess. 2.13), to suffering (1 Pet. 2.21), to peace (1 Cor. 7.15), to the peace of Christ (Col. 3.15), to freedom (Gal. 5.13), to sanctification (1 Thess. 4.7), to one hope of our calling (Eph. 4.4), to the inheritance of a blessing (1 Pet. 3.9), to the promise of eternal life (Heb. 9.15), to eternal life (1 Tim. 6.12), to God's marvellous light (1 Pet. 2.9), to God's eternal glory in Christ (1 Pet. 5.10), to the fellowship of his Son Jesus Christ (1 Cor. 1.9), to the marriage supper of the Lamb (Apoc. 19.9). Thus God's calling springs from his grace; he, the God of all grace (1 Pet. 5.10), calls in *Christ;* not because of the works of man, but because of God's calling (Rom. 9.12), in virtue of his own glory and perfection through his grace (2 Peter 1.3; Gal. 1.15), through the grace of Jesus Christ (Gal. 1.6), in a holy calling not because of our works but of his own prior decision and grace, which was given us by Christ Jesus before endless ages but is now made manifest through the appearance of our saviour Jesus Christ (2 Tim. 1.9—10; cf. Heb. 9.15; 1 Pet. 5.10). This call of God, manifested to us in the Gospel of the death and resurrection of Jesus Christ, is thus not only a word that *informs* us of our salvation in Jesus Christ, not only a word that *proclaims,* but a word that is *effective,* that *makes present.* Jesus Christ, the exalted Lord himself, acts by the power of the Spirit in his word, which is a call to salvation for all who believe in him.

All that is said here of the verb "call" can be confirmed by reference to the substantive *klesis,* which is similarly used with a specifically theological meaning. Here again we have vocation by God in Christ; "the supernatural vocation of God in Christ Jesus" (Phil. 3.14; cf. Rom. 11.29; 1 Cor. 1.26:7.20; Eph. 1.18:4.1,4; 2 Thess. 1.11; 2 Tim. 1.9; Heb. 3.1; 2 Pet. 1.10). Thus Christians are simply "those who are called" (cf. Rom. 1.6–7:8.28; 1 Cor. 1.2,24; Jude 1; Apoc. 17.14). Each individual is called; not, however, as an individual, but as a member of the one people, the one body; called in one body (Col. 3.15), *one* body and *one* Spirit (Eph. 4.4). Thus all Christians form the "chosen generation, a kingly priesthood, a holy nation, a purchased people: that you may declare his virtues, who hath called you out of darkness into his marvellous light: Who in time past were not a people: but are now the people of God" (1 Pet. 2.9–10). Thus all Christians have, in the Church, a share in the royal, priestly and prophetical office of Christ.

This, then, is the basis from which to understand the word *ekklesia*, which—even apart from its non-religious usage—is known to include, in its New Testament use, a content of religious meaning which is both complex and profoundly interconnected; it can mean the total community of the men of the New Covenant redeemed by Christ; the local Christian community; the Christian community in one household; and in particular, the community assembled for the liturgy. But in all these different ways, *ekklesia* means the community of the new people of God, called out and called together. The etymology of *ek* was hardly adverted to consciously any longer. The starting-point was the Old Testament; *ekklesia* had been used in the Septuagint to translate the Old Testament key-word *qahal* ("community") or *qehal Jahwe* ("community of God"). But after the unbelieving Jews had rejected the corner-stone, the young community had to consider itself as the true people of God of the last times, the true people of the Covenant which God had gathered to himself in Israel. It is this people of the Covenant, called and assembled by the word of the Gospel of Jesus Christ, which now represents the legitimate succession to the people of God in the Old Testament. Thus, according to the testimony of the Acts of the Apostles, it was first the primitive community in Jerusalem that was called *ekklesia;* here individual community and universal community, individual church and universal Church, were identical. But soon they are speaking of the *ekklesia* in Judea, in Galilee, in Samaria; and finally of *ekklesiai* in the plural. Each individual *ekklesia* was an image of the primitive community, each one represented the *ekklesia* as a whole. Paul uses *ekklesia* chiefly for the individual community (and especially for the liturgically assembled community), and often has it in the plural; but in the Captivity Epistles we find above all a quite new and profound use of *ekklesia* as the whole Church.

What the individual community and individual church is on a small scale, that the whole community, the whole Church, is on a large one; the gathered community of the people of God of the New Testament, called by God through the Gospel out of the world,

called together for Christ and in Christ. And at the same time it is
precisely this whose praises are sung in the Captivity Epistles as the
mysterion of God's saving work for men, the *mysterion* of Christ and
pleroma of Christ; his body, to be built up in baptism and the Eucharist, in faith, love and suffering; and his bride, still awaiting him
and yet already his own. Thus the whole *ekklesia* is the mysterious
gathering together of those who believe in Christ. She is—to use another word for it now—the great *concilium* of believers, whom God
himself has summoned through Christ in the Spirit.

All men on earth are summoned to this council, to be gathered in
the one Spirit, held together by the bond of love, in the power of the
word and the sacraments, under the leadership of the Apostles;
"all" as "one in Christ Jesus" (Gal. 3.28). This *concilium* closes the
gap which is, in Jewish eyes, the basic religious division, that between the people, who are called, and the sinful Gentiles; for God
has "called not only of the Jews but also of the Gentiles" (Rom.
9.24; cf. 1 Cor. 8.18). It closes what is in *Gentile* eyes the basic social division between free men and slaves; for God has called both
free men and slaves (1 Cor. 7.20–24). The Holy Spirit is to be
poured out upon all (Acts 2). The Gospel is to be preached as a witness to all peoples throughout the whole world, the whole *oikoumene*
(Matt. 24.14), and the word of the message has gone forth to the
ends of the *oikoumene* (Rom. 10.18). The *ekklesia* is indeed a *concilium oecumenicum*.

What, then, is the authentic ideological starting-point for a theology of the ecumenical council? It is to be found in the proposition
that I have just been briefly developing; the *Church herself* is the ecumenical council, the assembly of the faithful called together from
the whole inhabited globe, convoked by God himself through Christ
in the Spirit. This proposition now needs to be further developed
and brought in relation with what is *ordinarily* called an ecumenical
council, that is, the ecumenical council convoked by *men*. What is
the relation between the ecumenical council convoked by *men* and
the ecumenical council convoked by *God*—the Church? This can be
stated in a proposition which may be taken as the second fundamen-

tal one in a theology of the ecumenical council: the ecumenical council convoked by men is the *representation* of the ecumenical council convoked by God, which is the Church.

The ecumenical council convoked by men as a representation of the Church

This proposition has two functions, negatively critical and positively constructive:

(1) The ecumenical council convoked by men is *only* a representation of the ecumenical council convoked by God; the ecumenical council convoked by men is not simply the Church, but only a representation, projection and making-present of the Church. This has a double significance.

In the first place, the Church is essentially the ecumenical council convoked *by God;* as such she is not dependent in her very substance on this particular projection of her substance, the projection of herself in an ecumenical council convoked *by men.* The Church can exist without ecumenical councils. In actual fact the Church carried on during her first three vitally important centuries, and during many subsequent centuries, without any ecumenical councils. In actual fact the first ecumenical council of Church history goes back to the initiative not of the Church's leaders but of the pagan government, in the person of the Emperor, still a pagan and retaining the title, office and influence of Pontifex Maximus.

Secondly, if the *existence* of the ecumenical council convoked by men is not necessarily implied by the Church's nature as the ecumenical council convoked by God, still less is any particular *form* for it implied, given that it really does provide a representation of the Church. The ecumenical council convoked by men can manifest and represent the Church in the most various historical forms. The evidence of Church history shows that this variability affects principally the person and office of the man who convokes the council and presides over it, the range of those taking part, the subjects discussed, the procedure, and the necessity for explicit approbation. Hence, having regard in particular to the reunion of separated

Christians and possible future negotiations for union at some later council, it is extremely necessary not to turn questions of current law or ceremonial into questions of dogma. We should rather examine the law as it is at present to see what could be changed in it and what is really, on account of the Gospel of Jesus Christ, unalterable. The distinction between *ius divinum* and *ius humanum,* discerned according to the Gospel of Jesus Christ, is something which might be of absolutely fundamental importance for a council and reunion. It is not given enough attention, with regard either to the ecumenical council or to the Church's life in general. While the Protestant Churches have, as it seems to us Catholics, sometimes, in their ecclesiastical structure, dangerously weakened or even lost the framework, the Catholic Church has, for safety's sake, strengthened the structural frame and overlaid and cluttered it up here and there in various ways which often do more to impede the sight of the non-Catholic observer than the picture itself does to draw him to thoughtful contemplation.

(2) The ecumenical council convoked by men *really is* a representation of the ecumenical council convoked by God. The very first account of Church councils that we find in Christian literature gives extraordinarily clear testimony to the council's being understood in this way. Tertullian says: ". . . at certain places in the Greek lands those councils of all the Churches are held, by which at once matters of greater importance are dealt with in common and there is given a representation of the whole of Christendom of such a kind as must inspire reverence. And how fitting it is to gather together under the good sign of faith in Christ! Behold how good and pleasant it is for brothers to dwell together in unity!"[6]

When even two or three are gathered together in the name of the Lord, he himself is in the midst of them. Even in as small an assembly as that—and quite especially in the liturgy—communion with Christ is made present, the Church herself is present. This little assembly is not indeed simply and absolutely *the* Church; the Church is the *whole,* the whole of the people of God, of the body of Christ, of the temple of the Holy Spirit. But even this little assembly makes present, *represents,* the Church. And if even this little assembly does so, how much more must the great assembly, gathered to deliberate or decide on important questions affecting the whole Church, which therefore has behind it not just a few individuals but the whole, the *oikoumene,* the people of God from the whole inhabited world. The representation of the *concilium* of the Church as convoked by God which is offered by this *concilium* convoked by men from the whole *oikoumene* to deliberate and decide in common, and arrange and set in order the affairs of the Church, is not, indeed, of that most intensive sort provided by the common act of the liturgy, but neither, on the other hand, is it of that most general sort presented by the coming together of individual Christians; it is of an altogether special sort. The Church is here represented not only (great though even this is) in a *partial, particular way* but (and the whole is not merely "greater" than the part) in a total, all-embracing, in fact, *ecumenical* way. It is precisely thus that the ecumenical council convoked by men represents the *ecclesia una, sancta, catholica et apostolica.*

The assembling of the individual Churches scattered over the *oikoumene* and so different amongst themselves—Churches of every country and part of the world, of every race, language and culture, representing every form of state and society—makes present the visible-invisible *unity* of the whole Church as a particular, concrete event. But precisely because the unity which this assembly makes into a concrete event is a unity of various and mutually different *individual Churches,* it is plain that the council which makes this unity present as an event at the same time makes world-wide *catholicity* present as an event. Thus we have the ecumenical council convoked by men as the representation of the *ecclesia una et catholica,* but—*ecclesia sancta?* The history of the councils is enough to keep us clear of the illusory notion that we can count on an ecumenical council's being an assembly of particularly holy (as it might be, canonizable) men, a *concilium sanctorum.* On the contrary, the ecumenical council convoked by men is once again a true image of the ecumenical council convoked by God, in that in both cases it is *men* who are convoked, and consequently the *concilium* is never exempt from the human and sinful element. Yet in the Church's tradition not only the ecumenical council convoked by God but also the ecumenical council convoked by men is called holy and even *sacrosanctum*.

But we remember not only that in the earliest times the attribute "holy" was applied with striking rarity to the Church, but also that its primary sense was by no means that of the moral holiness of the members but of the Church's relationship to God (holy in the sense of "heavenly") and above all to the Holy Ghost (holy in the sense of "spiritual"); and again, that the original question asked at baptism in the apostolic tradition was not in the simplified form, "Do you believe in the holy Church?" but, very precisely, "Do you believe in the Holy Ghost *within* the holy Church for the resurrection of the flesh?"[7] It is because of the Holy Ghost that the Church of men and of sinners can be called holy.

So, if the ecumenical council convoked by men is to represent the ecumenical council convoked by God, it can only be in the power of that sanctifying Spirit who, as the Spirit of Jesus Christ, lives and works in the Church; who, Jesus promised, would remain in the Church for ever (Jn. 14.16 f.), would teach her all things and bring all things to her mind that Jesus had said (14.26), who would not bear witness of himself to any new truth, but to the truth of Jesus, and who would lead her into the fullness of that truth (16.13 f.). This is how the Holy Spirit works in the Church, according to Jesus' promise, and hence also how he works in that special event which represents her—the ecumenical council convoked by men. It is this that makes permissible the audacity of that by-no-means obvious or matter-of-course "and" which appeared, according to the Acts of the Apostles (15.28), in the decree of the apostolic Council of Jerusalem, and which acted as a guiding light to later councils and their decrees: "It has seemed good to the Holy Ghost *and* to us . . ." In the Holy Ghost, the ecumenical council convoked by men is a representation of the *ecclesia sancta*. And of the *ecclesia apostolica* too? We shall be discussing this almost immediately, but first there is something else to be pointed out.

A credible or an incredible representation?

Representation of the *ecclesia una, sancta, catholica* by the ecumenical council convoked by men implies not only a gift bestowed upon it but a task, and a severe task. Ecumenical councils never have been inoffensive periodical general assemblies meeting in quiet and peaceful times, but always gatherings of the Church in times of unrest and external danger. It was when the conscience of the Church had been shocked by heresy, or by tasks set her by history, not yet mastered and calling for a decision on the part of the whole Church, that the hour of the ecumenical council would strike. In such times of stormy unrest and new decision, it matters very much whether this representation of the *ecclesia una, sancta, catholica* takes shape only in a rough-and-ready sense or, on the contrary, *well,* that is to say *credibly* (for men both inside and outside the *ecclesia*). We may take warning today from the bitter words of Gregory Nazianzen, Doctor of the Church, quoted by Martin Luther in his work *On Councils and Churches*:[8]

> To tell the truth, I hold that one should flee from every council of bishops, since I have never known good to come of any council; not even the removal of abuses . . . but always ambition or quarrels over advancement. . . .[9]

It is *not* a credible representation of the *ecclesia una* when the council is merely an external (though perhaps very magnificent and impressive) manifestation of unity, something like a well-organized totalitarian party congress, where those in charge of the congress have a very good idea of how to employ various methods and tricks in the agenda and procedure so as to reduce free initiative to a minimum from the start, and where an uncritical, enthusiastic *placet* to the Führer's plans is the one badge of loyalty. The *ecclesia una* is given *credible* representation when unity at the ecumenical council is a genuinely interior unity of faith and love, thankfully embracing all the varieties of individual opinion in a genuinely biblical *koinonia,* which does not consist simply of a centralizing link between each individual and a visible organizational center, but above all in a brotherly *communio* of individuals *with one another* in the spirit of the glorified Lord of the Church.

The *ecclesia catholica* would not be given credible representation if the council did not really give utterance to all the individual Churches with their needs and requirements, their history and traditions; if some particular individual Church were to impose its special tradition (in devotion, doctrine, law) on the others; if decisions were not—according to the best conciliar tradition—reached by unanimity but by a forced transformation of minorities into majorities (as by over-representation of some individual Church in terms of votes, or by some all-too-pointed "hint from higher up"). The *ecclesia catholica* is given a *credible* representation when, on the one hand, all the individual Churches are able to integrate that which is their own into the decision of the whole council, so as to express the true tradition of the whole Church, of the *sensus ecclesia,* and so that what is given to the Church is not dispute and division but peace in freedom; and when, on the other hand, the council bears in mind in everything it does not only those who are represented there but also those who—even though they may be baptized Christians—are not taking part in the council, for reasons in which the *ecclesia catholica* is not guiltless.

The *ecclesia sancta* would *not* be given credible representation if, in the ecumenical council convoked by men, the real workings of the Spirit were crushed by party interests and diplomacy, if personal interests rather than revelation, human law rather than the Gospel of Jesus Christ, preservation of the *status quo* and opportunist politics rather than renewal of the Church, were to loom in the foreground. The *ecclesia sancta* is given *credible* representation when the council does the will of the Father who is in heaven, when it listens to Jesus Christ who speaks to the Church through the Scriptures, when it is open to the Holy Spirit, who breathes where he will, even outside any official ministry.

The ecumenical council convoked by men; a representation of

the *ecclesia una, sancta, catholica*—and *apostolica*? This brings us to an important point.

The ecumenical council and the laity

We now have to think about Martin Luther. After having twice appealed from the Pope, as being ill-informed, to a free council, Luther traced out a program for a reforming council in his address "To the Christian Nobility of the German Nation Concerning Reform of the Christian Estate" (1520).[10] He states here, as the third wall which the Romanists have erected for their defence: "Threaten them with a council, and they declare that none can summon a council save only the Pope."[11] In addition to arguments drawn from conciliar history, Luther counters this by bringing into play one of his fundamental insights into the nature of the Church, the universal priesthood of all believers.

> So, if need arise, and the Pope is a hindrance to Christendom, it is for anyone to act who most readily can, like a loyal member of the whole Body, so that there may be a true, free council held; and this none can do so well as the secular sword, especially since they too are Christians, they too are priests, they too are spiritual, they too have power in all things. . . .[12]

What does Catholic theology have to say about this? There are three points to be conceded:

(1) As far as concerns the person and office of the one who summons it, there is, as we have seen, nothing binding laid down by revelation about an ecumenical council as convoked by men (assuming that the Church is truly represented).[13] There is no tradition that the Apostolic Council (Acts 15.6) was convoked by St. Peter, and history shows us numerous instances of councils convoked by laymen.

(2) The doctrine of the universal priesthood is one of the fun-

damental truths of Catholic ecclesiology. We Catholics also believe that *all* Christians are summoned to the ecumenical council convoked by *God,* which is the Church as "a chosen generation, a kingly priesthood, a holy nation" (1 Pet. 20.9).

(3) As regards participation by the laity in an ecumenical council convoked by *men,* there is this to be said: Since the Church as convoked by God is the ecumenical council of the *whole* royal and priestly people of God, no dogmatic reasons can be adduced for ruling out, *a priori,* the participation of the laity in the work and decisions of the ecumenical council as convoked by men. The Council of Jerusalem did not consist solely of apostles; Acts 15.4 explicitly refers to the whole community as receiving the delegates from Antioch, and 15.22 to the participation of the community in the decision. But the pattern for the first ecumenical councils was set not so much by the Council of Jerusalem as by the regional synods of the second and third centuries, to which Tertullian refers. It makes no difference here what explanation one adopts of how these synods arose; whether as extended parochial assemblies (R. Sohm), or meetings modelled on the civil *concilium provinciale* (E. Friedberg), or as arising from the needs of the Church, for the discussion of difficult problems (K. von Schwartz), or as having grown out of the sense of unity and the lively contacts between the early communities, with representatives from several communities coming together to discuss and decide on matters affecting those communities in common (A. Hauck). In any case it would be hard to establish, according to the historians, that these synods originally consisted only of bishops. Remember once more the importance, in the concrete, of the relationship of the layman Constantine to the first ecumenical council; he formally ordered the bishops to hold the council, he determined who, and how many, should take part in it, the place of assembly and the subject of its deliberations; he appointed the organizing committee, he personally intervened in what was done, he pressed for the adoption of the Nicene formula, his recognition made it legally binding, he imposed penalties on those who refused to sign it; he published the decision on the

celebration of Easter, and made it obligatory for the bishops to observe it; finally, he bore a large part of the costs of the council.

Think, again, of the influence exercised by early medieval kings on the provincial synods which became so important at that period; when, for instance, history was made at the Synod of Sutri in 1046, where Henry III cleared the way for papal reform by banishing three rival popes. Even the papal general councils of the high Middle Ages included the secular powers as well as bishops, abbots and representatives of chapters; and these laymen had their part in the deliberations, though not actually the right to vote. At the councils of Pisa and Constance the number of bishops and abbots present in person was exceeded by that of the procurators for those who did not appear and representing various ecclesiastical bodies (universities, chapters, monasteries), and by that of the doctors of theology and canon law, who had full voting rights. Even at Trent and the Vatican it was not only bishops who took part; the Emperor and the Christian princes were invited to the Council of Trent as representing the laity, either to come themselves or at least to send representatives. The Vatican Council was the first occasion on which this was not done. Even in the present Code of Canon Law not only bishops but also cardinal-priests and deacons and the heads of orders have full rights of participation in the council, while those called in as experts in theology and law have a voice in discussion though not in the final decisions (cf. canon 223). This is the present position in canon law. But on the basis of our theological survey, we can say that no fundamental dogmatic reason could be brought against having the laity directly, and not only indirectly (through the bishops), represented at the ecumenical council, in a form adopted to contemporary conditions. The situation of the world and the Church being what in fact they are— the "hour of the layman," as it is being called—this is not something to be regarded as out of the question. Rather, it should be given serious consideration.

The council and ecclesiastical office

So what is valid in Luther's conciliar theology needs to be recognized on the Catholic side today. But at the same time there is a critical question to be put to Luther: Is the Church of Jesus Christ truly represented in a humanly convoked ecumenical council solely on the basis of the universal priesthood of all believers? We return here to the point whose treatment we postponed earlier; the representation of the *ecclesia apostolica*. How does the ecumenical council represent the *ecclesia apostolica?* Luther would answer, in so far as it assembles in the apostolic succession, meaning in the spirit of the Apostles, in an interior agreement with them. His answer is right. But we then have to ask: And when is a council in agreement with the Apostles? Luther would answer with the second great requirement of his conciliar theology, as expressed seven years before his death in his work *Of Councils and Churches* (1539)[14]: The council is in agreement with the Apostles if it is in agreement with Holy Scripture, which the Apostles have transmitted to us in the Church and to whose authority both Church and council do and must submit. Here, too, Catholic theology can be in accord with Luther's answer. For according to Catholic theology, too, the ecumenical council stands not above but under the word of God; it cannot proclaim any new revelation but only expound the old afresh; its words are not the inspired word of God but only human words spoken with the assistance of the Spirit. Being words with human limitations—though, thanks to the assistance of the Spirit promised to the Church, always teaching truth and not error—the words of a council can, even according to *Humani Generis,*[15] be clarified, supplemented and brought to greater perfection. St. Augustine goes so far as to use the word *emendare,* "to correct," in this connection.[16]

But the next question is: Who, then, is it who is entrusted with the full power of proclaiming the Gospel, and with the leadership of the Church which is summoned into being and gathered together by the Gospel? At this point, the subject of the humanly convoked ecumenical council raises the problem which is central to the

Catholic-Protestant dialogue today; the problem of ecclesiastical office and its function. Is it this same problem, perhaps, that lies behind the surely striking fact that, because of her form of ecclesiastical order, and despite all the misunderstandings and misuses of ecclesiastical office which have occurred and will always occur in her, it is the Catholic Church and she alone who is in a position to venture on an ecumenical council (at least in her own fashion) and thus continue the tradition of the early Church?

On the other hand, even Luther and Melanchthon were, at bottom, afraid to hold a Protestant Council in the later stages of the Reformation, since it could be expected to produce a weakening rather than a strengthening of unity in their Church. The question of office and authority in Church and council arose even then, as it arises today for the World Council of Churches, which does not set out to be a council in this sense. I am not here dealing with the problem of office. Catholic theology today is once more looking at ecclesiastical office in a more scriptural way; as a gift of the Holy Ghost, not at man's disposal, deriving from the glorified Lord for the service of the brethren, in order to put into operation, by the fullness of Christ's power, the work of atonement completed by Christ, in the proclamation of the Gospel, the administration of the sacraments, and the guidance of the Church. And hence it sees the succession of apostolic office not as an automatic transmission of office through ordination but as the outward sign of the free action of the Spirit who gives that gift, taking men into the service of the message of Christ in an act which both presupposes faith and demands an apostolic disposition of mind. But Catholic theology cannot at the same time fail to press Protestant theology for an answer on what it believes concerning the succession not only of apostolic belief and confession of faith, but also of the special apostolic office for the preservation of that belief and confession of faith; and on what it has to say about that giving of the Spirit in an apostolic vocation, blessing and commissioning, in association with the laying on of hands and prayer, to which there is clear witness in Scripture; of that

ordination which confers the grace of office and legitimizes it in
the eyes of the community and which, according to the pastoral
epistles, is something to be passed on to others. All these questions
call for long, patient discussion. But bit by bit we are coming to
understand each other better, even on these problems.

But the point here, in considering the theology of the ecumenical council, is this: The insight of the Catholic Church, with, on
this matter, not only the whole conciliar tradition of two thousand
years behind it but also the witness of Scripture (especially the account in Acts of the so-called "Council of the Apostles"), holds one
thing as indispensable; just as the Church convoked by *God* is not
something amorphous but a structurally articulated council, with
the special vocation of the Apostles playing a special part in it, so
the ecumenical council convoked by *men*, if it is really to represent
the Church, must not be an amorphous collection of individual
members at random but must reflect the structure of the Church.
This means that ecclesiastical office, and in this case most especially the *episkopoi* who represent individual local Churches, must
be asserted in an appropriate way, so that they shall be able, in
this humanly convoked ecumenical council, to carry out the task
laid upon them of proclaiming the Word and giving leadership to
the Church. The *episkopoi* who represent the individual Churches
do not have the powers and authority of their ministry as delegated to them by the people; it is the Holy Ghost who, in succession to the Apostles (Acts 14.22), has placed them as bishops to
shepherd the *ekklesia* of God, which he has purchased with his
own blood (20.28). Hence the *episkopoi*, though they do represent
the individual Churches, are not simply functionaries of the community, and the ecumenical council convoked by men, though it
does represent the whole Church, is not simply a parliament of
the Church. Conciliarism in this sense is incompatible with the
Scriptures. This especially needs to be clearly stated when one is
trying to recover the good elements in the conciliar theory, whose
sound beginnings go back not to Marsilius of Padua and William
of Ockham but to the twelfth-century canonists.[17] Because of this

spiritual office received from the Holy Spirit, it is the bishops who are pre-eminently (though not exclusively) called to represent their individual Churches, and thus the whole Church, at the ecumenical council convoked by men, and to do so, precisely because of their office, with individual responsibility, each taking, in conscience, his own personal decision, under the Word of God.

The council and the Petrine office

We come finally to the Petrine office. All the difficulties besetting both the reunion of separated Christians and the holding of a general council of the *whole* of Christendom, both the theological and dogmatic difficulties and the practical, existential ones, are apt either to begin or end at this point. It often seems to be a hopeless problem. I have gone into it in detail elsewhere.[18] As concerns the theology of the ecumenical council, two points need to be summarily indicated: (1) According to the Catholic conception, the Petrine office has the special function, in the ecumenical council convoked by God (the Church), of representing and guaranteeing the unity of the Church for the sake of charity and the strengthening of faith. Hence it is also fundamentally necessary that the Petrine office be recognized as having a special position in the ecumenical council convoked by men. (2) As in the Church, so in the humanly convoked ecumenical council, the Petrine office can be present in quite varying ways. The relationship of the Petrine office to Church and council, though having a permanent essential structure, is subject to historical change. No particular historical development (whether in a centralizing or decentralizing direction) can be regarded in advance as good or bad. It has rather to be measured by the standard of Scriptural revelation. With regard to the present situation, and to that reunion of separated Christians for which we long, there is this to be said: Both the witness of the primitive Church in Scripture and the history of the Church and the councils show that it is possible for the Petrine office, without compromising its essential nature, to remain very much in the background in relation to Church and council, and that precisely for the sake of the unity of the Church. There is a very definite distinction between the necessity for a center in the Church and papal centralism, between the necessity for the Petrine office and papalism. As J. Ratzinger has recently with justice pointed out,[19] Vatican I condemned not only extreme episcopalism but also extreme papalism. What Johann Adam Möhler of Tübingen wrote 135 years ago is still very much to the point:

> Two extremes are possible in the life of the Church, and both of them are really egoism: when either *everyone* or just *one* person wants to be everything. In the second case the bond of unity grows so close and love so warm that it is impossible not to suffocate; in the first, everything falls apart and it grows so cold that everyone freezes. Each of these egoisms gives rise to the other. In fact, neither one person nor everyone should want to be everything; it is only possible for all together to be everything, and for the unity of all to be the whole. This is the idea of the Catholic Church.[20]

One thing is certain: the removal of schism is going to call for sacrifices from *everyone* involved (none of whom, certainly, can be held blameless), even from the Petrine office. The one ecumenical council in Church history which succeeded at that time, with indescribable effort, in restoring unity at least to the Western Church, the Ecumenical Council of Constance, shows how great a sacrifice the Church can demand of the Petrine office for the sake of unity. The idea is widespread in our Church at the present time, and the Pope himself does not seem to be averse to it, that the onesided definition made at Vatican I, and the over-centralization connected with it, need to be corrected, chiefly at the practical level. Whether the Second Vatican Council will succeed in doing this remains to be seen. But even if (as I myself do not expect) it were to be unsuccessful in this respect, the fact that an ecumenical council has been convoked at all after the First Vatican Council is in itself an extraordinarily clear and irrevocable pointer in this direction. Just as it is the special function of the Petrine office to represent and guarantee the *unity* of the Church, so also is it the special function of the *episkopoi,* coming together in an ecumenical council convoked by men, to represent and guarantee the apostolically *collegiate* character of the Church and her leadership. The ecumenical council, which according to the present state of the law, *"suprema* pollet in universam Ecclesiam potestate" (canon 228), is thus an impressive demonstration that the leadership of the Church as a whole is not simply the affair of one individual but is at the same time, by God's convocation, the business of the *collegium apostolorum* or *episcoporum.* The *episkopoi* do not come together to speak with greater or less authority about the situation of their own dioceses, and thus indirectly about that of the whole Church; nor do they come together to give the Pope advice; they come together to decide, directly and authoritatively, as being the supreme level of the ministry, matters of importance for the whole Church, and so to exercise their part in the universal leadership of the Church.

The calling of an ecumenical council has brought up a number of long-standing questions, both for Catholic and Protestant Christians. For both Catholics and Protestants, the fact that they have been brought up is, even on its own, a great sign of hope for theology and for the Church. My present purpose is not to solve nor even to state all these questions. It is simply to work out the basic starting-point for a theology of the ecumenical council: The Church is the ecumenical council convoked by God, and the council convoked by men is the special representation of the Church. It seems to me that this is a starting-point, not merely canonical, nor merely historical, but authentically theological, which might be a help in leading both Catholic and Protestant Christians and theologians to further fruitful reflection. And it is reflection on ourselves that we all need so badly. Let us hope that this Second Vatican Council is not going to serve any proclamatory, self-assured extolling of herself by the Church, but rather a humble and practical Christian reflection upon herself, reflection which will work for a bold, large-scale renewal of the Church in the light of the Gospel of Jesus Christ, aimed at the unity of Christians, which the Holy Ghost alone will be able to achieve.

NOTES:

[1] On all that follows here, cf. the documentation and further discussion in H. Küng, *Strukturen der Kirche,* Freiburg, Bâle and Vienna (1962). (*Quaestiones Disputatae, 17.*)

[2] L. Mohler, Freiburg-im-Breisgau (1934).

[3] VII, 7, 5 (*PG,* 20, 651).

[4] *De Ieiunio,* 13, 6–7 (*CC, 2,* 1272); cf. *De Pudicitia,* 10, 12 (*CC, 2,* 1301); and later on Cyprian, *Ep. 75,* 4 (*PL,* 3, 1205 f.).

[5] Cf. Ernout-Meillet, *Dictionnaire étymologique de la langue latine,* Paris (1959).

[6] *De Pœnitentia,* 13, 6 (*CC,* II, 1272).

[7] Cf. P. Nautin, *Je crois à l'Esprit Saint dans la Sainte Eglise pour la résurrection de la chair. Etude sur l'histoire et la . . . théologique du Symbole,* Paris (1947).

[8] *WA,* 50, 604.

[9] *Ep. 130 ad Procopium* (*PG,* 37, 225).

[10] *WA,* 6, 404–65.

[11] *WA,* 6, 406.

[12] *WA,* 6. 413.

[13] The concrete implications of this will be developed in the next section.

[14] *WA,* 50, 509–653.

[15] Cf. *AAS* (1950), p. 566; C.T.S. edition, *False Trends in Modern Teaching,* p. 9, para. 16.

[16] *De Baptismo,* 2, 3, 4 (*PL,* 43, 128).

[17] See B. Tierney, *Foundations of the Conciliar Theory. The Contributions of the Medieval Canonists from Gratian to the Great Schism,* Cambridge (1955).

[18] See *The Council, Reform and Reunion,* pp. 132–142; *Strukturen der Kirche,* pp. 206–355.

[19] "Primat, Episkopat und successio apostolica," *Catholica,* 13 (1959), p. 264.

[20] *Die Einheit in der Kirche oder das Prinzip des Catholizismus,* ed. J. R. Geiselmann, p. 237.

5

Vatican II: a Good Start

IT IS NOT giving away any secrets to say that morale on the eve
of Vatican II, even in Rome itself, was none too good. Optimism
was not in evidence. There was nothing but problems, worries and
questions in all directions: How is anything going to work, with
these delegations and these schemata? Is not the "open" element
only an insignificant minority amongst this multitude of over two
thousand bishops? What is it possible to achieve here? Hasn't everything really been settled and finished in advance by all that any-
thing-but-reassuring process of preparation? The ghost of the Roman Synod walked again, and there was talk of a *concilio lampo,* a
lightning council with no real discussion. But the pessimists were
proved wrong; everything was better than anyone had expected.
Soon the first rays of light began to appear.

The Shepherd

It was not only non-Catholic Christians and those alien to the
Church who were put off by the opening ceremony, with its completely non-contemporary Baroque pomp. Many bishops, too, and
from different nations and continents, found it sad that papal ceremonial should be the very thing to remain totally unaffected by the
faintest breath from that movement of liturgical renewal which is
making itself felt throughout the Church. There was so much that
could have been dispensed with, whereas the one important thing
was lacking—the communion of the faithful. Participation by the

bishops, who had all had to celebrate their private Masses beforehand, was slight. The ancient formula of a conciliar concelebration
of all the bishops with the Pope had been carefully ignored. It was
one more case of having to deplore the passing over by traditional-
ists of good old Catholic traditions in favour of other ideas of no long
standing. Many Christians, both in and outside the Catholic
Church, had expected that at the same time as the invocation of the
Holy Spirit the Council would make a confession of guilt; a confession of guilt on the part of the Catholic Church, who bears her share
of responsibility for the wretchedness of the world and for the division of Christendom; a confession of guilt like that made by the German hierarchy in their pastoral letter for the opening of the Council, which commanded attention and awakened hope far beyond
the bounds of Germany. It was hardly surprising that no place for
any such confession of guilt could be found within the triumphal
framework of Baroque splendour.

But even here there was a bright spot: Pope John XXIII. No one
held him responsible for all this unseasonable décor. It had got
around that on this occasion, once again, the use of the *sedia gesta-
toria* had had to be simply forced on him. And anyone who saw that
old man, past his eightieth year, coming slowly down the *scala regia*
and only then, finally, mounting the *sedia,* had the immediate impression that for this humble and unassuming Shepherd the whole
mass of external pomp was a matter of profound indifference. Protestants who could take little pleasure in all the solemnity were
helped over much of what was unintelligible in the opening ceremony by the sight of the Pope's prayerful face; grave, withdrawn,
never for a moment distracted by all the religious "performance"
going on round him. Not until the Pope was greeting the cardinals
in turn, exchanging with each one a few informal, friendly words,
did the well-known smile appear on his face, beaming with simplicity, amiability and deep affection. Is it not a good omen for
Vatican II that it is being held under this particular pope, who
has so much more of an evangelical character about him than many
of his splendid predecessors?

Rejection of doctrinalism

The Pope's opening address to the Council has been described as colourless. This is a mistake. Only someone unequipped to hear with Roman ears and sort out the important from the unimportant could say such a thing. On the contrary, this speech was a bold and unmistakable confrontation of the greatest danger threatening Vatican II, along with so many earlier reforming councils: the doctrinalizing of the Council. Reactionary tendencies in doctrine constitute the greatest danger for the Council. But could there have been a clearer disavowal of such tendencies than the Pope made in his opening speech? "The salient point of this council is not, therefore, a discussion of one article or another of the fundamental doctrine of the Church, which has repeatedly been taught by the Fathers and the ancient and modern theologians, and which is presumed to be well known and familiar to all. For this a council was not necessary." What the Pope is looking for is rather a proclamation of all this in a way adapted to our times: "A step forward towards a doctrinal penetration and a formation of consciences, in faithful and perfect conformity to the authentic doctrine, which, however, should be studied and expounded through the methods of research and through the literary forms of modern thought." As against those who suspect "modernism" in every fresh formulation and renewal of doctrine, the Pope says: "One thing is the substance of the ancient doctrine of the *depositum fidei,* and another is the way in which it is presented; and it is this that must be taken into great consideration, with patience if necessary, everything being measured in the forms and proportions of a *magisterium* which is prevalently pastoral in character."

But are there not errors in existence today, too, and do not these errors have to be fought? It is precisely the Church, ruled as she is by the Lord's abiding truth, who has no need to get excited over the often swiftly changing opinions of men, or to lose patience with them; she can meet the errors of the day and rise calmly above them: "At the outset of the Second Vatican Council, it is evident as always that the truth of the Lord will remain forever. We see, in fact, as one age succeeds the other, that the opinions of men follow one another and exclude each other, and often errors vanish as quickly as they arise, like fog before the sun." In any case, in the present situation a different kind of combat against error is called for, not the method of condemnatory severity but that of helpful compassion: "Ever has the Church opposed these errors; frequently she has condemned them with the greatest severity. Nowadays, however, the spouse of Christ prefers to make use of the medicine of mercy rather than that of severity. She considers that she meets the needs of the present day by demonstrating the validity of her teaching rather than by condemnations." And when men themselves already perceive that these things are errors, it is not necessary for the Church to let herself go in repeated condemnations and moralizing admonitions: "Not, certainly, that there is a lack of fallacious teaching, opinions and dangerous concepts to be guarded against and dissipated, but they are so evidently in contrast with the right norm of honesty, and have produced such lethal fruits, that by now it would seem that men of themselves are inclined to condemn them, particularly those ways of life which despise God and his law, excessive confidence in technical progress, and well-being based exclusively on the comforts of life." It is precisely by following this course of mercy and not severity that the Church can show herself as ecumenical in breadth: "That being so, the Catholic Church, raising the torch of religious truth by means of this Ecumenical Council, desires to show herself to be the loving mother of all, benign, patient, full of mercy and goodness towards all the children separated from her." The speech, striking a note of hope throughout its length, came to a climax in a call for unity among Christians and all men.

Is not this a new strain? All this is a clear rejection of any purely negative, polemical anti-Protestantism; of any negatively static, moralizing anti-modernism; and it is also (the Pope's silence on this point excited general attention) a rejection of that southern European type of anti-Communism which, while tolerating appalling social abuses, has sought (in vain) to combat Communism (when freely chosen, not under duress) with rhetoric, negative safeguards and unenforceable decrees of excommunication, instead of overcoming it by preaching the Good News to rich and poor alike and by a positive, constructive social and economic policy.

The ecumenical slant

The presence of other Christian communions at the Second Vatican Council is more significant than any number of ecumenical proclamations. It is generally known that there were several circles in Rome who did not wish to have non-Catholic observers. When one thinks of how long Rome had more or less ignored the other Christian communions, and in particular the World Council of Churches at Geneva, and had maintained no official relations with them, it is easy to register what a tremendous change is implied in the presence of Orthodox and Protestant observers at an ecumenical council of the Catholic Church.

Many of the observers had expected that they would be allotted some fairly unobtrusive place for the opening ceremony. Instead, they had the place of honor immediately beside the papal altar, plainly visible to all. Countless millions who were following the ceremony on television had this fact impressed on them. It is the same thing again at the sessions of the Council itself; the best place in the *aula*—immediately next to the *praesidium* and the Council secretaries, immediately opposite the College of Cardinals—is the observers' tribune. From this spot, assisted by interpreters from the Secretariat for Unity, they follow all that happens in the Council, seeing and hearing everything; good speeches and bad, progressive and conservative, short and long; the unrestrained murmurs and the liberating bursts of laughter; attacks in good Latin on the Latin of the Church, and defences of it in bad Latin. They are there when a curial cardinal is cut short, amidst applause, for overstepping his time; they are there when a projected decree is given tentative praise or subjected to violent attack, when it is accepted or rejected. They arrive at and depart from the basilica with the Fathers of the Coun-

cil and the theologians; they meet them in the Council's famous cof-
fee-bar, a place of innumerable exchanges of views and important
contacts. They receive the schemata to be discussed just as the
Fathers of the Council do, and have access to all conciliar documents. And, unlike the Fathers, they are even allowed to report to
their brethren of their own faith on the doings of the Council.

Certainly, the observers cannot be in agreement with everything
that goes on in the *aula*. But there can scarcely be one of them who
has not spoken in praise of the confidence that has been placed in
them. The presence of these representatives of non-Catholic Christendom (about half of all Christians are non-Catholics) stands as a
perpetual admonition to the Fathers of the Council not to forget the
unity of Christians in all that they do and leave undone, but to use
every means to further it and realize it. The course of the debates
has shown, to an increasing degree, that their presence is anything
but useless. The observers make the task of the Fathers all the easier
for them by the fact that they follow what is done not only as outsiders but with intimate understanding and great discretion. Of
course they know that the Catholic Church cannot, any more than
anyone else, achieve everything in a single day. They are aware of
inadequacies and weaknesses, but also of the tremendous ecumenical awakening and the swift progress made even during the first
weeks of the Council. The Catholic Church is now ecumenically
oriented. That is something irrevocable.

The Council as a real personality

All the fears felt that Vatican II would merely constitute a huge
appendage and extension of the Roman Curia, completely dependent on the Curia's preparations and management, have been dis-
proved. In the first hour of the first session the Council established
itself as having a personality of its own. Historically, the credit for
this goes, as is well known, to Cardinals Liénart of Lille and Frings
of Cologne and the bishops who ranged themselves with them. The
selection of names for the commissions had been badly prepared.

Those who prepared them had expected that, for lack of other possibilities, the Council would simply endorse the lists of names of those who had been appointed, exclusively by the Curia, to the preparatory commissions. But just as the voting was supposed to begin came the two short speeches of the two cardinals, calling, amidst rapt and strained attention, for a postponement of the election and better preparation. The episcopate roared its applause, and the Council had found itself. The Fathers discovered, to their astonishment, the truth of the statement made in canon 228, § 1 of the Code of Canon Law: "Concilium oecumenicum suprema pollet in universam ecclesiam potestate"—"The ecumenical council enjoys supreme power over the universal Church."

From now on the Council firmly went its own way, even in face of opposition. Neither quotations from the Code nor papal encyclicals nor disciplinary decrees of earlier councils or of the Curia (e.g., *Veterum Sapientia*) had any power to check or put a brake on the apostolic freedom with which the Fathers pursued their discussions of the needs and worries and hopes and expectations of the Church and the world. But the Pope himself holds the collegiate episcopate of the Church in respect, as it grows more and more conscious as time goes on of its power as the apostolic community; and he safeguards the freedom of the Council with wise interventions which the Council itself welcomes. Linked to the Council by television, he takes a delight in the lively discussions, and says with a chuckle in public: "Chi va piano, va sano e lontano!—Who goes slow, goes safe and far!" Is it to be wondered at that John XXIII, unlike Pius IX during Vatican I, enjoys the sympathy of the entire conciliar assembly?

World-wide Catholicity

The desire of Rome was that there should be no committees of bishops in connection with the Council: "No small councils round the great Council!" But they became necessary as early as the improved preparations for the elections. Thus it was shown from the start that the Catholic Church consists not only of the universal Church but at the same time of local Churches. The committees and meetings of bishops were of decisive importance throughout all those weeks. This is where questions were talked out, theologians gave lectures on the problems under discussion, and numerous contacts were made.

This did not lead to some sort of nationalist grouping or federalist separatism. On the contrary. It was only in this way that all-embracing catholicity became a concrete reality. The committees of bishops made it possible to have a truly Catholic representation of the various local Churches on the conciliar commissions. It was in fact the episcopate of central and northern Europe (Belgium, Germany, France, Holland, Yugoslavia, Austria, Poland, Switzerland and Scandinavia) who had worked out a really ecumenical list, on which other countries and continents too were represented. It is thanks to this list, to which widespread assent was given, that the election did not lead to any overwhelming of minorities by the majority but to a just apportionment of seats on the commissions.

It deserves special notice that the West-East conflict, the thing that overshadows everything that goes on in the world, has so far been kept out of the Council. It was surely something of an event that the episcopates of West Germany on the one hand and Poland and Yugoslavia on the other, states which maintain no diplomatic relations with each other, were able to get together on one common list for the commissions. This world-wide catholicity is something that the world can see from outside: the impressive representation of different continents, different countries, different colors of skin, different rites; the alternating succession of presidents—the Cardinals of Cologne, Lille, Utrecht, Palermo, Toledo, Antioch, New York, Sidney, Buenos Aires . . . the list of the bishops who speak, which ranges over the entire globe.

The bishops themselves experience this same world-wide catholicity from within. It comes home to them directly that the unity of the Catholic Church does not consist only (as was at one time apt to be thought) in the lines joining everybody to the one center, but at the same time, and just as strongly, in the unity of the bishops and the local Churches with each other. Innumerable links between countries and continents have been forged here, with an exchange of worries and interests, problems and solutions, theories and experiences. The *collegium* of the bishops, the solidarity of local Churches with each other, is a reality which has today been strengthened by being experienced afresh.

Renewal according to the Gospel

The first tome of decrees prepared for the Council contained, as its beginning, a number of dry theological schemata. Was this to be the starting-point? The Council firmly insisted on beginning elsewhere. In full accord with the Pope's opening address, it wanted, right from the start, to give its work not a rigidly doctrinaire but a hopeful and pastoral bent. This was the point of the message, not envisaged by those who did the preparatory work, which the Council decided upon, at the suggestion of the presidents, before the discussion of the first schema.

It gave eloquent expression to the necessity of renewing the Church according to the Gospel:

In this assembly we wish, under the guidance of the Holy Spirit, to seek out *how we are to renew ourselves so that we may correspond more and more closely to the Gospel of Christ.* We wish to proclaim the truth, in its fullness and purity, to the men of our time in such a way that they will understand it and willingly agree with it. Because we are shepherds, we are striving to meet the demands of all those who seek for God, "if haply they may feel after him or find him: although he be not far from every one of us" (Acts 17.27). Therefore, while obeying the will of Christ, who delivered himself up to death "that he might present to himself a glorious Church, not having spot or wrinkle or any such thing, but that it should be holy and without blemish" (Eph. 5.27), we wish to concentrate all our powers and thoughts in order so to renew ourselves, as lead-

ers, and the faithful entrusted to us, that the lovable face of
Jesus Christ will shine out upon unbelievers, as it shines in our
hearts "to give the light of the knowledge of the glory of God"
(2 Cor. 4.6).

The Church's task of serving the brethren in Christ is stressed
with unusual clarity and underlined with the words "the Church
is not here to rule but to serve." Hence the Council will in its deal-
ings be mindful of all who are in need, and therefore calls urgently
for peace among nations and for social justice.

The Council has the task of renewal according to the Gospel, and
thus of preparing for reunion. This was given clear expression by
the fact, along with the Council's message, that it began its work
not with the decrees on doctrine but with the program of renewal
of the liturgy.

Freedom and frankness

In recent years a great deal has been written about freedom in
the Church; not infrequently, with regrets for its absence. At the
Council, its presence was demonstrated day after day. There has
been no reluctance to call grey grey and black black. At bottom,
everyone has been taken by surprise by the degree of freedom of
expression, but everyone practises it; not only in their official utterances in the *aula* but outside the *aula* too, in all the innumerable
conversations, discussions and get-togethers which make up daily
life for the Council Fathers. The most trivial but perhaps most
amusing item in this freedom consists in the endless series of Council jokes which make the rounds of the Fathers and of Rome at
large: such as the two cardinals, well-known conservatives, who
hailed a taxi to take them "to the Council," and found themselves,
by a natural oversight, being driven not to St. Peter's but towards
Trent.

For everyone taking part in it, the freedom of the Council is a great and decisive experience. There are so many who, experiencing for the first time in their lives this free companionship of the bishops, have found things which they had felt, more or less instinctively, being here explicitly formulated; things which they had only dared to think privately being shared by the vast majority of the Church; things which one used only to say quietly to one's friends being spoken aloud in the face of the whole Church, and without any of the usual diplomatic safeguards and wariness. And thus a virtue came into its own again which had for long been almost forgotten in the Church; the virtue of apostolic frankness. And everyone felt what a liberating thing this frankness was, a liberation from fear, from sham, from inaction. This fearless assertion of freedom in the Council is indeed what is needed if there is to be a true renewal of the Church and a reunion of separated Christians.

The Council's freedom has not expressed itself in negative, destructive carping and rebellion, but has kept pressing on to constructive proposals. The Council has thus so far manifested an astonishing openness concerning the needs of the Church and the world and the great tasks which cry out for fulfilment today. There are indeed, as in every reforming council, a conservative wing and a progressive wing. But so far, even after violent debates, it has always been possible to re-establish communications, and that in a fundamentally frank and open relationship. It is no secret that it is the central European episcopate and central European theology which have so far, intellectually, led the field. This has only been possible because the great majority of the bishops of North and South America, Africa and Asia, have been working on the same lines. This alone can explain the result of much of the voting; this alone can explain the fact that it was almost without exception the German and French bishops who got the largest numbers of votes in the election of the commissions. Many of us Europeans had to make a thorough and very positive revision of our notion of the Church in, say, South America. The open readiness for bold reforms of the episcopates of continents outside Europe is one of the great and joyful surprises of Vatican II. It is thus that the "magnificent minority," as it was thought of at the beginning of the Council, has established itself as the Council's "overwhelming majority."

Such was the beginning of Vatican II: a good beginning, better than anyone had ever expected.

6

Procedural Differences

CONCILIAR PROCEDURE and order of business is a matter of the greatest importance for the outcome of Vatican II. Formal decisions on procedure are capable of deciding in advance, to an important extent, about actual concrete matters. It can be a matter of procedure whether a question is dealt with in one way or another way, or even whether it is dealt with at all. It is indisputable that much of the method of procedure worked out for Vatican II was in many respects imperfect, and to some extent more suited to some sort of Roman diocesan synod than to an ecumenical council with serious discussion on its hands. Procedure had to be altered several times during the Council by the Pope. But even this had its advantages. If, for instance, the original standing orders had included an article providing for closure of debate, this would probably, with memories of Vatican I, have been interpreted as a Curial check on freedom of discussion. After the Council itself had discovered how, what with the large number of the Fathers and the contributions they made, a discussion was apt to work itself to death, they were glad to accept a procedural amendment in this sense. There are, of course, various questions about the proceedings which have still not been sufficiently clarified. In dealing with the questions set me here, I shall be as frank as I need to be, but without damage to the conciliar secret.

Voting

Article 39 of the Council's standing orders lays down that in general congregations and on the commissions (apart from elections) a two-thirds majority vote of all the Fathers present is required to give the force of law to any decision. What is the point of this two-thirds majority? It is there as a procedural improvement on the position at Vatican I, when only a bare majority (one-half plus one) was required. The improvement is welcome on both theological and practical grounds. The ecumenical council convoked by men has the great and exacting task of representing not only the external unity of the Church but her profoundly internal, spiritual unity, her unity in the Spirit; and to give it credible representation. It is the *consensus Ecclesiae* that is to be given expression at the Council: the common feeling, the common thinking, the common decision of the whole Church. The common feeling, thought and decision are expressed, in the ecumenical council convoked by men, by *unanimity,* in mind and, so far as can possibly be achieved, in voting, on conciliar decisions, at least so far as binding matters of faith are concerned.[1] The ecumenical council is not a democratic parliament, where it only matters that some sort of numerical majority, the very barest, perhaps, should be found for or against any decision. The ecumenical council is, rather, the representation of the Church and her unity, and this is given credible expression only in unanimity of decision such as is effected by the Spirit. The presence of the Holy Spirit of unity is made manifest not by the larger size of one faction but by the unanimity of all.

The early Church was very conscious of the significance of unanimity in conciliar decisions. No characteristic is so persistently and multifariously referred to in the acts of the synods as that of unanimity. At the medieval general synods there was a similar striving for agreement amounting to moral unanimity. At the Ecumenical Council of Constance, not only was voting taken by nations instead of by individuals, in order to make it impossible for the Italians to form a majority, but unanimity among the nations was also required. At the Council of Trent, Pius IV emphasized, as far as concerned the treatment of important dogmatic questions, that "he desired to define only what was decided with the unanimous consent of the Fathers." This ruling was quoted at the First Vatican

Council by that considerable number of bishops who protested vigorously against the alteration of procedure so as to require only a bare majority, and who never left this question alone right up to the time when the Council broke up.

It goes without saying that moral unanimity (like *certitudo moralis*) is by its very nature not a *positively* applicable norm which can be stated with *precision,* i.e., with mathematical precision. It cannot always be asserted mathematically that here, because of this one particular negative vote, comes the point at which moral unanimity ceases to exist. But it is in any case at least an extremely important *negative* criterion. True, it is not possible to maintain (at least in the present constitutional situation of the Church) that the opposition of a minority can call in question the *legal* force of a council's decisions. But this indirect juridical consideration does not in any way settle the whole question. The decisive question here is of the *moral* obligations which the Fathers of the Council have in this matter. And it is just here that the principle of moral unanimity is important. This principle can be used to establish that in a given case it is *not* possible to speak any longer of unanimity in a *good* sense. The importance of this can, in certain circumstances, be decisive. It is a question of whether the unity and unanimity of the Church is to be given credible representation by the Council. And this is not done when the numerical majority imposes itself on a substantial minority of individual Churches (which is something very different from an heretical or schismatical sect which has in practice been written off and excluded even before the Council), against their expressed will, so that the true *consensus Ecclesiae* is called in question. In such a case the approprate thing would be for the majority, in accordance with Pius IV's rule, which was often applied successfully at Trent, to refrain, in the interests of the Church's unity and unanimity, from imposing itself on the minority. This, moreover, is the only way of averting the danger of schism. It is only thanks to the loyalty towards the Church of the minority bishops at the First Vatican Council that the tragic schism which followed on the definition of infallibility did not have more far-reaching effects. The question readily suggests itself whether, if the proceedings had been less partisan and more marked by understanding and a spirit of unanimity, schism might not have been avoided altogether.

It is a matter for rejoicing that so far all the decisions taken at Vatican II have been taken with the kind of majority that entitles one to speak of moral unanimity. There has only been one exception, much discussed both by the Fathers and by the press. The first schema of the theological commission, on the subject of revelation, had been strongly attacked on account of its partisan, doctrinaire, unpastoral and unecumenical character. The voting on this schema gave a drastic demonstration of the fact that it is possible to apply the rule about the two-thirds majority in a nonsensical way, i.e., not in favour of but against the majority; to turn it into its opposite by putting the question in an artificially negative form. On this schema, the presidential committee decided to apply for the first time the sound and important distinction (which had actually not been envisaged in the standing orders) between a general or introductory debate and a special debate on a particular matter, and to close the general debate with a vote. The right wording of the question would have been: Those *for* the schema and in favour of discussing it further (in a special debate) vote *placet*; those *against* the schema and against continuing the discussion vote *non placet*. The result would have been about 800 *placets* and 1400 *non placets,* so that the schema would have been rejected and sent back to the commission; the overwhelming majority would have got its way.

What happened in fact, however, was that the question (I cannot go here into the background to this) was put the wrong way round, by a seemingly small alteration hard to sort out at the dramatic moment when the vote was being taken: Those in favour (not of the schema, but of *breaking off the discussion*) vote *placet*; those against (not the schema, but of breaking off the discussion) vote *non placet*. The resulting switch-round had important consequences; those opposed to the schema and against continuing the discussion had to vote *placet* instead of *non placet* (i.e., about 1400); those in favour of the schema and of continuing the discussion had to vote *non placet* instead of *placet* (i.e., about 800). What did the alteration involve? Instead of the *supporters* of the motion having to find a two-thirds majority (as would make sense according to Article 39), it was the *opponents* of the motion who had to produce the two-thirds majority. They just failed to do so. So the discussion of the whole inadequate schema had to go on, against the will of the large majority of the Council (who were also its progressive element). The rule on the two-thirds majority, intended to produce as nearly as possible moral unanimity, led paradoxically, through this artificially negative framing of the question, to the victory of a one-third minority over an almost two-thirds majority.

The case is of immensely far-reaching importance in principle. To go on applying Article 39 in this nonsensical way would mean that any minority of the one-third plus would be able, by a negative framing of the question, to impose any schema or decree on the almost two-thirds majority and so in practice dictate everything to it! In justification of putting the question the negative way round, it may be said that where a proposal has already been accepted by the preparatory commission, the principle applies of *melior est positio possidentis*—the schema was provisionally *in possessione*, had provisionally been accepted, so that it was for its *opponents* to establish a two-thirds majority. But this is an obviously false conclusion. Certainly the proposal was *in possessione* as far as the *preparatory commission* was concerned, but certainly not as far as the *Council itself* was concerned. The Council is quite evidently not the executive organ of the commission; the commission is the servant of the Council. The Council has the sovereign right to decide whether or not it will accept a proposal prepared by a commission as a suitable basis for conciliar discussion. This is precisely the point of the general or introductory debate and the voting that follows it. It is this general or introductory debate which decides whether a given proposal is *in possessione* for the *plenum* or not. *That* is what is to be voted on, *placet* or *non placet*. Acceptance of a schema requires a two-thirds majority.

If it should be maintained in this connection that a schema pre-sented to the Council is as such approved by the Pope and cannot be rejected by the Council, then this is wrong too. That preliminary, very general approval does not in any way imply approval of the *schema itself,* which is still to be discussed; to say it did would make discussion in the Council practically superfluous. Approval means no more than approval that the schema *be presented.* The Pope is simply saying quite generally that this schema can be presented to the Council for discussion, acceptance, rejection or alteration.

The fact that John XXIII, of all people, does not want by any means to force any schema on the Council, is shown by his famous intervention immediately after the extraordinary vote on that first schema of the theological commission. After various Fathers had called on him, he ruled that the vote was for practical purposes annulled, that the schema was withdrawn from discussion, and that it was to be referred back not to the theological commission but to a mixed commission for thorough revision. The necessity of giving the schema an ecumenical orientation was underlined by the Pope's having the new commission drawn from the theological commission (elected by the Council) and the Secretariat for Christian Unity, all constructive co-operation with which had been strictly avoided by the theological preparatory commission (appointed by the Curia). Thus the Pope's intervention does not represent, as it might seem to do, an overriding of conciliar procedure and the conciliar majority, but a sensible application of conciliar procedure and the protection of the progressive majority, which had been overborne by the negative framing of the question. The whole of John XXIII's wise and moderate behavior during this debate provides a demon-stration of the value of the primacy in the Church; for this, when rightly understood, consists not in absolutist dictatorship but in an exercise at the highest level of mediation and the settlement of disputes for the sake of the unity of the Church. The Council was not sparing of its applause for this service by the Pope.

Unquestionably, it would have been possible to avoid the whole muddle over this vote if conciliar procedure had provided for what is rightly taken for granted in any parliament—the direct proposal of a motion on a point of order. In any parliament, motions of this sort can be proposed at any point in the debate, and have to be decided before any decision is taken on the matter under discussion. In this way, a correction of the form of the question could have been demanded before that vote was taken. Thus the Council's procedural rules stand in need of completion by making possible the proposing of a direct motion on a point of order. However, most of the Fathers of the Council might not find it too easy, in what might well be a dramatic situation, to propose such motions, unprepared, in Latin. This brings us to another question.

Latin as the language of discussion

There is no point here in going over the grounds *for* Latin as the language of discussion; they are mostly of a traditional kind. Since Article 33, § 3 of the Council's regulations fortunately limits each individual speaker to ten minutes, Latin will no longer be needed to ensure brevity in the speakers; besides which, it has been shown that it is possible even in Latin to use many words and say little. But a theology which, in the second half of the twentieth century, was only capable of achieving clarity and avoiding misunderstanding by using a dead language would be in a bad way. On the other hand, the use of living languages might be just what would compel a fresh examination of certain Latin terms which have become fossilized into formulae. A council which is explicitly concerned with adaptation to modern times cannot but be concerned (as was indeed very much emphasized by John XXIII in his opening address) with contemporary utterance in contemporary language. Can one altogether blame the press for finding more amusement than edification in some of the really almost comical Latin circumlocutions for modern technical devices (as in the schema on the press, films, television, etc.)?

But even apart from the necessity for contemporary utterance in contemporary language, many of the Fathers rightly felt that the

use of Latin as the language of the Council had some very considerable practical disadvantages.

(1) Latin is a hindrance to *intelligibility* in the discussions. It is
impossible for anyone to ignore the fact that the world-culture at
present in process of construction is not going to be Latin-Occiden-
tal in character, and that knowledge of Latin has shrunk consid-
erably even in Europe, even in Italy, in consequence of the shift of
emphasis in education. But never before in the history of the Church
has the number of non-Europeans and those not of the Roman
world been so great at a council as it is at Vatican II. Hence it is
not to be wondered at that the standard of Latin makes it possible
for many of the Fathers to follow the discussion only with great
trouble and effort, and not with that absolute precision which is
called for. Even for those with a good knowledge of Church Latin,
listening to Latin speeches for hours on end is extraordinarily tiring.
The considerable variations in Latin pronunciation are certainly
fascinating, but again do little to improve the intelligibility of the
speeches. One wonders whether a German's Latin is as difficult for
a Portuguese to understand as the Latin of a Portuguese is for a
German. Certainly, many a Latin-speaking German finds an Eng-
lishman's English easier to understand than his Latin. The low
intelligibility of Latin has led to having technical announcements
in the Council, for the sake of better intelligibility, repeated in
French, German, English, Spanish, Arabic and sometimes even
Italian. It is somewhat paradoxical to be more concerned about
exact understanding of technical announcements than about exact
understanding of the actual speeches in the Council.

(2) Latin is a hindrance to the *living* quality of discussion. The
criticism has frequently been made that the individual speeches of
the Fathers have little reference to each other and are basically just
a series of long-prepared monologues. But if a speaker is to make
any direct spontaneous reference to the speaker before him, whether
positive or negative, by cutting short what he himself has to say or
expanding it, he has to be able to speak a language in which he can
express himself directly without lengthy linguistic and grammatical

preparation. Is this why Article 29 allows the use of the principal modern languages in the commissions, in contrast to the plenary sessions of the Council?

(3) Latin is a hindrance to the *freedom* of discussion. Anyone with a less-than-curial facility in curial Latin is at a disadvantage against members of the Curia when unforeseen difficulties arise. This applies particularly when presidents and cardinals have occasion for any direct spontaneous intervention. It will also apply, if the situation arises, to motions on points of order which have to be formulated on the spot. Consider the difficult business already described involving the two-thirds majority; how many of the Fathers of the Council are capable of framing a juridically and theologically satisfactory motion in Latin, without written preparation, calling for the question to be put in another form?

The Pope himself, when he speaks spontaneously, without preparation, never talks Latin but, to the delight of many of the Fathers, Italian. And even the Curia uses Latin much less than is often supposed; many of the official documents received by the Fathers (lists, voting-cards and so forth) have been in Italian.

Many advantages would certainly spring from the Council's doing its work in the principal languages of the world. It would be a manifestation of broad catholicity, of unity in multiplicity. It would also be an ecumenical act. It is not for nothing that Patriarch Maximos IV of Antioch, who understands Latin extremely well, has always talked French. For the Easterns, the privileged position of the Latin rite in the Catholic Church, theoretically dead and buried but in practice still maintained, is simply something hard to bear. A council which is supposed to be preparing the way for the reunion of separated Christians could surely show more generosity here, with respect both to the Easterns and to Protestants.

The practical solution is the adoption of the system of simultaneous translation which has proved itself satisfactorily in the United Nations and at many congresses dealing with questions of the utmost difficulty. Various forms of it are possible. If the radio version of it were chosen, which is the simpler kind, then of course it would be possible for the proceedings to be picked up on a receiver outside the walls of the basilica. Would that be such a terrible thing? This brings us to the much discussed question of the conciliar secret.

The conciliar secret

This is something that seems to have been an invention of Vatican I. It was meant, so far as possible, to guard against intervention in the council's affairs from outside. In the nineteenth century, at a time when *political* intervention was possible, this was doubtless more necessary than it is today. It may well be that Vatican II is the first council in the history of the Church which has nothing to fear from interference by political powers. On the contrary, because of the positive objective that the Pope has given to the Second Vatican Council, the attitude of world opinion is open and sympathetic. Are we not really missing a great opportunity by trying to put an artificial screen round the Council? Has damage been done to the Catholic Church or the Council by its becoming known that quite serious differences of opinion have been uttered in the *aula*? Have not the very freedom of discussion and seriousness of argument brought it home to many people, most impressively and sympathetically, that the Catholic Church is not, as is often stated, a totalitarian, absolutist system? Would not public discussion in the Council be a unique opportunity to familiarize people with the religious problems of the Church today? Should we not accept the risk of a few misreports in the press, such as would correct themselves in the course of debate?

The press, including especially the Catholic press, has repeatedly complained of the news policy of the Council's press bureau. Both at the numerous press conferences and, especially, in connection with the conciliar debate over modern means of communication, the journalists were reminded over and over again of the duty of truthful reporting. Their answer to this could well be that it was the news policy of the press bureau that was making truthful reporting impossible for them, or at least difficult. In fact the conciliar secret encourages tendentious reports, rumours, mischievous conjectures, bold speculations and the invention of false news for the want of true. On top of which the keeping of the conciliar secret in Rome has been the purest theory. Basically, nothing of any importance remained secret, and Italian newspapers in particular kept reporting things that were in themselves *sub secreto*. If one was a regular reader of *Il Messagero, Le Monde,* the *Neue Zürcher Zeitung* and the *Frankfurter Allgemeine Zeitung,* one was kept very well informed about all the "inner happenings" and much of what was said, word for word, by the Fathers in the *aula*. According to malicious tongues, the only people in Rome who kept the conciliar secret were the non-Catholic observers.

For all these reasons there are many who wish that the conciliar secret, more of a nuisance than a help, and an illusion in any case, should be dropped. It would also be a demonstration of confidence towards the press, which has so far, in general, reported the Council with great accuracy and understanding. Above all, it would be a significant gesture towards the *populus Dei,* which is the Church; the people of God, whose Council it is, and who have a right to hear what their representatives are saying, discussing and deciding, and when they murmur and when they applaud. So there is applause in the Council, is there?

Applause in the aula

Applause in the *aula* was frequently deprecated by the General Secretary of the Council. But reports of applause came again and again. The argument from the holiness of the place, making applause inadmissible, was scarcely convincing, since this was St. Peter's, where the Pope is always greeted with clapping. Further, applause was forbidden neither by the Pope nor by the Council's rules of procedure.

For the individual bishop in the great conciliar *aula,* anxious to have some indication of the mind of the *plenum* amidst the many and often opposed statements that he hears, spontaneous applause when important things are said is a sign by which he can evaluate that mind. Why forbid it, so long as it does not lead to unpleasant disturbances or organized demonstrations? Spontaneous applause belongs to the earliest conciliar tradition. Acclamations are reported sparingly in the case of Ephesus, but abundantly for Chalcedon and the later councils. Their number was constantly recorded with great care. Behind this lay the Fathers' idea, theologically an important one, that the Holy Spirit, under whom it is that the Council speaks, manifests himself only in unity. The unity of the Spirit manifests itself in applause. The stronger and more unanimous the applause, the more clearly it showed, for the Fathers, the presence and action of the Holy Spirit. Applause in the *aula,* as a spontaneous sign of agreement and unity in the Spirit, can still have meaning today.

With procedure as it is at present, it is generally difficult to form an opinion about the attitude of the *plenum* until a vote is taken. One hears the speeches, whether more affirmative or more negative. But the proportion of those *speaking* for or against a schema is liable to be very different from the proportion of those *voting* for or against it. Speakers for or against can even be multiplied by arrangement. How are the Fathers, and in particular the commissions, who have to be guided by the speeches, to form any clear idea of the opinion of the *plenum* or of its majority?

There are already various bishops who speak in the name of groups of bishops, or even of one or several bishops' conferences. They are given more attention than if they spoke only in their own name, and at the same time they enlighten the *plenum* and the commissions on the state of opinion in their group. Could not this procedure be given a place in the standing orders of the Council, by letting those who are spokesmen for one or more bishops' conferences speak first (though not exclusively), and give an objective picture, supported by figures, of the views within their bishops' conferences? Every parliament has methods of procedure on these lines in connection with the parties in it. It would be a great help both to the *plenum* and to the relevant commission in forming an accurate opinion. At the same time it would shorten debates. It would certainly in no way exclude the individual vote of each Father of the Council according to his conscience. The most important thing of all (and one that was not generally done) would be to have the schemata that are to be discussed printed in good time, distributed in good time to those taking part in the Council, and put on the agenda in good time. Improvisations must remain the exception. A good discussion of an individual schema is ensured only if the discussion can be prepared well and unhurriedly in advance. This is another point at which the Council can learn a great deal from secular parliaments.

The Council's rules of procedure were initially very imperfect. They were improved in many ways. Further improvements, for the sake both of the Council and of the Church, are desirable.

NOTES:

[1] Cf. the fuller treatment in *Strukturen der Kirche*, pp. 39–46.

Part III

CARRYING OUT THE PROGRAM

7

Liturgical Reform in the
Light of History

Present-day reform of the Mass

ONE OF THE TASKS before the Second Vatican Council is that of the renewal of worship and the liturgy. This is a task of great moment in the history of the Church. What the present council has to decide in this respect will be no less important for the Church and for Christianity as a whole than the decisions regarding liturgical reform which faced the Council of Trent after the decline of the late Middle Ages. It is precisely for this reason that it is extremely important for us to examine the historical background, since it is only when they are viewed in this perspective that the decisions confronting the present council can be properly understood and evaluated. All the same, it is quite likely that the opinion may be voiced, both in the Council and perhaps afterwards, too, in many dioceses and parishes, that the Council's proposed liturgical renewal is in fact no more than a series of innovations which are in direct contradiction to the good old Catholic tradition. There are, alas, far too many people who, because of a basic lack of knowledge, see the "old tradition" as one and the same thing as what happened in their younger days, although, in comparison with the 2000-year-old history of the Church and her liturgy, those younger days are young indeed! Such people, however, proceed very easily from this assumption to make those three odd-sounding statements by which— once again, because of lack of knowledge and sometimes even for

the sake of convenience—they dismiss all liturgical reform in the
Church: (1) "It has always been like that!" (2) "It has never been
like that before!" and (3) "I don't think we'd take to that sort of
thing!"

It is, however, possible for anyone who really understands what
is meant by the good old tradition of the Church and her worship
to use these three sentences as well, but in quite the opposite sense
—that is, not in opposition to a renewal of the liturgy, but in support of it. In the light of history, one can say perfectly seriously,
in connection with many of the things which should be introduced
today as "new," that "It has always been like that!" Similarly, one
can say of other things which ought today to be given up or at least
put into the background, that "It has never been like that before!"
And finally, of those many things which tend to obscure true tradition and which are basically only favorite practices of a temporary,
personal or local nature, "I don't think we'd take to that sort of
thing!"

It is necessary here to point out straightaway that the renewal of
the liturgy which is under discussion in the Council is fully supported by the very best of the old Catholic tradition, that what
seems to be new today is basically of the greatest antiquity and
that what may have to go is, in fact, not part of the old tradition
but of relatively recent innovation. We are not going into this
simply because it is of historical interest—the Council is concerned
with something which has little to do with pure research into liturgical history. Our examination of the historical background is based
far more on pastoral considerations, since what this council has in
mind is the renewal of the Church as a preparation for the reunion
of all separated Christians, with ecclesiastical worship as the central
point of this renewal. And this renewal of Christian worship in conformity to the prevalent conditions of a new age can only be good
if it is derived from the Gospel of Christ, from its origins. In the
Catholic Mass, what ultimately matters is simply that the Lord's
command, "Do this in memory of me," is obediently carried out. Do
this, and not this, that or the other, however beautiful, impressive or

long-established it may be. But is it not true to say that this very
thing that our Lord commanded us to do has become obscured
over the centuries? Has it not in fact been said, half jokingly, half
seriously, that if the Apostle Paul himself happened to go into the
average Catholic church while High Mass was being celebrated,
he would have great difficulty in understanding, unless somebody
explained it to him, that what was taking place here was the fulfilment of the Lord's command to "do this in memory·of me"? What
the present reform of the liturgy aims to do is once·again to make
the original structure of Christian worship, which derives from the
Gospel, more clear and understandable for the people. The pattern
of the liturgy of the ancient Church cannot, of course, be slavishly
copied. What the ancient liturgy can provide, however, is a model
which brings the organic structure of Christian worship well to the
fore and which can, in this sense, also be adapted to modern needs.

In such a short exposition it is impossible to make a complete survey of the entire history even of the Roman Mass, let alone of the
many other rites, which are, in fact, not being dealt with directly by
the Council. For this the reader must consult J. A. Jungmann's *Missarum Sollemnia,* which has become a widely accepted standard work
on the subject in almost every major language in the world and must
provide the basis for any detailed account of the historical development of the Mass.[1] All that I can do here, in connection with the
schema on the liturgy which is under discussion in the Council and
the decisions which will result from these discussions, is to make the
reader aware of a few salient points so that he will recognize what
is essential in this historical development and understand the background facts of the present scheme. To this end, I shall briefly re-
view four typical images of the Mass throughout the centuries. None
of the examples which follow are poetic fabrications. They have
been chosen because they conform closely to the most recent research into the history of the liturgy.

First Example: Mass celebrated in a house in the second century. Let us
imagine that we are back in the earliest Christian times in Rome,

during the oppression and persecution of the Church. Christians form an ever-decreasing minority. We are looking into a room. It is a dining-hall. The Eucharist would have been celebrated, a short time ago, in this room, the celebration taking place, just as it did during the Last Supper, while the meal was in progress. Now, however, the dining-room has become an assembly hall. All the tables have disappeared except one. The leader of the assembly, a bishop or priest, who is dressed in the clothes of a Roman citizen, is standing at this table. He is facing the people.

Perfectly ordinary bread and wine have been brought along. The bishop now begins, in Greek, not in Latin, the prayer of thanksgiving, the *eucharistia*. The biblical words of consecration are inserted into this single prayer of thanksgiving. At the end of the prayer all those who are present say "Amen" and receive—standing—the gifts, which are now no longer bread and wine, but the body and blood of Jesus Christ. This is the Mass as it has been handed down to us by Justin the Martyr (*c.* A.D. 150)—an extremely simple celebration, consisting of a single "prayer of thanksgiving" and the meal or communion of all those present, and for this reason called the "Eucharistia." The oldest Roman eucharistic formula that has been preserved comes from Hippolytus of Rome (*c.* A.D. 215). This gives us a very fine idea of what the ancient Mass looked like. The gifts are placed on the table and the Mass, or prayer of thanksgiving, begins. Together with the priests who are present, the bishop extends his hands over the gifts and begins: "The Lord be with you." The people reply: "And with thy spirit." "Lift up your hearts!" "We have lifted them up to the Lord." "Let us give thanks to the Lord!" "It is meet and just." Then the bishop continues:

We give thee thanks, O God, through thy beloved servant [*pais, puer*] Jesus Christ, whom thou hast sent to us in recent times as our saviour and redeemer and the herald of thy new dispensation. He is thy undivided Word, thou hast made everything through him, and it was well pleasing to thee. Thou didst send him from heaven into the womb of the Virgin and, carried in the womb, he became flesh and was revealed as thy Son, born by the Holy Spirit of the Virgin. In that he fulfilled thy will and won for thee a holy people, he extended his hands in suffering, to redeem from suffering those who believe in him. And since he was handed over, a willing victim, to suffering, to deprive death of its power and to break the chains binding us to the devil and to trample hell underfoot and to enlighten the just and to mark an epoch and to proclaim the Resurrection, he took the bread and, giving thanks to thee, said: Take and eat, this is my body, that is broken for you. Likewise he took the chalice, saying: This is my blood, that is shed for you. Whenever you do this, do it in my memory. Mindful also of his death and resurrection, we offer the bread and the chalice, giving thanks to thee for deeming us worthy to stand before thee and serve thee. And we ask thee to send the Holy Ghost down upon this offering of thy holy Church. Bringing her together in unity, do thou bestow on all thy saints who receive it the fullness of the Holy Spirit, to confirm our faith in truth, so that we may praise and glorify thee through thy servant Jesus Christ, through whom is praise and honour to the Father, to the Son and to the Holy Ghost, in thy holy Church, now and for ever and ever. Amen.[2]

Communion followed immediately after this, the faithful receiving the offerings, taking the bread in their open hands. At quite an early date, although it did not always take place, a Service of the Word was held in association with the celebration of the Eucharist, in imitation of the synagogue service. A series of texts from the Old and New Testaments were read, without a break, and explained, there were communal prayers and psalms were sung. What can we learn from this ancient form of the Mass?

(1) The basic structure of the Mass is quite simple and easy to understand. It consists essentially of the prayer of thanksgiving, which incorporates the commemorative words of consecration, and the eucharistic meal. This basic structure was preserved throughout the

centuries, despite frequent later additions and accretions. In its essence it does not depart from the Last Supper as we know it from scriptural sources.

(2) In its early form, the Mass was quite flexible. Only the essential outlines of the celebration were fixed. Each bishop or priest used his own discretion in shaping the liturgy. The language was the vernacular of the period; thus, the language used in the celebration of the oldest form of the Roman liturgy known to us was not, as many believe, Latin, but *koine* Greek, the current vernacular of the Roman Empire. The entire service was an intimate communal feast, during which the people prayed and sang together.

(3) All those who were present at the meal also received the sacrament in both kinds, bread *and* wine. It would have struck these early Christians as completely absurd to be present at a meal without eating, or to receive the sacrament either before Mass or before the eucharistic prayer was over. It would have seemed preposterous to them if several Masses were celebrated simultaneously in the same place. If more than one priest were present, then concelebration took place, all the priests saying a single Mass together with the chief celebrant.

Second Example: Mass celebrated in a basilica in the fifth and sixth centuries. Christianity has by now spread throughout the entire Roman Empire. Let us imagine ourselves to be present in one of these splendid Roman basilicas of the period. Here, too, the wooden table, or altar, is placed well to the fore and the priest celebrates the same Mass, once again facing the people and once again dressed in the clothes of a Roman citizen. But there have been many changes during the intervening centuries.

Everything has become longer, grander and more solemn. Various intercessions, for the living, the dead, special petitions for the Church and so on, have been inserted into the simple, ancient eucharistic prayer of thanksgiving. These intercessions are linked with the names of martyrs, to whom more and more honor is now—since the time of Christian persecution—being paid. Furthermore there are, in addition to the prayer of thanksgiving, three important new elements: the singing of a psalm, accompanied by a prayer, on the entry of the clergy into the basilica (the introductory psalm or Introit), a second psalm while the faithful bring their offerings of bread, wine and other gifts (the Offertory), and a third psalm during the communion of the faithful (the Communion chant). At the same time, the Mass has above all been, as we would say now, *solemnized*. A whole set of ceremonies have been borrowed from the Byzantine-Roman court ceremonial, including many which the earliest Christians had rejected as heathen practices—genuflections, bowing, kissing, such things as incense, candles and so on and such marks of distinction as the stole or the ring. As a result of this solemnization of the Mass, a more artistic form of chant was gradually replacing the earlier, simpler singing of the people. What, then, can we learn from this example?

(1) It goes without saying that the liturgy of this period had adapted itself to the change which had taken place in the vernacular. Since the people of Rome no longer used Greek, but Latin, the liturgical language had changed from Greek to Latin. Latin had been in liturgical use since about A.D. 250.

(2) A whole host of involved ceremonies, which take place particularly in solemn High Mass and which today have a disturbing effect upon people who prefer to aim at simplicity and straightforwardness, in that these ceremonies distract from what is essential, can be traced directly to the Byzantine-Roman court ceremonial, and thus cannot be regarded as part of the unchangeable essence of the Mass.

(3) The adaptation of the Mass to the celebration of special feasts in honour of the saints is closely connected with the then prevalent cult of the martyrs and is thus a later development.

Third Example: Mass during the high Middle Ages. The center of world civilization had by this time moved northwards away from Rome, and political leadership had, in the eighth and ninth centuries, passed into the hands of the Frankish emperors. A parallel movement took place at about the same time in the case of the liturgy, which had hitherto been confined to Rome and its environs (and its sphere of influence, as, for example, the mission to the Anglo-Saxons). Not only the ordinary parochial liturgy, but also the solemn papal liturgy, were transferred to the Frankish empire, with many serious consequences.

Until this time, there had been no such thing as silent, low Mass. All the prayers of the Mass, including the words of consecration, had, for obvious reasons, been spoken aloud, as they were by Christ. Now, however, many silent, or quietly uttered, prayers were added to the Mass, once again close to the beginning (the Gradual), during the preparation of the offerings and at the Communion. We find the priest saying prayers continuously at the altar, even during the actions of the Mass. At this time too, we find the practice of silent, or quietly spoken, priestly prayer gradually spreading even to the oldest prayers of the Mass, including the ancient prayer of thanksgiving (the Canon) and the words of consecration incorporated into it. One obvious reason for this is that the people no longer understood Latin.

One consequence of this was, of course, a gradual estrangement between the people and the altar. This arose because the language of the liturgy was no longer understood by the people, because the various solemn, ceremonial actions, such as genuflection, signs of the cross and the use of incense, were rapidly increasing in number and in importance, and, finally, because the choir, where the clergy assembled, was separated from the nave of the Church, where the people were. A "high altar," placed right up against the apse, replaced the older altar which used to stand close to the people. Again, we find the priest now no longer celebrating Mass facing the people, but facing the wall, and, what is more, no longer able to see over the superstructure of the altar, because it has become so high. As the Mass is no longer visible and understandable, it has to be interpreted in a new and allegorical way for the sake of the people, and they begin to see it as a dramatic representation of the life of Jesus—as a play or spectacle. The original meaning of the Mass as a celebration in thanksgiving and in commemoration of the Last Supper is often lost. The people do nothing. They simply see the action of the Mass, and that is why the traditional garments, or vestments, which had been preserved since the time of Rome's supremacy, gave way at this period to similar vestments which changed in colour according to a definite plan. It is for the same reason that, despite violent opposition on the part of the ecclesiastical authorities, the practice of the priest's elevation of the sacred body and blood and his adoration by genuflection was introduced for the first time in the thirteenth century. The reception of the Sacrament in Communion became the exception rather than the normal rule, but the people wanted at least to be able to see the sacred species. At the same time, ordinary bread disappeared from the altar and was gradually replaced by the "host," which was unleavened and snow-white and, in appearance, quite unlike ordinary bread. Moreover, whereas in the ancient Church all the priests who were present celebrated one and the same Mass together, we find each priest now saying his own Mass separately, and, to permit this practice, more and more side-altars being built adjacent to the original single altar. Finally, what can we learn from this third example?

(1) This period saw the emergence of a deep gulf between the priest and the people. This is very far from the original mind of the Church, but the gulf has persisted throughout the centuries and can often only be overcome nowadays after a long and sometimes painful struggle.

(2) During this period, too, Communion became a separate rite, and was administered, moreover, more and more frequently, in one kind only. Earlier in the history of the Church, Communion during Mass was the norm; during this period of the Middle Ages, however, it was exceptional. Before this time, the Bread of Life was, as Jesus commanded, eaten. Since then, it has more often been beheld and adored. The recent introduction of the monstrance bears witness to this.

(3) Whereas there was previously only one altar in any given church and only one Mass celebrated at any given time, from this time onwards many Masses could be celebrated simultaneously at

many different altars in the same church. The "private" Mass had come into being.

Fourth Example: Mass since the Tridentine reform of 1570. This is, to all intents and purposes, the Mass which we have today. In the first place, the reforms made by the Council of Trent cut out the rank and monstrous excesses which had, particularly during the later Middle Ages, crept into the Mass. In the second place, the Council's reforms had regularized the Mass down to the last detail, thus doing something which had never been attempted before. For this reason, the post-tridentine Mass is often called the "Mass of the rubrics." As literally everything had been regulated down to the last word and the tiniest detail of the position of the celebrant's fingers, and, what is more, since the people were still given no opportunity of taking an active part in the celebration, their private and personal piety began to express itself with great energy and accompanying emotion in an ever-increasing number of different devotions. What happened all too frequently was that the Mass was regarded as just one among many devotions, although it probably remained the most important. More candles were lit during these various devotions than at Mass itself. Meanwhile, in Europe, what has been called the "exodus" had come about. Sunday Mass was no longer fully attended. In many different European countries, the fact that only a small number of the faithful regularly went to Sunday Mass was recognized with horror. This, of course, had the most far-reaching effects on the religious life of the people as a whole. It is not true to say that it is exclusively the form of the Mass which is at fault here, though it is certainly one of the causes which can be blamed. It is thus not difficult to understand why many countermeasures have been introduced since that time by the Church leaders, beginning with Pius X, who urged frequent Communion and the active participation of the people in Christian worship, right down to Pius XII and the most recent reforms. It is basically a question of overcoming the thousand-year-old gulf between the people and the priest at the altar, and of once again making clear to the people the original structure of the Eucharist.

The Mass of the future

The task with which the Second Vatican Council is confronted is a great and splendid one. The Council should set about it without hesitation, though not without careful reflection, and see it through to the end. The most important consideration in all liturgical reform must be that the pattern of the Eucharist, as laid down by Christ as binding on the Church when he shared the Last Supper with the Apostles, should emerge powerfully from the eucharistic celebration today, and thus concentrate attention more intensely on what is essential in the Mass and make the rite correspondingly more intelligible. The foregoing can be stated thus in concrete terms:

(1) With regard to the sacrificial part of the Mass, the eucharistic prayer, including the words of consecration, should be said intelligibly and aloud. This implies a simplification of the present Canon with the preface according to the pattern of eucharistic prayer used by Hippolytus and excluding the mementos and so on (the same would apply to the various intercessions made during the preparation of the offerings).

(2) With regard to the Service of the Word, this should be a meaningful service of communal prayer and singing, together with an intelligible reading aloud, and at least a short exposition, of the biblical texts. In the latter case, far more serious consideration should be given to the whole of Holy Scripture. This could be done by replacing the present annual cycle of passages from the Bible which are read on Sundays by a six-year cycle, and introducing a continuous reading, particularly of the New Testament, into weekday Masses.

In both parts of the Mass, the following should be observed: The use of vernacular, celebration facing the people, the full and active participation of the people, a clear distinction between the simple and more solemn forms of the Mass, the introduction of new forms for the celebration of feasts (incorporating singing by the people and the choir in the vernacular, orchestral accompaniment and a renewal of the method of singing the Psalms), the relegation of features of secondary importance (such as the merging of various feasts of the saints, no unnecessary repetition of prayers, fewer genuflections and less bowing and kissing, a more sparing use of incense and the omission of the last Gospel and the Gradual) and, finally, an active promotion of those reforms which have already been introduced into Holy Week and the Easter vigil.

The ultimate aim of all this is the active participation of all the faithful in the worship of the Church, by means of a bold and vital share in the priest's celebration of Mass—praying and singing together, giving thanks for, commemorating, offering up and eating together the Body of the Lord. To achieve this, it is necessary to go back to the very oldest of the Church's traditions, to go back, in fact, to what it has "always been like." This is not simply a return to the past for its own sake, but a vital reshaping of the liturgy to conform to our present needs, a reshaping in the light of our knowledge of the Gospel and in the very best Catholic tradition. Is there anyone who lacks the courage to take part joyously in this work? It is indeed not a matter of furthering some pet theory or private fancy, but of fulfilling, exactly, faithfully and meaningfully, the will of Christ: "Do this in memory of me!"

NOTES:

[1] J. A. Jungmann, *Missarum Sollemnia. Eine genetische Erklärung der römischen Messe.* Vienna (1949), 2 vols. (English translation: *The Mass of the Roman Rite, its Origins and Development,* New York, Benziger, 1961). For a shorter introduction to the subject by the same author, see *Vom Sinn der Messe als Opfer der Gemeinschaft,* Einsiedeln (1954); *Das eucharistische Hochgebet. Grundgedanken des Canon Missae,* Rothefelser Series 1, Würzburg (1956); *Der Gottesdienst der Kirche,* Innsbruck, Vienna and Munich (1955). English translation, *Public Worship: a Survey,* Collegeville, Liturgical Press (1957).

[2] This quotation is taken from J. A. Jungmann, *Der Gottesdienst der Kirche,* p. 104 f.

8

Importance of Liturgical
Reform for Christian Unity

A deviation from the original aim of the Council?

THE EXTRAORDINARILY OUTSPOKEN DISCUSSIONS which have taken
place in the Council on the subject of liturgical reform have now,
for the time being, been closed. More than a thousand proposals
as to how the liturgy might be improved were put forward by the
Council Fathers. These are at present being considered by the
Commission on the Liturgy, and will be submitted as soon as possible to the *plenum* and put to the vote. As a result of this, many
questions still remain open at present.

It is very difficult for an outsider to assess the real implications
of these discussions, in which to some extent quite conflicting views
were expressed. Many Christians, in particular Protestants, are
quite understandably wondering what all this really has to do with
the original aim of the Council. Was the Second Vatican Council
not summoned, they ask, with the aim of preparing the way for
reunion with separated Christians, and is not this discussion about
the reform of the Liturgy in reality no more than a purely domestic
matter, of Catholic interest only?

It is quite true that the Pope did summon the Second Vatican
Council for the purpose of preparing for reunion. His very first
proclamation expressed this aim quite clearly, and it was precisely
because of this that the Second Vatican Council, unlike the first,
was publicly acclaimed with such joy and hope in every quarter

of the globe. Both the Pope and the bishops have had this fundamental aim constantly in mind, and the observers from the great
non-Catholic communions, who attend all the Council's discussions
and have a close-up view of all the proceedings, serve, by their
very presence, as a reminder to the Council Fathers not to lose sight
of the Council's ultimate aim— the reunion of separated Christianity. But the real question is, *how* is this reunion to be achieved?
Only on condition that *the Catholic Church herself is renewed*: in conformity with the legitimate demands of the other communions—
the legitimate demands of the Orthodox, the Evangelical, the
Anglican and the Free-Church Christians, in the light of the Gospel
of Christ. It is the Gospel which must act as judge in our disputes
over what is and what is not legitimate in each claim that is made.
It goes, of course, without saying that we Catholic Christians sin-
cerely hope that other Christians will meet us half way, by renewing
themselves as well and, once again, by carrying out the legitimate
requests of the Catholic Church, also in the light of the Gospel.

Acting in the spirit of ecumenical *rapprochement,* the Second Vatican Council aims to give a powerful, fresh impetus to the renewal
of the Catholic Church, which was begun, in a very conservative
way, and more in the nature of a restoration, at the time of the
Counter-Reformation, and was continued at the turn of the century, principally by Leo XIII, in a far more constructive and
creative way.

It is against this backcloth that the present discussions on the
subject of liturgical reform have to be seen. But has liturgical reform
really any *ecumenical* significance? One might almost go so far as to
say that the fact that a *beginning* has already been made with the
reform of the liturgy is in itself of ecumenical importance.

Why should liturgical reform be given priority?

The first section of the first volume of schemata which were prepared by the commissions is devoted to four schemata on dogmatic
theology. The fifth section and the second section from the end are

devoted to the schema on the liturgy. Going contrary to certain trends which pointed in other directions, or were less in line with ecumenical considerations, the Council decided to deal with the liturgical sections first. From the ecumenical point of view, this decision has two important consequences:

(1) *A concentration on the practical needs of pastoral care.* In this way the Council has, for the time being at any rate, avoided the danger of becoming too preoccupied with doctrine to the exclusion of everything else. The danger which constantly threatens the World Council of Churches, which is unable to assume any unity either in the message or in the teaching of its individual members—or at most only a minimum of unity—is that of becoming preoccupied with pragmatic considerations, with the result that practical work is overemphasized and too little value is placed on the importance of doctrine. On the other hand, the danger facing the Council of the Catholic Church, which can in fact assume unity in its message and teaching, is that doctrine is overstressed and practical work receives too little attention, since the Church always tends to be immersed in doctrinal problems. Catholic theologians especially— this fortunately applies to a far lesser extent in the case of the bishops —are always inclined to overestimate the need for constant elucidation of the Church's teaching. Would it be of any value at all today, to the Church or to the world, simply to restate old doctrines? "There is no need to summon a Council to do this," John XXIII himself said in his inaugural address to the Council. Would it, moreover, benefit either the Church or the world to pass judgement upon all those whose teaching is in error? The Church "prefers to use the medicine of mercy rather than severity, and she believes that she can demonstrate the value of her teaching by aligning herself more closely to the needs of today rather than by using the weapon of judgement and condemnation," the Pope said, with certain innate tendencies on the part of the Church to overemphasize doctrinal questions clearly in mind. The settlement of doctrinal differences between individual Catholic schools of theological thought never has been, and is not now, the task of a council. It would also

not be opportune to try to settle differences in doctrine between the individual Christian denominations—these will have to be gone over slowly and thoroughly by the theologians, from the exegetical, historical and dogmatic points of view. The Council cannot replace the work of the theologians, and, in any case, a premature attempt to resolve highly controversial issues of doctrine would do the gravest disservice to the ecumenical cause.

Liturgical reform and a concentration of effort upon the practical aspects of pastoral care—these are the important, positive features in all attempts towards reunion. The schema on the liturgy which is before the Council does not set out to lay down anything dogmatically. Thus it is evident that it is quite possible for the Church to be renewed, and for a positive forward thrust to be given to the movement towards a closer understanding between the various Christian communions, without previously clearing up every theoretical question. Undoubtedly the most promising approach to ecumenical approximation today is to smooth the way, by a practical renewal, based on the Gospel rather than on one particular theology, for later theological discussions.

(2) *A concentration on central problems.* The Council has, so far at least, avoided the danger of allowing itself to be sidetracked in discussion from the central problems. The First Vatican Council dealt with many questions of ecclesiastical discipline which were peripheral, and consequently not the concern of an ecumenical council. There are similarly many questions for discussion by the present council which are certainly important—for example, the problems raised by the films, television and the press, problems of ecclesiastical trusteeship and allied questions. But all these are, in comparison with the intrinsic task of the Church, no more than fringe problems. It is Christian worship which is, and must always be, central in the life of the Church. If success is achieved in renewing the Church's liturgy, the effects of this renewal will be felt in every sphere of activity within the Church. If Catholic worship is successfully refashioned in a more ecumenical form, the effect on the whole movement towards reunion with the separated Chris-

tians will be decisive. The Protestant Reformers, too, regarded liturgical renewal as a task of central importance, and it was one of their most insistent demands. The Council of Trent carried out considerable reforms in the sphere of Catholic worship by removing many appalling abuses and by rearranging the form of the Catholic liturgy. But the Tridentine reforms were in fact more in the nature of a restoration of the medieval *status quo* than a truly constructive and creative renewal of Christian worship in the light of the Gospel and arising from a need to adapt worship to the requirements of a new age. It must be remembered, however, that the Council of Trent did not have all the findings of modern historical and liturgical research at its disposal, as the present Council does—we have only come to a true knowledge as to how the Mass has developed throughout the centuries since the appearance of J. A. Jungmann's epoch-making work, *The Mass of the Roman Rite, its Origins and Development*. One of the facts which emerge from this work is that no positive answer could be given to many of the demands made by the Reformers at the time of the Council of Trent, and that even now these questions are still unresolved. From this point of view as well, then, it is of the utmost importance in the cause of the reunion of separated Christianity to give precedence to liturgical reform and to concentrate on the central problems of renewal.

But does the liturgical reform, in the form in which it is at present being debated within the Catholic Church, really point in an ecumenical direction? It would certainly not be true to claim that the nineteenth-century renewal of the liturgy, consisting largely of restorative measures and carried out in a traditionalistic spirit and under the influence of the Romantic movement, ever really had the interests of the Reformers or their legitimate demands in view. This claim can, however, definitely be made in the case of the Second Vatican Council. Certain basic structural elements can be singled out here and, from them, several individual questions emerge. It is, however, at the present moment very difficult to foresee exactly how far the individual points of the radical renewal advocated by the contemporary liturgical movement can be brought to bear upon the Council itself.

Should Protestant claims be taken into consideration in liturgical reform?

(1) *A closer approximation to the pattern of the Last Supper*. One of the main objections of the Reformers was that the Mass had developed into a pure "ceremony" which had basically little to do with the Last Supper. Indeed, they claimed that it had become so overgrown with rank abuses and misinterpretation that it had become idolatry.

We Catholics, on the other hand, maintained that the essential element of the Mass—"Do this in memory of me"—has always been preserved, though it cannot be denied that the original and inherent fundamental structure of the eucharistic element in the Mass has become overlaid and obscured by non-essentials over the centuries. In its original form, the Mass was a simple and universally intelligible celebration, consisting of thanksgiving and the sacred meal. The essential elements of the Mass were the *eucharistia*—a single prayer of thanksgiving, often freely improvised, in the course of which the words of consecration were repeated—and the partaking of the consecrated gifts. The language of the Mass was the language of the people and the signs were quite clear—ordinary bread and ordinary wine were used, and everyone present received both the body *and* the blood of the Lord. This original basic structure of the Mass became partially obscured with the passage of time—by the insertion of new elements into the eucharistic prayer of thanksgiving and by numerous extraneous additions, by the continued use of an incomprehensible liturgical language and by the practice of praying the most important parts of the Mass silently, by the unnecessary multiplicity of external details, by an increasing "solemnization" in the form of public worship which was often extremely ill-adapted to pastoral needs, by the gradual neglect of the commemorative aspect of the Mass, and so on.

The aim of the contemporary movement for liturgical renewal

is to make the Church's celebration of the Eucharist conform more clearly and more closely to the Last Supper which Jesus celebrated with his apostles, by reforming the entire rite, by bringing what is essential well to the fore, by suppressing what is inessential, by shortening the rite, by eliminating all unnecessary repetitions, by accepting once again all that is good in the ancient tradition of the Church, and so on. A very important feature in any renewal of the liturgy, and one which is particularly desirable and most urgently needed, is the restoration of the ancient eucharistic prayer and, in conjunction with this, the reform of the Canon of the Mass. Any attempt to make the celebration of the Eucharist approximate more closely to the Last Supper must be of the greatest ecumenical importance.

(2) *The hearing of the word of God.* Another of the reproaches which the Reformers levelled against the Catholic Church was that the word of God was no longer heard in Catholic worship. The message, they held, was proclaimed in an unintelligible language, the biblical texts were not elucidated and preaching was seriously neglected.

From the earliest period in the history of the Catholic Church, the reading of Holy Scripture had an honourable place, and at a very early stage a Service of the Word, consisting of readings, prayers and singing, was held in conjunction with the eucharistic celebration. At that time, the entire Scripture was read aloud and commented upon in public services. St. Augustine, for example, spent weeks and months expounding the Psalms, Genesis, the Gospels and so on, verse by verse, to his community. In the Middle Ages too, the word of God was proclaimed by the Church, though it cannot be denied that, by this time, the preaching of the Word was in a sorry condition. The people no longer understood the language, comparatively short extracts were read from the whole of the Old and New Testaments, and the essential task of the Church to proclaim the word of God was frequently not treated very seriously. The contemporary movement for liturgical renewal aims at giving the preaching of the Word a new importance within the framework of public worship, by introducing the intelligible reading of Holy

Scripture in the vernacular, by arranging a new cycle of passages from Scripture, covering several years rather than, as now, only one, and thus providing for the reading of those texts which have hitherto been neglected, by giving greater emphasis to the sermon, by restoring the ancient form of the Service of the Word, which can be conducted by a deacon or a layman who has been authorized by the bishop, and held independently from the celebration of the Eucharist (this would be particularly useful in those districts where there is a shortage of priests), and by allowing the spirit of Holy Scripture to penetrate the whole of the liturgy, including the hymns and various devotions. Non-Catholic Christians will surely agree wholeheartedly that, if these new measures for the word of God to be heard and taken more seriously in Catholic worship are carried out, the effect on the whole work of renewing the Church and her preparation for reunion with separated Christians will be decisive.

(3) *Worship by the entire priestly people.* A further criticism made by the Reformers was that the liturgy of the Middle Ages had become, like the medieval Church herself, sacerdotalized. The people were, to a very great extent, excluded, and only the priest played an active part in religious worship.

In the early Church, the people contributed a very active part to the liturgy—there were communal prayers and singing, the Body of the Lord was eaten and the Blood of the Lord was drunk, together. When the regional liturgy of Rome was imposed on the Frankish Empire, the consequence was, without doubt, a strict exclusion of the people. They did not understand the Latin language. Their share in the liturgy was restricted to watching passively. The Mass, divorced, as far as they were concerned, from its words, was given an allegorical and quite arbitrary interpretation. The essential features of the Mass became more and more obscured by the ever-increasing solemnization of the ceremonial. The altar table, which had originally been situated close to the people, was elaborated into a "high" altar and placed away from them in the apse, where Mass was celebrated facing the wall, instead of facing the people, as before. The clergy, in the choir, were separated from the people in the nave by the rood-screen. The practice of general Communion among the people ceased because of an exaggerated reverence for the Sacrament, and an unnecessary insistence on the moral conditions, fasting regulations and so on. All these are undeniable facts, and because of them the people, who had once actively participated with the priest in co-celebrating, singing and giving thanks together, had become passive and dumb. It was not until 1897 that the lay missal was removed from the Index of Forbidden Books.

It is the aim of the movement for liturgical renewal so to remodel religious worship that it may once again become the worship of the entire priestly people. For decades, the chief aim of those who are working for a renewal of the liturgy has been to secure for the people an active share in the whole liturgy. This, they claim, could be achieved by reshaping the liturgy so that it becomes fully intelligible, by introducing communal prayer and singing and a communal partaking of the eucharistic feast, including Communion in both kinds, by re-introducing the vernacular, by suppressing "private" Masses, by renewing church music and giving it, by means of a completely new approach to the singing of the Psalms etc., a powerfully pastoral slant, and so on. All this provides a positive answer to the genuine demands of Protestant Christians.

(4) *Adaptation to the needs of the various peoples within the Church.* Another of the Reformers' criticisms was that the Church, and consequently her public worship, had become excessively "Romanized." Her liturgy was insufficiently suited to the needs of the different peoples and races within the Church. This criticism was applied to the whole spirit of the liturgy, as well as to its structure, language, music, gestures and movements.

In the early Christian period, almost every local Church worked out its own individual liturgical pattern, with the result that an impressive number of Eastern and Western rites came into being within the one Church. The same, yet a different, Mass was celebrated according to the Greek, Roman, Ethiopic, Armenian, Syriac, Mozarabic, Slavonic or other rites. It was towards the end of the sixth century that the liturgy of Rome was passed on, by the Roman monks, to the Anglo-Saxon mission. In the Frankish Empire, however, it was the Frankish princes and prelates themselves who suppressed the older, native Gallician liturgy and introduced the liturgy which had previously been in use only in Rome and her immediate environs. The motives behind this were clearly cultural and political rather than pastoral. The Roman liturgy underwent many changes when it was transferred from Rome to the Frankish Empire—one of the most notable being the emergence of the Gregorian chant, which we sing nowadays, not according to the early Roman tradition, but in the form in which it has been handed down to us by the Franks. The fact remains, however, that the liturgy as a whole was in many respects a foreign one to the peoples north of the Alps. The foreign language itself was sufficient to prevent the Roman rite from becoming a genuine people's liturgy among the Germanic tribes. The same problem arose at a more recent date, in an even more acute form, when the local liturgy of Rome was transferred from Europe to other continents with totally different cultures. If a wrong decision were to result from the present unhappy controversy over the liturgy, it might become impossible for the liturgy ever to be adapted to the needs of the Asiatic peoples.

The present-day aims in liturgical renewal include the complete readaptation of public worship to the needs of every individual racial group, so that the liturgy of the Church may once more become a genuine liturgy of the people. If what the movement for liturgical renewal stands for could be summed up in a phrase, it would be "unity, but not uniformity." It should be perfectly possible to adapt the liturgy to suit the needs of each race or people by adapting the language, gestures and movements of the liturgy, the form and content of the prayers, the singing and the arrangement of the music, and the entire structure of the rite. All this presupposes, of course, a far greater degree of autonomy on the part of the episcopates of each individual country, and an extensive movement of decentralization away from the Roman Curia. It is also quite possible to envisage the introduction of new rites in the missionary territories. The conscious development of genuine people's liturgies certainly meets the legitimate claims of Protestant Christianity.

Old controversial issues

The general structural principles, which have been outlined above as applicable to the whole of contemporary liturgical reform, also hold good for every case of detailed reconstruction in the liturgy. But the same general principles can also be effectively applied when any of the centuries-old points of controversy between Catholic and non-Catholic Christians are brought up for discussion. It may also be that the time has at last come for a positive and constructive solution to be found to these questions.

(1) *The Vernacular.* The use of the vernacular in communal worship was one of the Reformation's greatest attractions—German hymns played a particularly important part in the rapid spread of the Reformation in Germany.

In the early Church, of course, the vernacular and the liturgical languages were one and the same, and this led to the development of many different rites within the Church. In Rome, Mass was originally not celebrated, as we have said, in Latin, but in Greek. It was only with the re-emergence of Latin as the language of the people of Rome that Latin was re-introduced, round about A.D. 250, into the Roman liturgy. The Anglo-Saxons and later the Franks used Latin, as a foreign language, in the liturgy, whereas, at a later period, despite criticism on the part of the Franks, SS. Cyril and Methodius, leading the mission to the Slavs, used the vernacular in the liturgy. In this they received the full protection of Rome. In addition to the Latin rite, there are still in existence many other rites, each using its own language liturgically. To the present day, these rites still enjoy, at least theoretically, a status equal to that of the

Roman rite. Even within the Roman rite itself, considerable progress has been made in recent years in the use of the vernacular, especially in the administration of the sacraments.

It is the aim of the modern liturgical movement to secure at least the gradual introduction of the vernacular into the Mass itself. The movement is convinced that it will be possible to meet the majority of the genuine claims of Catholics and of the separated Christians only when the vernacular has been introduced in this way—when the eucharistic celebration is more similar to the pattern of the Last Supper, when the word of God is both heard and understood, when worship has become the worship of the entire priestly people and when the liturgy has been adapted to the widely differing needs of the different races and peoples.

(2) *Communion under both kinds.* The ban on the people's reception of the chalice was regarded by the Reformers, and strenuously attacked by them, as a particularly clear example of how the liturgy had become the exclusive concern of the clergy and as a contravention of the Lord's command, "Drink *all of you* of this."

In the early Church, it was the universal practice for the people to receive Communion under both kinds, but their reception of the chalice ceased in the twelfth and thirteenth centuries, as Communion generally became less and less frequent. Before this, however, various expedients had been tried out, in an attempt to overcome the practical difficulties. The statement of the medieval theologians, that Christ was entirely present under either kind, was in itself correct, but it was nonetheless largely to blame for the decline of the practice of the people's Communion under both kinds and the consequent loss, in the celebration of Mass, of its aspect as a eucharistic meal. It was only later, however, that the people were expressly forbidden to receive the chalice, at the time of the Church's conflict with the Hussites in particular, though the practice still continued until a much later date, being permitted in Bohemia until 1433 and in Germany until 1564. The ban was reinforced, as a consequence of the movement for Catholic restoration, for example in Austria in 1584. In 1621 the ban was extended to cover the entire Latin rite, though even today Catholics of the Latin rite are permitted to receive the Eucharist under both kinds in a celebration of the Mass according to the various Eastern rites.

Those who are working for liturgical renewal aim to secure permission for the people once more to receive the chalice, at least in principle, during the celebration of Mass according to the Latin rite and to introduce, at least gradually, the practice of Communion under both kinds. In this way, it may be possible to settle, in a changed theological climate, one controversial issue which has divided Catholic and Protestant Christians for so long.

(3) *Concelebration.* The reformers also protested against the celebration of "private" Masses, in some quiet corner of the Church, without lay participation, frequently even while a "main Mass" was being celebrated, for the people, in the body of the Church.

The celebration of the Eucharist was always the affair of the entire community in the early Church. Individual Masses were, of course, celebrated in private houses, but individual members of the Church participated fully in these Masses, and they were not celebrated concurrently with the public worship of the community or parish. "Private" Masses can be traced back to the religious communities of the early Middle Ages. Motivated by personal piety, the monks made strenuous efforts to "say" as many Masses as possible, with the result that too little attention was given to that essential feature of the Mass, its aspect as a communal eucharistic meal. To begin with, oratories adjoining the monastery church were used for the celebration of several Masses at the same time. Later on, it gradually became customary to set up several altars—side-altars—in the one church, and to allow several Masses to be celebrated simultaneously in the same church—a practice which would have been unthinkable in earlier times. A growing desire for votive Masses gave a very powerful impetus to the celebration of these private Masses. Concelebration is, however, practised today in the Eastern rites of the Catholic Church and is also the normal practice in the Latin rite during the Mass of the consecration of priests.

It is one of the aims of the modern liturgical movement to revive the ancient practice of the Church in this respect—to make it possible for several priests to concelebrate with the one celebrant, so that they adequately participate in one and the same Mass. At the same time, the movement hopes that the practice of "private" Masses will gradually be suppressed.

It would be possible to mention several other reforms, especially in connection with the administration of the sacraments and many of the prayers which priests say on various occasions, all of which point in the same direction. But the foregoing should be sufficient to show that what is at stake in the course of the present council's discussions is of the utmost importance in the cause of ecumenical Christianity. And, though the discussions have brought widely differing viewpoints to light, when seen as a whole they reveal a truly refreshing frankness. Even if it proves impossible for everything to be achieved all at once, each single, positive step forward is significant in itself, and is bound to lead to others later.

Certainly a great deal of fresh thought needs to be given to the theology of the Eucharist as well, and in particular with reference to its commemorative aspect, to the doctrine of transubstantiation, to the sacrificial aspect of the Eucharist and the problems involved, etc. But, here as elsewhere, this should not be the exclusive concern of Catholics alone.

It is to be hoped that Christians outside the Catholic Church will not simply take note of the efforts which the Catholic Church is making at present to advance the cause of Christian reunion, and remain content to refer rather complacently to the reformation which has already taken place in their worship. A reaction of this kind would, in the Catholic view, imply a one-sided attitude on the part of Protestant Christians. It is rather to be hoped that those Christians outside the Catholic Church will make every effort to examine their own position very carefully and to approach the Catholic Church more closely from their side, too, in a constructive and ecumenical spirit. The central point of controversy alone—that of the priestly office and function and its significance in the sphere of public worship—provides sufficient basis for serious ecumenical thought. It should be possible to prepare the way for the reunion of separated Christianity along these lines, in a constructive and positive manner, so long as this is done by both Catholic and Protestant Christians.

9

Latin—the Church's
Mother Tongue?

IT IS A remarkable fact that there are few problems of ecclesiastical reform which can excite such an emotional response in Catholics as that of Latin in the liturgy. All kinds of people—both those who understand Latin and those who do not—become quite passionate in their defence of Latin, although they always voice their arguments in their own language. The reasons put forward in favour of Latin in the liturgy are, however, generally of a cultural or aesthetic kind rather than of a pastoral nature. It is often forgotten, too, that all the arguments which a classics master may, with complete justification, put forward in support of the preservation of Latin in secondary education cannot be used to make out even an adequate case for the preservation of Latin in worship.

There seem to be a great number of emotional factors at work here, which make us view the whole question of Latin in the liturgy in the wrong proportions and in a false perspective. The arguments in favour of Latin are frequently exaggerated, and any discussion of the subject tends to be lifted up onto a quasi-dogmatic plane. Again and again one hears the same catch-phrases—Latin is *the* language of the Church, Latin is the language of the *mysterium tremendum,* Latin is the sacred language of Catholicism, Latin is the Catholic Esperanto, and so on. What is the best way to reply to these arguments? Undoubtedly the most suitable thing to do—and, bearing in mind the task facing the present Council, there is also an urgent need to do this—is to draw attention, in the most matter-of-fact and unemotional way possible, to certain obvious facts. Let us take, then, the one catch-phrase which sums up and includes all the others: "Latin is the mother tongue of the Church." For Latin to satisfy all the conditions contained in this sentence, it must have been spoken since the earliest times in the Church, it must be universally spoken within the Church, and it must at all times be intelligible.

Latin has not been spoken since the earliest times

(1) It is important here not to overlook the obvious, but nonetheless decisive, fact that the founder and head of the Church, Jesus Christ himself, did not, either in speech or in prayer, or in his sermons, use Latin (like the Romans, with whom he was acquainted), nor did he use Greek (like the priests of the Temple, who had become hellenized and thus completely alienated from the ordinary people), nor did he use Hebrew, the "sacred tongue" of the Old Testament, which he certainly understood. Christ used Aramaic —the ordinary colloquial language of the people.

(2) In the mother Church of all the Churches in the world, the Church of Jerusalem, the mother tongue and the liturgical language were also one and the same, that is, not Latin but the vernacular (Aramaic).

(3) The sacred Scriptures of our Church were, moreover, not written in Latin but in *koine* Greek—the vernacular language of the Roman Empire.

(4) As we have seen in a previous chapter, the most ancient liturgical language of the Roman Church, too, was not Latin but Greek —the oldest formulae of the Mass, those of Justin and Hippolytus, have been handed down to us in Greek. It was only round about the year 250 that the gradual transition from Greek to Latin began to take place. It was evidently the community itself which demanded this change of language, because Latin was becoming more and more the spoken language.

(5) Furthermore, even in the case of the other early Christian communities, the liturgy was not conducted in any special Latin liturgical language but, once again, in the vernacular.

How is it then possible for one language to be the "mother tongue" of the Church, if this language was not used either by the founder and head of this Church or by the Church's oldest community, or by either the Roman or any other primitive Christian community as an ecclesiastical language? At that time, no one felt the need for a "sacred language," intelligible only to the "initiated." The very opposite was in fact the case, and the Church felt that she existed for the "little ones"—the simple and the uneducated—and that she was committed to become Greek for the Greeks and barbarian for the barbarians.

Latin is not universally spoken within the Church

The claim that Latin as an ecclesiastical language acts as a "bond of unity," uniting all the various sections of the Church in the world, cannot be substantiated.

(1) During the first centuries of her history, the Church succeeded, to a phenomenal extent, in bringing about a real unity within herself, and Latin did not play the slightest part in this achievement. In the original task of building up the far-reaching but decentralized federal structure of the early Church, Latin was, quite simply, never a necessary instrument for the Church in her need to manifest her unity.

(2) Both before and after the relatively late emergence—in Rome —of Latin as the language of the Church—and it was only possible for Latin to become a liturgical language because it was also a vernacular—the early Church recognized a large number of official ecclesiastical and liturgical languages which were also, as in the case of Latin in Rome, at the same time vernacular languages. Among these can be listed Aramaic, Greek, Syriac, Egyptian (Coptic and Ethiopic), Old Slavonic, Armenian, and so on.

(3) All these languages are still officially recognized liturgical lan-

guages within the Catholic Church. Latin is simply one language of worship among many, although the most widespread. To this very day, during papal High Mass in Rome, the Scriptures are read in Greek as well as in Latin. (This is, of course, a survival from the original papal liturgy, conducted in Greek.) For many pilgrims in Rome, the greatest experience of the world-unity of the Catholic Church in St. Peter's is certainly not the Credo sung in Latin. During the singing of the Credo, those Catholics who are not "Latin" in language or culture are obliged to remain silent, while the exact significance of the Creed can only be guessed at by those Catholics who may be "Latin," but who no longer really understand the language and can, in any case, certainly not translate it accurately. This goes too even for the average Italian! No, the greatest experience for most pilgrims, of all races and colours, is the praying aloud of the Our Father in countless different languages during the great people's audiences in Rome, and the singing of the people in many languages.

(4) In furthering the cause of reunion with the separated Eastern Churches, Rome certainly does not insist that Latin should be accepted as the only liturgical language, even for the sake of "unity." On the contrary, the other liturgical languages have been particularly encouraged, especially since the time of Pius XI. What indeed is constantly borne in mind in Rome is that the various attempts to Latinize the Eastern Church (linguistically *and* culturally) played an essential part in her separation from Rome and in the widening of the schism later on, especially during the time of the Crusades.

(5) As far back as 1615, permission was granted for the conduct of the entire liturgy, including the Breviary, in Chinese, and this permission has never been officially rescinded. In 1949, permission for the celebration of Mass, exclusive of the Canon, in Chinese, was renewed. In Israel, too, some priests have been given permission to celebrate Mass in Hebrew.

To sum up, the Church has no need for any external and purely formal unity based on one single liturgical language. Her unity is primarily a spiritual unity—in the one Lord and the one Spirit, in the one Faith, in the one baptism and the one Eucharist, in the one charity and hope and under the one leader. Hers is a unity in multiplicity. She is the *one* Church of *many* languages. This is the miracle of Pentecost.

Latin is not intelligible

(1) Latin replaced Greek as the liturgical and ecclesiastical language of the Roman Church because Greek was no longer understood by the people. In the same way, Greek, which had become more and more confined to the sphere of scholarship and learning, gave way, in the eastern part of the Roman Empire, to Syriac, Armenian, Coptic and so on: that is, to the languages of the people. In every case, these changes took place because the new liturgical languages were universally intelligible.

(2) The discipline of the *arcanum,* which was exercised for a certain period by the early Church in order to protect the sacred mystery of Christian worship, made no division between the clergy —that is, the educated, who understood—and the Christian people —the uneducated, who did not understand—but only between the Christians and the *heathens.* In the cause of general intelligibility, even bishops and popes who were educated in the classical tradition, such as Ambrose, Augustine and Gregory the Great, expressly condemned the use of *classical* Latin and declared themselves in favour of a language which, though not debased, was closer to that of the people.

(3) The structure of the Mass at that time, and of the individual parts of the Mass, was distinct and clearly discernible. It was unencumbered by features of secondary importance. The movements and gestures were intelligible and had no need of explanation. The liturgical prayers were, to a great extent, simpler, more straightforward and of a more popular kind—indeed, the priest frequently used improvised prayers. All this helped the people enormously to understand the spoken word and the entire service.

(4) Nowadays—that is to say, since the Middle Ages—Latin is

understood only by an ever-decreasing number of scholars and priests, and even in their case there is often a serious deficiency of knowledge. How many scholars are there today who can follow and understand every reading of St. Paul's epistles simply by listening? And how many priests are there who can easily read the difficult patristic homilies in their breviaries? Latin can only be compared to Esperanto, the "language which is understood internationally," in that it too is often spoken about but very seldom spoken. One might be given a sensible answer to a question in Latin in one or two Catholic sacristies, but in the highways and byways of the world the only answer one would receive would be a blank look of incomprehension.

(5) There has been, in recent years, a considerable increase in the number of complaints about the use of unintelligible Mass-books in Latin. Especially with the spread of the so-called *Betsingmesse,* and the corresponding use of the missal in conjunction with this form of Mass celebration in the German-speaking countries, more and more people are beginning to feel that Latin has no place any more in the Mass. There would certainly be no lack of protests if a funeral service or a marriage were conducted in those countries entirely in Latin, or if the Epistle and Gospel of the Sunday were read only in that language! Catholics did not admire Pius XII because he was able to make superb speeches in Latin—it was, in fact, quite depressing to observe how the Italians who were present in St. Peter's Square during those speeches chattered and laughed among themselves because they did not understand what was being said—but because he was able to make himself perfectly understood in the vernacular languages of the various people he addressed. Who would dream of using Latin when he wanted to say something in church that really needed to be understood—such as, for example, an announcement or a statement about the collection? Nowhere in the entire Catholic world, from St. Peter's down to the most obscure village church, is it the practice to use Latin in such cases. No one can possibly deny that our people do not understand Latin, and no one can call a vague inkling of what is being said full "understand-

ing." Should anyone wish to dispute this fact, he should first of all ask a number of young people and adults what is meant by, for example, a few of the individual articles of the Latin Creed, which is, after all, intended to be a confession of faith, e.g., "Et in Spiritum Sanctum, Dominum et vivificantem, qui ex Patre Filioque procedit, qui cum Patre et Filio simul adoratur et conglorificatur, qui locutus est per prophetas." Why should it be a matter of complete indifference, in the Catholic's profession of his faith and his normal conversation with God in adoration, thanksgiving and petition, whether what is said is either precisely understood or else only more or less vaguely guessed at? What are we to make of the command to "adore God in spirit and in truth"?

(6) We seem to have completely forgotten the enormous instructional and missionary significance of the Mass in former times. For many centuries, the Mass was practically the only means of popular Christian instruction. Previously, the Mass was used to explain the Faith. Now, however, countless hours have to be devoted to teaching both children and adults the Faith, and these lessons have to be constantly repeated, in order to explain the Mass in its present complicated and no longer immediately intelligible form. Here, too, no one will deny what most liturgical scholars advocate, that the ideal form of public worship is one which requires a minimum of additional explanation and at the same time conveys a maximum of religious instruction and is also fully conducive to prayer. It is certainly not possible to regard a form of worship which, in order to be fully intelligible, requires the worshipper to learn a foreign, dead language, as ideal. The suggestion, which is frequently made, of instructing the people in Latin—some idealists have even proposed that Latin lessons should be given on the Vatican Radio!—is no less naïve-sounding. Surely our pastors have enough to do, trying to bring the Gospel home to present-day Christians, without having to put the additional burden of Latin on to the shoulders of their flock?

(7) Serious though the difficulties with regard to Latin may be in Europe, the position is even worse in those countries outside

Europe, where there is absolutely no tradition of Latin at all and where the native languages are not Indo-Germanic and are thus basically different from Latin in every respect. I was once told by a man who had made a special survey for Rome in Japan that he had come across many priests there who told him that they found saying the Breviary in Latin worse than any kind of lowly, menial work. "Yes," this man told me, "what if Peter and Paul had gone to Tokyo first? What should we have done, if we had been obliged to conduct our official conversations with God in a language that was spoken round about two thousand years ago in Japan, but is dead now? It would be most desirable if all our European fellow-Christians who are so keen on Latin were compelled to pray and conduct the liturgy for at least a year in Japanese—in fact, in the earliest form of Japanese and using the Japanese characters." The enormous impetus of the early Christian mission, which had only the most primitive tools at its disposal, was essentially due to the use of a liturgy which was intelligible and open to adaptation. Our present-day missions are carried out with great dedication of purpose, and every modern aid and method is used, but, taken as a whole, the results are minimal. In India, only 1.4% of the population is Catholic, in China 0.5%, in Japan 0.23%. Between 1880 and 1958, the total Catholic population of the world increased by only 0.14%. Many people who are competent to judge attribute the collapse of the Church's mission in Asia, if not entirely, then certainly in a very great measure, to the fault of a liturgy which is not adapted to the needs of those countries. No less a person than Cardinal Celso Constantini, who was for many years the secretary of the Propaganda Fide, wrote on 25 January 1940, in the *Osservatore Romano:* "During the first centuries of Christianity, the missionaries established the Church with a native hierarchy and, for liturgical purposes, they made use of whatever language they happened to find there—Syro-chaldaic, Greek, Latin, Old Slavonic, and so on. What we have tried to do is to christianize the East with a foreign hierarchy and with Latin. But the East has not been christianized." It was Constantini, too, who coined the phrase that the evangelization of China was not checked by the Chinese Wall but by the Latin wall. It is true that the missions are the very place where there are particular difficulties in introducing the vernacular because universal national languages are not (for the moment!) available. Here, too, the same rule could serve; let the Gospel be proclaimed (or the liturgy celebrated) in whatever language is used for announcements about collections and other matters which are really meant to be *understood*.

(8) Even in our extensively dechristianized Europe, the liturgy could be given a completely new missionary impetus. A living liturgy in the Church is never simply an abstract act of worship performed in God's honour; it is also always, and at the same time, something which is done to bring about the sanctification and edification of the faithful. In addition to its basic function as an act of worship, the liturgy also has, at the same time, an important catechetical and pastoral task. The language of the liturgy plays a decisive part here. It would, of course, not be true to say that people do or do not attend public worship simply because the vernacular is or is not used. Whether they attend or do not attend depends more upon whether their faith is alive or not, and upon the general state of the Church. But this depends essentially upon whether the liturgy which we celebrate is *intelligible* and intimately related to the people's needs. Such a liturgy can undoubtedly strengthen and put new life into a weak and ailing faith. How frequently one hears people say that they do not like going to Low Mass or High Mass, and how much they like going to a community Mass, during which the whole congregation sings and prays together. Many priests can testify to an increased church attendance and an increased number of communicants when this form of Mass is celebrated. It must also surely be counted as a positive advance that people should often be heard to say, after a Mass of this kind, that they thought it was *beautiful*. The most far-reaching effect is, however, the way in which the *experience* of this kind of Mass-celebration knits the people firmly together as a single community—this

experience is also powerful enough to move even those who would otherwise just stand around or kneel inattentively in church. A large proportion of the congregation goes without missals from the very first. It should, of course, be possible to conduct an international celebration of Mass in Latin, and to achieve the necessary degree of "intelligent understanding," in so far as circumstances permitted, by means of translations and additional explanation. But would a celebration of this kind ever become an *experience?* And, at the end of such a celebration in Latin, would many people not be justified in asking: "Why were we given translations to look at? Why were we not allowed to speak, and be spoken to, in our own language?" It is a well-known fact that it is often very difficult indeed to translate Latin accurately and intelligibly because of its special syntax and its participial constructions. Finally, it must also be obvious that, even if the circumstances made it possible for a *reader* to translate for each language-group, he would be a disturbing intermediary, coming between the people and the priest at the altar. The translator-reader can only be a temporary solution to the problem, which will disappear as soon as the priest himself at the altar is permitted, once again as in the past, to speak directly to the people in a language which is intelligible to all of them.

(9) We should not allow ourselves to be swayed in our choice of a liturgical language in a given linguistic zone by the fact that tourists or foreign workers constitute an exception to the general rule. There should be no question of withholding an intelligible liturgy from the fixed population of a Christian community merely because of the presence of a few exceptional individuals, especially as these probably understand as little of the liturgy in their own counry as they do in the country they are visiting or living in. The much repeated saying that the Catholic "feels at home anywhere" in the Catholic Church means basically that he really understands as little of what is going on in church everywhere as he does at home. In order to make up for this lack, however, active pastors in very many towns are already providing facilities for worship in various lan-

guages. It is certainly not in order for a Catholic to be given a translation in his own parish, though this can be perfectly appropriate in the case of a tourist who happens to be present in the church.

Latin is not a matter of faith

Is it not possible, however, that an extensive use of the vernacular may lead to liturgical confusion? It stands to reason that no intelligent pastor wants chaos in the liturgy. But is there really any grave danger of this, in view of the post-tridentine rubrication of the Mass? Let us rather consider the possible danger which threatens from the other side. J. A. Jungmann, perhaps our greatest liturgical scholar, writes:

> The liturgical life of the Church emerged from the reorganization of 1570 in a refined and clarified form. But, at the same time, a certain rigidity was introduced into the Roman Mass in that, in the first place, the new Missal was promulgated as the standard form and its use declared to be binding on the whole Church and, in the second place, any kind of local initiative was forbidden. It was, however, never laid down that such rigidity should be a permanent condition. Instead of improving upon what was already in existence, a juridical and casuistical paraphase of what had been established by the Council was introduced and a new, specialized branch of learning, the rubrication of the liturgy, was developed. For this reason, that period of liturgical history initiated by Pius V has been termed the "epoch of rubrication" or the "epoch of stagnation in the liturgy."[1]

It is most undesirable that all subjective values and all the variety of individual experience, which were once inherent in the Mass, should find refuge in a host of devotions outside the Mass. What we must try to find here is a middle course between chaotic arbitrariness and a rigid uniformity which is alien to human life and experience—in a word, a unity in multiplicity, but a genuinely Catholic multiplicity. Or, as Hofinger says:

A genuinely Catholic form of worship must not only reflect the radiant unity of the *Una Sancta*—it must also leave room for individual variety and for the particular qualities of the many races and nationalities which should be able to find a true home in the one Church. National and racial character ought to be allowed somehow to express itself in worship as in other spheres, without destroying the underlying unity of the Church. This can most easily be made clear by a comparison between the unity of worship and that of faith. Within the Catholic Church there can, of course, be only one Catholic faith, which is one and the same for the German as for the Chinese Catholic. But the Chinese Catholic does not have to shed his Chinese nature before accepting the Catholic faith in order fully to become a Catholic. He believes as a Chinese, he matures in the faith as a Chinese and he reacts to the Christian revelation as a Chinese. If it is his duty to proclaim the Christian revelation, he is bound to do this as a Chinese. Surely this applies too to his worship as a Christian?[2]

Latin as a liturgical language is not a matter of faith but a question of practical and pastoral expediency. Although Latin did satisfy this need during an earlier period of the Church's history, it cannot be said that it does so now. Even the Council of Trent expressed itself very cautiously on this point, despite the violent debates among the Reformers and their sometimes rather rash reforms. The first version of the chapter in question contained a reference to the basic suitability of Latin as a standardized language which was incapable of further development. The decree which was subsequently accepted, however, confined itself to the conclusion that no advantage would be derived from celebrating Mass in the language of the people *passim,* that is, everywhere without a strictly regularized form, and thus from abandoning the "long-established form."

But it has perhaps already become superfluous to comment at such length on this topic. During the present Vatican Council,

Mass has been celebrated so often in a different rite and in a different language, thus providing the Council Fathers with visible proof of the manifestation of the unity of the one Faith and the one Eucharist in a multiplicity of different rites, forms and languages. This repeated experience of catholicity in the liturgy has undoubtedly played a decisive part in encouraging and inspiring among the Fathers an open-minded approach towards liturgical renewal, including the question of liturgical language.

When it is remembered that the Council has the task of breaking the habits of more than a thousand years, then it is not difficult to grasp why it proceeds only step by step and makes general regulations, while leaving particular decisions within this general framework to the episcopates of the various countries.

NOTES:

[1] *Missarum Sollemnia*, vol. 1, p. 179 f. (*The Mass of the Roman Rite, its Origins and Development*, New York, Benziger, 1961.)

[2] J. Hofinger and J. Kellner, *Liturgische Erneuerung in der Weltmission*, Innsbruck, Vienna and Munich (1957), p. 437.

10

The Renewal of the Canon

The universal prayer of the Church

UNLESS ALL APPEARANCES are deceptive, we can look forward
with confidence to the reinstatement, in the renewed liturgy of the
Mass, of the prayer that was in general use in the earliest days of
the Church, that survived later in various forms, and is still preserved in the present-day Roman rite in the solitary word *oremus*
just before the Offertory chant. This prayer will thus, if our expectations are fulfilled, be inserted once more into the liturgy after
the reading of the Gospel, and the sermon. The prayer, known as
the "Universal Prayer of the Church" (*oratio communis*) or the
"Prayer of the Faithful" (*oratio fidelium*), is a prayer for the whole
Church and for all its members, but in particular for those in holy
orders. The priest prays for the Church, for the Pope, bishop and
clergy, and for all the faithful, for secular rulers, or all who are in
need, who suffer affliction or are ill, and for all who are exposed
to danger. He prays, too, for the unity of the Church and for
peace in the world, as well as for special intentions. The people
respond: "We beseech thee, hear us!" or "Lord, have mercy upon
us!" It will be possible to formulate, within the framework of this
universal prayer of the Church, intercessions for the special problems of the times or for the local needs of the community or parish, and to pray for the living and the dead in the communion of
saints. It must surely be a positive advantage in the celebration of
Mass, if special petitions, which have hitherto been allowed to find

expression only in various Catholic devotions—and then very often in a highly questionable form— are incorporated into the celebration itself and expressed in the communal prayer of all the faithful present. It might also even be possible to integrate into the body of the Mass, and thus give greater significance to, the particular intention expressed by masses for the dead, which, since the Middle Ages, have become unduly prominent in Catholic practice. What comes particularly to mind here is that a special intercession could be made for one individual deceased person on the day of the funeral. This would be preferable to the present practice of repeatedly directing an entire Mass to this single intention, which is, after all, of secondary importance only, compared with the intention of the Mass as a whole.

If the universal prayer of the Church is re-introduced into the Mass, will this not give rise to an unnecessary repetition, since the very same intercessions are voiced in the Canon—for the Church, the Pope, bishop and all the faithful, the living and the dead and for various intentions, as well as commemoration of the martyrs? And is it not true that the main aim, in any reform of the Mass proposed by the Council, should be to revise the entire rite, shortening and simplifying it, with the result that repetitions are avoided, what is unessential is suppressed and what is essential is brought into prominence?

The eucharistic prayer

All this only goes to prove that the Canon itself is in urgent need of reform. Not the least important reason for the disappearance of the Universal Prayer of the Church from the Roman rite is that the intercessions were inserted into the Canon itself. The unity of the ancient and extraordinarily homogeneous eucharistic prayer was destroyed by these later, heterogeneous insertions. It is very difficult nowadays to thread one's way through these various intercessions and piece together the fragments of the single great prayer of thanksgiving which at one time, in conjunction with the

reception of the sacramental gifts, constituted the entire Mass. It
is because of these later additions and the gradual spread of the
practice of silent prayer that the Canon has now really lost its
original character as a prayer of commemoration, thanksgiving
and proclamation. Very little of what St. Paul says in I Cor. 11.26
can be found today: "For as often as you shall eat this bread and
drink this chalice, you shall *shew* [= herald, proclaim] the death
of the Lord, until he come."

The probable re-introduction of the *oratio communis* will make it
relatively easy to restore the ancient, homogeneous eucharistic
prayer in its original character. All that has to be done is to leave
out of the present Canon the intercessions which are already included in the *oratio communis*. In this way, the structure of the
ancient prayer of thanksgiving emerges clearly. What becomes immediately apparent is the close similarity that exists between the
present eucharistic prayer and the earliest known version of the
eucharistic prayer in the Roman liturgy, that of Hippolytus of
Rome (*c.* 215):

Eucharistic Prayer	*Eucharistic Prayer Today*
"The Lord be with you!"	"The Lord be with you!"
"And with thy spirit!"	"And with thy spirit!"
"Lift up your hearts!"	"Lift up your hearts!"
"We have lifted them up to the Lord!"	"We have lifted them up to the Lord!"
"Let us give thanks to the Lord!"	*"Let us give thanks to the Lord* our God!"
"It is meet and just."	"It is meet and just."
"We give thee thanks, O God, through thy beloved servant *Jesus Christ,* whom thou hast sent to us in recent times as our saviour and redeemer and the herald of thy new dispensa-tion. He is thy undivided word, thou hast made everything through him, and it was well pleasing to thee. Thou didst send him from heaven	"It is truly meet and just, right and for our salvation, that *we* should always and everywhere *give thanks to thee,* almighty Father, everlasting *God, through Christ* our Lord. It is through him that the angels praise thy majesty, the dominions adore it, the powers fear it. The heavens and the heavenly hosts and the blessed

into the womb of the Virgin and, carried in the womb, he became flesh and was revealed as thy Son, born by the Holy Spirit of the Virgin. In that he fulfilled thy will and won for thee a holy people, he extended his hands in suffering, to redeem from suffering those who believe in him.

And since he was handed over, a willing victim, to suffering, to deprive death of its power and to break the chains binding us to the devil and to trample hell underfoot and to enlighten the just and to mark an epoch and to proclaim the resurrection, he took the bread and, giving thanks to thee, said: *Take and eat, this is my body, that is broken for you.* Likewise he took the chalice, saying: *This is my blood, that is shed for you.* Whenever you do this, do it *in my memory.*

seraphim join together in one hymn to celebrate their joy. We beseech thee to let our voices join with theirs and humbly confess thee, saying: Holy, holy, holy, Lord God of hosts! Heaven and earth are filled with thy glory. Hosanna in the highest! Blessed is he who comes in the name of the Lord! Hosanna in the highest! Therefore, most gracious Father, we humbly pray and beseech thee, through Jesus Christ, thy Son, to receive and bless these gifts, these offerings, these holy, unblemished oblations. We pray thee, God, deign to make this offering wholly blessed. Approve it and ratify it, making it just and acceptable, so that it may become for us the Body and Blood of thy well-beloved Son, our Lord Jesus Christ.

He, on the day before he suffered, took bread into his holy and venerable hands and, with his eyes lifted up towards heaven to thee, God, his almighty Father, he gave thanks to thee, blessed it, broke it, and gave it to his disciples, saying: *Take and eat all of you of this, for this is my body.* In like manner, when he had supped, taking also this excellent chalice into his holy and venerable hands, and giving thanks to thee, he blessed it and gave it to his disciples, saying: *Take and drink all of you of this, for this is the chalice of my blood, of the new and everlasting covenant,* the mystery of faith, *which shall be shed for you and for many so that sins may be remitted.* Whenever you shall do these things, you shall do them *in memory of me.*

Mindful also of his death and resurrection, we offer the bread and the chalice, giving thanks to thee for deeming us worthy to stand before thee and serve thee. And we ask thee to send the Holy Ghost down upon this offering of thy holy Church. Bringing her together in unity, do thou bestow on all thy saints who receive it the fullness of the Holy Spirit, to confirm our faith in truth,

Therefore, Lord, we, thy servants, and also thy holy people, *mindful of the blessed suffering of the same Christ, thy Son, our Lord, likewise of his resurrection from the dead and his glorious ascension into heaven, offer* to thy sublime majesty, *from thy gifts and presents, a pure sacrifice,* a holy sacrifice, an unblemished sacrifice, the holy bread of everlasting life and the chalice of eternal salvation. Be pleased to look down upon them with a gracious and serene countenance, as thou wast once favourably disposed to accept the offerings of thy just servant Abel, the sacrifice of our patriarch Abraham, and that which thy high priest Melchisedech offered to thee. Humbly we ask thee, almighty God, command these things to be carried up by the hands of thy holy angel to thy altar on high, before the face of thy divine majesty, so that those of us who, by partaking in the sacrifice of this altar, shall have received the most sacred body and blood of thy Son, may be filled with every grace and heavenly blessing. Through the same Christ our Lord. It is through him, Lord, that thou dost always create all these good gifts, sanctify, vivify and bless them, and bestow them upon us.

so that we may praise and glorify thee *through thy servant Jesus Christ, through whom is praise and honour* to the Father, to the Son and to the Holy Ghost, in thy holy Church, now and for ever and ever."
"Amen."

Through him, and with him, and in him, *is to thee, God,* almighty Father, in the unity of the Holy Ghost, *all honour and glory.* For ever and ever."
"Amen."

The theological emphasis

What strikes us particularly in an examination of these parallel texts of the two eucharistic prayers is that the various points of theological emphasis are more equally distributed according to the original sense and significance of the Eucharist in the case of the early eucharistic prayer of Hippolytus. (It should be noted in this context that this was only one of the many rites used by the Roman community.) It is possible fully to understand the entire eucharistic prayer only if it is regarded as a fulfilment, in obedience, of the Lord's command: "Do this in *memory* of me." The fundamental aspect of the eucharistic prayer is its commemorative quality. In contrast to all natural religions, the Christian faith, as a historical religion, is always essentially related to concrete soteriological acts which took place in the past, so that it may be at the same time orientated towards the future—we call to mind the death and resurrection of the Lord until he comes again. It is for this reason that we are mindful of the Lord. This is the reason for our *memoria Domini,* our *anamnesis.* We commemorate all the saving acts of God which he brought about in Jesus Christ—Christ's life, death and resurrection. This is all to be found in the present form of the eucharistic prayer in the Roman rite, and especially in the crucial words which follow the words of consecration (*"Unde et memores . . ."*): "Therefore, Lord, we . . . are mindful of the blessed suffering of . . . thy Son, likewise of his resurrection from the dead and his glorious ascension into heaven." In the *praefatio communis,* commemoration of God's acts of salvation in Christ has been whittled down to the single phrase *"per Christum Dominum nostrum."* In the prefaces of the Holy Trinity and the Apostles, it has completely disappeared. In earlier times, the *prae-fatio,* that is, what was spoken, or prayed, before God and the community, was not simply an audibly prayed or sung introduction to the Canon in the narrowest sense of the word. It was, on the contrary, the whole eucharisic prayer, and was thus prayed aloud in its entirety. The *memoria Domini* of the eucharistic prayer of the ancient Roman rite thus embraces, in the fullest dimensions, everything that God has brought about for our salvation in Jesus Christ and at the same time reminds us of the Apostles' Creed. It is still possible for us to recover, even now, this original, all-embracing quality of the eucharistic prayer, if the relevant passages from the special prefaces of Christmas, the Holy Cross, Easter, the Ascension and Pentecost are considered together.

The commemoration which takes place in the celebration of the Eucharist is, of course, not simply a question of calling-to-mind in the purely historical sense. How would it be possible to be mindful of God's saving acts in Christ, without being spontaneously carried on from *thinking about* these acts to *thanking* God for them? The word "eucharist" itself means "thanksgiving," a prayer of thanks, the celebration of thanksgiving. What is expressed in the Creed in the form of a confession of faith is *proclaimed,* in joyous gratitude, in the eucharistic prayer. How would it be possible to commemorate God's saving acts in Christ gratefully, without proclaiming them aloud in gratitude and joy? Thus the celebration of the Eucharist is a powerfully effective celebration of both commemoration and thanksgiving, and the eucharistic prayer is the proclaiming aloud of a prayer of commemoration and thanksgiving by the whole priestly people and their special servants in holy orders: ". . . *nos servi tui, sed et plebs tua sancta*" (". . . we, thy servants, and also thy holy people"). The eucharistic prayer, in which the plural form is always used throughout, is certainly not a private prayer of the priest, as seemed to be the case when so many prayers in the first person singular were introduced for the first time into the early Roman rite during the Carolingian period. It is, on the contrary, the prayer of commemoration and thanksgiving of the whole Christian community. It is the people, too, who, together with the priest, bring up, or present, their gifts, as a visible expression of their mindfulness of and gratitude to God, the Father (*offerimus,* in its original sense, means, "we bring up," "we present," hence "we offer"). In the secular sphere, too, a vote of thanks is often followed by the presentation of a complimentary gift. The presentation of these gifts (our spiritual "offering" or *sacrificium laudis* consists in the bringing up of gifts in homage—there is no question of destroying or annihilating them) is at the same time an expression of our attitude of obedience and surrender to God's will, which should correspond to the attitude of obedience and surrender of our High Priest, who made the ultimate act of submission on the Cross. The rite indeed makes a veiled allusion to the fact that when the priest, celebrating with the people, reaches the climax of the eucharistic prayer—that is, when he says the words of consecration—he is not only, by virtue of his words and actions, the spokesman of the people in the congregation, but also actually stands in place of the one who is present and is in reality acting here—Christ himself. The offering of the Church can only be fully understood when it is seen as the result of Christ's complete surrender of himself. The gifts which, by being offered in thanksgiving, are consecrated into Christ himself, are received in the communion of the sacred meal. The prayer of commemoration, offering and thanksgiving finally culminates and achieves its aim in the eucharistic meal, a communion which all Christians share together with Christ: "For we, being many, are one bread, one body; all that partake of one bread" (1 Cor. 10.17).[1]

Many very difficult theological questions concerning the doctrine of the Eucharist emerge in this connection. The theology of the Counter-Reformation was in many ways biassed and of a very dubious nature, especially where its teaching on the Eucharist was concerned. For example, the commemorative aspect of the Eucharist and its character as a feast, both of which were still in prominence in the Middle Ages, were neglected, whereas its sacrificial aspect was subjected to overemphasis. Now, it is the concept of the sacrifice, and the way in which it should be presented and brought home to the people, that pose numerous questions which have still to be resolved. In any renewal of the Canon, the original proportions of the eucharistic prayer and its earliest perspectives would have to be taken carefully into account in the light of Holy

Scripture. On the other hand, it is obviously neither strictly necessary nor, for that matter, even remotely possible, for all the theological problems to be solved before embarking on a renewal of the eucharistic prayer for practical purposes of pastoral care. This applies similarly to many other questions concerning the liturgy and its renewal.

During the present Council, Pope John XXIII has introduced the name of St. Joseph into the Mass, thus changing a Canon which has never been changed since the Tridentine reforms. This must surely be a sign to the Vatican Council that it need have no fear of altering or reforming the Canon. The Council's morning Masses in particular have adequately demonstrated how many of the non-Latin Catholic liturgies have preserved the eucharistic prayer in a much clearer and more distinct form than the Latin liturgy of the Roman rite. What has particularly impressed a great number of Council Fathers is that the eucharistic prayer, including the words of consecration, is said aloud in many of these non-Latin rites, and in some cases even sung, and that the prayer is concluded by the "Amen" of the people. This example of the non-Latin rites should surely inspire the Council to go ahead with the reform of the eucharistic prayer, where the Roman rite is most urgently in need of renewal. Our worship would be so much more intelligible and meaningful, and the Mass would make a much greater impact, were the Canon restored to conform more closely to the model of the earliest Roman rite. This could be achieved if the Canon were prayed aloud, if its structure were made more homogeneous and, provided that care was taken not to sacrifice its total significance in the plan of salvation, if it were more closely adapted to the annual cycle of the liturgical year. To embrace the best Catholic tradition in this way would in itself be an ecumenical action. Any reform which stops short at the Canon, and does not attempt to provide the Eucharist and the words of consecration with the new form of expression which they need, would be, for non-Catholic Christians as well, a superficial reform. A renewal of

the Canon would make the Mass correspond more closely to the
Last Supper and give greater depth to the meaning of the words
of our Lord: "Do this in memory of me," and thus confer a great
blessing on the Church and the Christian world.

NOTES:

[1] See also in this connection J. A. Jungmann, *Das eucharistische Hochgebet. Grundgedanken des Canon Missae,* Rothenfelser Reihe 1, Würzburg (1956).

11

Reform of the Breviary
in the Light of History

The problem

IF I MAY BE perfectly frank at the very outset of this chapter, I
must admit that I do not very much care for this subject in the
form in which I have to deal with it. Can there, in fact, really be
such a thing as reform of the "Breviary"?

The task confronting the Second Vatican Council is that of the
renewal of the Church as a preparation for reunion. The central
point of this renewal is the reform of religious worship, and it
would be impossible to renew the Church without renewing those
who are in holy orders. This, in turn, would be impossible without
renewing the priestly life of prayer, which has clearly to be carried
out according to the Gospel, and in particular, in accordance with
Christ's commandment: "And, when you are praying, speak not
much, as the heathens; for they think that in their much speaking
they may be heard. Be you not therefore like to them; for your
Father knoweth what is needful for you, before you ask him" (Matt.
6.7 f.).

Is it therefore not simply a question of reforming the Breviary,
but of renewing the entire life of prayer of the priest? This would,
of course, envisage a far more radical and comprehensive renewal than that of the Breviary alone, since the Breviary is

in fact no more than one special, historical form of priestly prayer.

Many different forms of liturgical prayer are interwoven into the fabric of the Breviary. Before any thorough renewal of the Breviary is attempted, it would be necessary to distinguish three basic forms:

(1) The Service of the Word of the whole of the Christian people.

(2) The priestly prayer of the secular priest.

(3) The canonical hours of the monk.

In all these three forms of prayer, three fundamental structural elements play an essential part: (*a*) the reading of Holy Scripture; (*b*) the prayer of the Psalms; (*c*) certain prescribed formulae of prayer.

The three structural elements are common to the three forms of prayer, and thus provide a clear link connecting all three in the liturgy. Very many of the structural defects which exist in present-day liturgical prayer have come about because insufficient care has been taken in the past to distinguish clearly between the three forms, and to understand the different layout and plan of the universal Service of the Word, the prayer of the secular priest and that of the monk. In practice, the monastic canonical hours have overshadowed the prayer of the secular priest and both have obscured the Church's universal Service of the Word. A true renewal, rather than a mere patching up of certain historical anomalies, will only be brought about on condition that we are prepared to deal separately, but with equal emphasis, with each of these three forms. Many bishops and priests are aware of the need for this approach. At this point, however, we should refer to the recent findings of liturgical research, in order to see more clearly, in the light of the historical development of the Breviary, not only the present position, but also the relevant sections of the schema on the Breviary which is before the Council.[1] I shall first of all consider the development of the Divine Office and then consider the various attempts to reform it.

The development of the Divine Office of the Church

Phase I: a voluntary and private observance of the hours of prayer (from the first to the third century).

For several centuries, no rule concerning prayer was imposed exclusively upon one definite group of persons within the Church, nor was there any law which formally laid down that any such prayer should be obligatory. Nevertheless, it has been recorded that, since the time of Hippolytus of Rome, thus from the year 200 or thereabouts, Christians, doubtless under the influence of Judaism, prayed daily together, and that these prayers were held at certain fixed hours (*horae*) on each day. The hours of the Breviary still correspond to these original times—in the morning (Lauds) and in the evening (Vespers), at the third, sixth and ninth hours (Terce, Sext and None) and at midnight (Matins). The hours of the Church, then, began as voluntary and private prayer which was practised by *all* the faithful.

Phase 2: a voluntary, but public observance of the hours of prayer (fourth century).

At this time there was a transition from the private prayer of the hours to their public, communal observation. This came about, on the one hand, in episcopal churches—the pastoral clergy holding the morning and evening hours for the entire people. In this case, the hours consisted principally of a reading from Holy Scripture with commentary, psalms and prayers. A change also came about, on the other hand, first in the case of groups of monks and later in entire monastic communities. Here, the monks communally observed not only the morning and evening hours, but also all the private day and night hours. It was at about this period that Prime and Compline were introduced for the first time.

Phase 3: an obligatory observance, binding on all "canons" (eighth century).

The "canons" of the early Middle Ages, who lived together in enclosed communities and observed the rules of canon law, assumed, from the monasteries, the duty of saying all the day and night hours, in Latin. The rest of the clergy, whose duties were mainly pastoral, generally speaking continued to try to observe only the morning and evening hours.

Phase 4: an obligatory observance, binding on all priests (twelfth and thirteenth centuries).

When a monk was prevented from being present in the choir, he was expected to say in private whatever part of the Divine Office he had omitted. This also presumably applied to the canon. Eventually it came about that any priest, such as a chaplain to a household, who was living outside the religious community and thus could not come under the direct organization of canon law, was obliged to fulfil the obligation concerning the recitation of the Divine Office to the same extent as any canon living in a community. This duty, which had its origins in the monastic way of life, became binding on *all* priests in the twelfth century. In the thirteenth, it was laid down in more precise terms for all clergy of the order of subdeacon and above. Thus, the number of those who recited the Office privately rather than publicly became greater and greater, especially since more clergy were undertaking pastoral work and fewer took part in the public prayer of the hours in choir. Throughout the whole of the Middle Ages, apart from a few hymns and so on, sung during the major feasts, the vernacular was never used in any part of the liturgy. Within the monastic communities, however, the continued growth of the practice of prayer in choir was helped by the transference of all physical work, originally carried out by all the monks, to lay-brothers. At this period, too, the Little Office of our Lady and the fifteen gradual psalms were introduced, and it became customary to pray the Our Father silently. This form of Divine Office could only be managed successfully by contemplative orders, and the entire situation stood in urgent need of reform. All proposed reforms aimed, in general, at a simplification and abbreviation of the Divine Office and the adaptation of what was primarily a monastic form of prayer to suit the needs of the secular clergy. It is possible to trace several attempts at reform throughout the course of the second millennium, but none of these have yet succeeded in achieving their aims. This is precisely why it is most necessary for the Second Vatican Council to take up the matter again and devote itself to the task of reforming priestly prayer.

Attempted reforms

Phase 1: the appearance of the "breviary" (from the tenth to the thirteenth centuries).

The various books which were necessary for the observance of the hours of prayer in choir were grouped together to form the (shortened) Breviary. The *breviarium* was originally a single page showing the order of sequence of the fixed parts of the Office. Now it is, of course, the book which provides the entire text of the Office, for the use of the individual priest. The earliest examples of different versions of the Breviary in the form of a "pocket edition" date from the tenth and eleventh centuries. In the thirteenth century, it was particularly the breviary of the Roman Curia, the members of which were obliged to travel frequently, which began to gain in importance. What is especially regrettable is that the cuts which were made in the compilation of the Breviary were made at the expense of the scriptural readings. Until the eleventh century, the principle that the whole of Scripture should be read in the course of each year was strictly adhered to, but later these readings were whittled down to the small fraction of Scripture that is read nowadays in the Breviary.

Phase 2: the sixteenth-century reforms.

The *devotio moderna,* a pious movement originating in Holland, did much to popularize the practice of a methodical, contemplative approach to the Breviary, especially among the religious orders. Cardinal Quiñones' breviary of 1535, commissioned by Clement VII, introduced a far-reaching reform in the method of private recitation. The rubrics were simplified, all the elements which derived from the once communal character of the Breviary, such as the responsories and chapters, were left out, and the hymns and antiphons were cut down. Most of the Old Testament and the whole of the New were read in the course of the liturgical year. The psalms were reduced to three for each hour. This breviary, which was excellently suited to its period, went through about a hundred editions in a short space of time, but was banned by the reactionary Pope Paul IV, on the grounds that it was "untraditional." In 1568, Pius V had another breviary published, and its use was binding on the clergy. This breviary restored the traditional form—the reappearance of the communal "choir" elements, for example, clearly marking a retrogression. The principal cuts were made in the additional sections—the Little Office of our Lady, the Office of the Dead and the penitential psalms, for example, were omitted. The frequently apocryphal readings from the lives of the early saints gave way to some extent to New Testament readings. But countless new feast-days of the saints were introduced into the Roman breviary in the period which followed, and the ferial office became more and more obscured.

Phase 3: the twentieth-century popes (Pius X–XII).

Pius X shortened the Sunday Office of Matins, cut out many repetitions in the Breviary, and so arranged the psalter that all the 150 psalms could, as a general rule, be said in the course of each week. In 1945, after the deficiencies of the translation from the Vulgate had been generally recognized, Pius XII approved the new Latin translation of the psalter which had been made by the professors of the Pontifical Biblical Institute and authorized the publication of the breviary containing the new psalter. In 1955, a further reform was introduced into the rubrication of the Breviary. This was generally regarded as the first step towards a fundamental reform.

Practical possibilities today

All the reforms that have so far been attempted, especially those of the Council of Trent and the present century, suffer from the fault of having always been merely external adaptations, and never fundamental renewals, carried out in the spirit of the New Testament and going right to the heart of the matter. Will the Second Vatican

Council succeed in bringing about this *fundamental* renewal which is so urgently needed? It should hardly be necessary to stress the fact that, at present, priestly prayer, measured against the yardstick of Matt. 6.7 f., is in many ways in an appalling state. Instead of providing spiritual sustenance, the Breviary is often no more than an additional burden which the secular priest is scarcely able to bear. Instead of providing an inducement for prayer, the Breviary, because of the need to get through an enormous number of words, all too frequently makes really good, deeply engaged prayer impossible. It would be most unfair to blame our pastors, who in the course of their duties often work themselves to the point of exhaustion, for this situation. No human being, it is true, is entirely free from the tendency to be slothful and to forget his duties, but the fault lies in this case with the Church's official arrangement of priestly prayer, which makes it to a very large extent impossible, under the circumstances which normally prevail in the sphere of pastoral work today, for even the best priest regularly to pray really well.

If a real improvement, rather than simply a change, is to be made (there have, after all, been many changes already), and if an end is to be made to the tendency, which has increased far more than many suspect among priests, to apply "self-help" and to introduce quite arbitrary reforms of their own, then a reform of the rubrics alone will certainly not be sufficient. What has to be reformed is nothing less than the whole of the Church's liturgical prayer. It will be necessary to make a clear distinction between the three basic forms of which we have already spoken at the beginning of this chapter and then to bring about a renewal which is closely adapted to each of these three different forms. At the same time, care must be taken to preserve the structural elements—the reading of Holy Scripture, the prayer of the psalter and the prescribed formulae of prayer—which are common to all three forms. In concrete terms, the following are required:

(1) *A renewed service of the Word of the entire Christian people.* We have already seen, in the case of the reform of the Mass, that it is necessary to differentiate clearly between the Service of the Word and

that of the Eucharist. It ought, however, to be possible to effect a renewal, within the framework of the reform of the Mass, of the Service of the Word in association with the eucharistic celebration and, at the same time, to restore the ancient Service of the Word which was originally independent of the eucharistic service, in the form in which it has already been described in the section on the early phases in the development of the Divine Office—in this case, with particular emphasis on the morning and evening hours. A Service of the Word of this kind would, like the ancient service, have to consist of scriptural readings with a short exposition, the singing of psalms and prayers. It could be held particularly on Sundays and feast-days, on the vigils of the major feasts, in Advent and Lent, and on all special occasions. It would be particularly beneficial if Services of the Word of this type were to be conducted, circumstances permitting, on Sundays and feast-days in those districts where there are no priests, by an authorized layman. If the priest himself were to take part in such a Service of the Word of the whole people, he should then be released from the obligation to say his private, priestly prayer.

(2) *A renewal of the monastic canonical hours.* Since the Divine Office in its present form is principally suited to monastic use, the best solution would be to allow monks in particular to continue in this tradition. It is possible for them to do what secular priests cannot do— they are able to keep to definite hours of prayer throughout the day and, what is more, they can observe these hours regularly as a community. A reform of this monastic prayer is, however, necessary. The Office should be both simplified and shortened and, perhaps most important of all, a scriptural reading, in the form of a *lectio continua* embracing the whole of the Bible, should be introduced. Those monastic communities whose rule is firmly established in tradition are bound to be more concerned than others with the preservation of Latin in their canonical hours.

(3) *A renewal of the priestly prayer of secular priests.* In the case of the prayer of the secular priesthood, there is no question, as there is in the case of the monastic orders, of striving to preserve a monastic

tradition in the Divine Office. The present trouble has arisen precisely because a form of prayer which was quite suited to the monastic communities was simply imposed upon the secular priesthood in the course of history. It follows then that no satisfactory solution will be achieved merely by simplifying or shortening the Office. As we have seen, the Breviary has already been shortened quite often in the past, and this has not, in our experience, resulted in a better form of essential prayer, but simply in shorter prayer, and sometimes even in a loss of essential elements.

The secular priest's prayer should not necessarily be shorter, but better, deeper and more recollected, and if he is to achieve this, he must have time for prayer, a time of peace and quiet, during which he has no need to hurry, but can be quite free for God. According to Matt. 6.7 f., prayer does not consist of saying a great number of words, but of being peaceful, and free for God. In concrete terms, this means that what is necessary is a regulation concerning prayer which prescribes this quiet, recollected time for God. And regulation which prescribes a *definite number of words* will, even if the prayer is in a shortened form, lead again and again, in the pressure of life and pastoral work today, to a hurried approach to prayer, which is unsound and deadening in its effect upon the priest's relationship with God. It is not a regulation of this type which is required, but one which concedes to the secular priest, who is compelled to live and carry out his pastoral duties under the pressure of modern conditions, this *necessary time* for God. It is imperative for us to arrive at a realistic appreciation of the situation in which the secular priest has to carry out his pastoral work nowadays, and so to view this situation that we do not make demands of the priest which are lofty and pious-sounding, but in practice absolutely impossible to fulfil.

What has to be worked out is a meaningful form of prayer for this "necessary time for God," into which the whole of the priestly life of prayer is integrated. It is important, too, for us to rid ourselves of the illusion which claims that it is necessary for the priest, besides fulfilling his obligatory priestly prayer, which in itself frequently de-

mands a heroic effort, to go on practising other, voluntary forms of
spiritual exercise, such as meditation, in addition. Surely it should
be possible to incorporate the legitimate part of this claim into the
whole of the priestly prayer?

How could all this be achieved in concrete terms? Several different practicable arrangements are possible, each giving priority to
what is essential in priestly prayer. Assuming that a period of prayer
lasting for three quarters of an hour each day were laid down as obligatory for the secular priest, then the following pattern could be
prescribed (the exact sequence is, of course, not of first importance):

The first quarter of an hour: *A consecutive reading* (lectio continua) *of
the Bible,* beginning with Genesis, continued as far as the Apocalypse, and then beginning again at Genesis. Those able to could
use the language of the original biblical text. It would be scarcely
possible to estimate the effect that a quarter of an hour spent regularly every day with the word of God would have on the priest's personal holiness, and on his sermons, instructions and pastoral work,
or to measure the extent of his knowledge of the Bible after he had
been doing this for twenty or thirty years.

The second quarter of an hour: *Meditation or spiritual reading.* The
method known as the *devotio moderna* seems to be very well suited to
the particular conditions of modern life and pastoral work and to
have achieved excellent results, though it goes without saying that
on no account should any one definite form or technique of meditation be imposed. An especially profitable form of meditation is
that which is based on an unhurried, recollected reading of spiritual
authors. It should be possible for the bishops, in conference, to issue,
and from time to time to revise, lists of good spiritual reading-mat-
ter, consisting both of "classic" works, in particular those of the
Church Fathers and the medieval spiritual writers, and, perhaps
more important, of good modern spiritual books.

The third quarter of an hour: *Morning and evening prayers,* thus going
back to the original tradition by which the priest, whose duties were
mainly pastoral and in the world, dispensed with the other, fixed

hours of daily prayer. These morning and evening hours should consist principally of psalms; these and other suitable prayers should replace the Latin hymns, which are often incomprehensible. There is a great treasure of such prayers, both by "classical" authors, such as SS. Augustine, Bernard of Clairvaux and Teresa of Avila, and by more recent writers, such as Cardinal Newman, and they should not be neglected. The morning and evening hours should also be arranged to change each day according to the liturgical season and various special occasions, and they should be in the vernacular. In this way, the Catholic priest would learn, indirectly, to pray the Psalms by heart in his own language, and he would thus be able to use them, as the Protestant minister is generally expected to do, on every possible occasion, both in public worship and in his pastoral duties, especially in ministering to the sick and the dying. It should be the task of the bishops in conference, acting in accordance with a general skeleton legislation prepared by the Council, to give instructions for the compilation of a suitable manual of prayer, consisting of these morning and evening hours, for the use of the secular clergy.

A renewal of liturgical prayer in all its three forms would have a significant effect on the renewal of the Church as a whole, and there is no need for a lengthy explanation to show that it would also play an essential part in the movement towards Christian reunion.

NOTES:

[1] See especially J. Pescher, *Das Stundengebet der römischen Kirche,* Munich (1954), and article on the Breviary in *Lexikon für Theologie und Kirche,* Freiburg (1958), vol. 2, pp. 679–84; J. A. Jungmann, *Der Gottesdienst der Kirche,* Innsbruck, Vienna, and Munich (1955), pp. 167–98.

Part IV

MATTERS OF DOCTRINE

12

"Early Catholicism" in the New Testament as a Problem in Controversial Theology

THERE WAS A TIME when Catholic theology, under various kinds of pressure from scripturally based Protestant theology, had the idea that there were important points on which it needed to withdraw behind the ramparts of ecclesiastical tradition. That time is past. Not only because Catholic theology is making itself at home once more in Scripture (with dogmatic theology rather slow and hesitant and keeping its distance, but still following along resolutely in the more daring footsteps—more daring over all difficulties, external and internal—of exegesis) so that today it often represents Protestant requirements as emphatically as does Protestant theology.[1] Nor only because Protestant theology—and not only dogmatic theology, but also and indeed especially that exegesis which has undergone the effects of form criticism—has become conscious in a new and undreamt-of fashion of the importance of tradition,[2] while historical research today is more disposed than was the age of the Reformation itself to take a positive view of the pre-history of the Reformers' Church and their theology.[3] The chief reason of all is that Protestant theology today—or exegesis, at any rate, to whose findings, however uncomfortable, dogmatic theology has to accommodate itself—has been supporting Catholic theology in an astonishing way, in so far as it has been doing what Catholic theology has always done; discovering "Catholicism" *in the New Testament itself.*

This has not made the dialogue of controversial theology any easier, but on the contrary harder, and hence all the more exciting.

It is striking how Protestant theology, under pressure from the facts yielded by historical research, has been driven to place the beginnings of "Catholicism" (meaning "Catholic decadence," a decline from primitive evangelical Christianity) further and further back in time. The Reformers still felt themselves at one with the Church of the first thousand years; for them "Catholicism," at least in any form that mattered, set in in the Church of the Middle Ages. Later Protestantism still felt at one with the Church of the first centuries; "Catholicism" began after the *"consensus quinque saecularis";* or perhaps the turning-point came earlier, with Constantine. At the beginning of this century, Harnack saw the apostolic Church as ending with the first century, "Catholicism" as already beginning in the second century with the influx of the Greek spirit into primitive apostolic Christianity: "The influx of Hellenism, of the Greek spirit, and the union of the Gospel with it, form the greatest fact in the history of the Church in the second century, and when this fact was once established as a foundation, it continued through the following centuries."[4] So the second century already presents us with "the Christian religion in its development into Catholicism."[5] This was the starting-point during the next few decades for a good deal of discussion of this hellenistic-Catholic fall from grace, by which "early Catholicism" was introduced during the post-apostolic period. To this early Catholic period belongs the emergence of the typically Catholic notion of office: "The struggle with Gnosticism compelled the Church to put its teaching, its worship and its discipline into fixed forms and ordinances, and to exclude everyone who would not yield them obedience. . . . If by 'Catholic' we mean the church of doctrine and of law, then the Catholic church had its origin in the struggle with Gnosticism."[6]

But did not pushing back "Catholicism" as far as this already mean arriving, in practice, at the New Testament? Surely even for Harnack the line of demarcation between New Testament and post-New Testament writings had become fluid? It is the special contri-

bution of the school of Bultmann (at the same time as confirming
many of the findings of liberal exegesis) to have stated the problem
now confronting us with all the requisite clarity: "Catholicism" begins even earlier; "early Catholicism" is there in the New Testament
itself. As a measure of how far we have come, it is only necessary to
compare the judgement made of Church order in the Pastoral Epistles in Paul Feine's *Theologie des Neuen Testaments*[7] with that in Rudolf
Bultmann's book of the same title.[8]

"Early Catholicism" in the New Testament confronts Protestant
theology with some difficult decisions. Catholic theology needs to
take an accurate view of this new state of the problem, which indeed
it shares. I have already tried to do this in another connection.[9] The
same problem will be developed here from a somewhat different an-
gle. I hope I may be permitted, during this Second Vatican Council with its ecumenical aim, to speak in a special way as belonging
to that theological faculty in which Johann Adam Möhler and his
colleagues began for the first time, from the Catholic side, to do constructive ecumenical theology. I should like to treat the problem as
a discussion with two representative Protestants from among my
colleagues at Tübingen, the first being of the school of Rudolf Bultmann and the second of that of Karl Barth. But this should not be
allowed to obscure the fact that a good deal will here be said of extreme importance to an understanding of the debate in the Council
on Revelation, which was fortunately interrupted, and, more than
ever, of the debate *de ecclesia*. It would be a great achievement in itself if Catholic theology and the Council were to become fully aware
of the enormous difficulties of the problem in the New Testament,
and were hence to summon up courage to be restrained and moderate in all dogmatic theological statements. I should like to start
my first section with the question:

Is the canon of the New Testament the foundation of the unity of the Church?

This is the question sharply and explicitly posed by Tübingen's
Protestant New Testament scholar, Ernst Käsemann; and as

sharply negatived.[10] What are his reasons? He adduces three, supported by numerous examples which we can only indicate here.

(1) *The variability of the New Testament kerygma itself.* The most obvious sign of this variability, according to Käsemann, is the fact that the New Testament Canon includes not one Gospel but four, all "strikingly divergent in their arrangement, selection and presentation." [11] And this not only because of the different characteristics of the Evangelists, not only because of the different traditions they sometimes use, but especially because of "the different theological, dogmatic attitudes of the Evangelists." [12] Thus, starting from the glorified Kyrios of faith, different views are taken of Jesus;[13] again, the common confession of Jesus' divine Sonship is interpreted in different ways according to theological tendency.[14] This being the case, the Evangelists are capable of freely criticizing each other.[15]

(2) *The extraordinary abundance of theological positions in primitive Christianity, ranging beyond the limits of the New Testament.* The canonical writings of the New Testament present us with "an abundance of unsolved and no doubt partly insoluble historical and theological problems which cannot be overlooked." [16] This is partly due to the "fragmentary character" [17] of our knowledge of the history and preaching of primitive Christianity; it is the very abundance of different traditions, for instance, that makes it so extraordinarily difficult to sort out the authentic Jesus-tradition in the New Testament.[18] It is also due to the "dialogue character" [19] of most of the statements in the New Testament; they do not constitute a Summa of *dicta probantia* but aim to give answers to concrete questions, exhortations and encouragement to concrete human beings, defence againt concrete errors; thus they take certain premises for granted and leave open a variety of conclusions. The voices that make themselves heard in the New Testament Canon form "an insignificant minority in comparison with all those who transmitted the message without leaving any written deposit and hence any lasting memorial. Why should we be justified in supposing that the many others had nothing different to say, or did not say it, from what was said

by the New Testament writers?"[20] The Canon of the New Testament gives us "only shreds of the dialogue that was being conducted within primitive Christianity." [21]

(3) *The partially visible incompatibility between theological positions within the New Testament.* The variability within the New Testament is so great that "we are confronted not only with considerable tensions but not infrequently with irreconcilable theological contradictions." [22] This applies even to the Gospels,[23] and still more to the rest of the New Testament.[24] Even in the Gospels we see not only a continuity but also a gap between Jesus and the disciples: "Even the oldest community of all includes misunderstanding as well as understanding. It obscures as well as manifesting the majesty of its Lord. Its faith, too, was carried in the earthen vessel of its humanity, its right-thinking was as precarious as all orthodoxies always are." [25]

What conclusion does Käsemann draw from these three observations? He is quite unambiguous about it: "The canon of the New Testament as such is no foundation for the unity of the Church. As such, i.e., as a datum accessible to the historian, it is, on the contrary, a foundation for the multiplicity of sects."[26] The different confessions in existence today all appeal to the New Testament—and they are right. For even in Christianity as it was at the beginning there was a multitude of different confessions alongside each other, combined with each other, over against each other.

Does Käsemann, then, stand for indifferentism on Enlightenment lines? On the contrary, what he stands for is *discernment of spirits.* "The connection and the distinction between letter and spirit must be observed. What Paul applies in 2 Cor. 3 to the Old Testament must not be restricted to the Old Testament; it applies in precisely the same way to the Canon of the New Testament." [27] For not even in the New Testament have we got God tied down; as a bare datum, as sounds and letters, the New Testament ceases to be the word of God. It becomes it and is it only when *through* the letters (no pseudo-mystical breaking-away from them) the Spirit manifests himself and, ever present, leads us anew into all truth. It is only in

the Canon as understood according to the Spirit that God speaks
and manifests his presence. This means that "the Canon is not
simply identical with the Gospel, and is the word of God only in
so far as it is and becomes the Gospel. Then, to that extent, it is also
the foundation of the unity of the Church. For it is the Gospel alone
that is the foundation of the one Church in all ages and all
places." [28]

This, then, is the meaning of "discernment of Spirits"; the understanding of the Scriptures from their real center outwards, from the
message of which they are a precipitation.[29] Hence a critical understanding of the Scriptures based on the *"Gospel,"* which is neither
separable from the Scriptures nor simply to be identified with them.
What is needed is, starting from this center, to walk the middle way
of the Reformation, between pseudo-mystical Enthusiasm on the
left (to be regarded as including the Protestantism of the Enlightenment), which tries to get beyond Scripture so as to seize hold on the
Gospel, and Catholic traditionalism on the right (including to a
large extent orthodox Protestantism) which regards the Gospel as
simply available and accessible in Scripture without measuring it
constantly by the critical standard of the Gospel. The Scriptures
and the Gospel, the Canon and the Gospel, are in a dialectical
tension which represents the permanent task of Protestant theology;
a continually new apprehension of the Gospel in the Scriptures,
which is what gives to those Scriptures, in themselves only a venerable historical document, their authority for believers.[30]

What is "the Gospel," according to Käsemann? This question
cannot, according to him, be answered simply by an historian, but
only by a believer, in so far as he listens to the Scriptures under the
conviction of the Spirit. The believer hears the Gospel, which is
proclaimed to him and encounters him as the *justification of the sinner.*
The justification of the sinner is the center of the Scriptures:

The Bible is neither God's word in an objective sense nor a
system of doctrine, but a crystallization of the history and
preaching of primitive Christianity. But the Church, which

made it the Canon, declares that it is precisely in this sense the bearer of the Gospel. She declares this because she sees the history here contained and proclaimed as subordinated to one aspect, the justification of the sinner; and it is only to this extent that she can declare it. But since her declaration is a testimony and a confession of faith, she is thus at the same time summoning us to put ourselves and our own histories in subordination to this event of the justification of the sinner. This means that we are brought to a point of decision, not only on whether we will accept this justification or not, but also on whether this confession of faith does represent a true grasp of the central point of the Scriptures.[31]

Such is Käsemann's answer to the question of whether the Canon of the New Testament is the foundation of the unity of the Church. It is an answer which testifies to his profound seriousness and radical honesty as an exegete. It would be false and unjust to regard the critical and destructive element, which leaps to the eye, as the thing that he is really after; which is what has been done by certain of his inquisitorial brothers in religion (there is such a thing as an Inquisition from below!). To lay oneself open to the encounter of the Gospel is the central aim of this theologian, who has given proof of his evangelical faith not only in years of service as a pastor but also under persecution. It may be because of his experiences in the Church of the Confession that Käsemann stands out, amongst the Bultmann School, for his interest in ecclesiology.[32] And what he desires theologically is not the multiplicity of confessions but the unity of the Church. But a unity of the Church which rests upon the Gospel, and as such is never plainly detectable but only present to faith: "The unity of the Church is, like the Gospel, never something recognized by the *beati possidentes* but only by the insecure and the tempted, within the confessions and in spite of them, and both with and in face of the New Testament Canon itself; recognized in so far as they are hearers and believers of the Gospel."[33]

But can we be satisfied with Käsemann's answer? Contradiction can be heard from the Protestant side, and of a kind to be taken

seriously. Under the title "The Unity of Scripture," Tübingen's
Protestant dogmatic theologian Hermann Diem has not only set
forth an important section of his dogmatic theology but has also
tried to enter into debate with Käsemann.[34]

The unity of Scripture

Diem is in sympathy with his colleague's stating of the problem
as presented by the New Testament. He also agrees with a large
part of Käsemann's answer. For Diem, this much is certain: the
writings assembled in the Canon of the New Testament do not form
a "unity of doctrine." [35] It was not the Reformers but the confessional Churches, Lutheran and Reformed, which began to teach
a dogmatic unity of the Scriptures: a dogmatic system of Scriptural
statements, drawn from the whole of Scripture, whether rather
according to a biblical or to a dogmatic system; which began to
understand the Scripture as a "principle" and *"summa"* of theology
instead of as a text from which to preach, and consequently to assert
its verbal inspiration and divine character. Thus it was they who
ceased to be content with the mere fact of the Canon as something
given in practice, and made a principle of its being finally closed.
This has done damage to preaching and to faith.[36]

Hence Diem thoroughly welcomes the fact that historico-critical
scholarship has compelled the Church and theology to re-examine
their doctrine of Scripture. For the present state of the discussion,

> it is significant that New Testament historians who have be-
> come especially active in this matter cannot so easily be
> regarded as intruders in theology as was perhaps more obvi-
> ously possible at an earlier period. The reason for this is, first,
> that present-day New Testament scholarship on the basis of
> its critical conclusions stresses in general the proclamatory
> character of New Testament writings, and hence stands with
> the Reformers and confirms the rightness of their use of
> Scripture. Further, its main objection to the prevalent use of
> Scripture is that the latter allows dogmatics to guard the in-

terpretation of Scripture, and thus modern criticism makes its voice heard just in connection with that process by which, as we established, the Reformation degenerated into classical Protestant dogmatics. Hence from this point of view it will have to be seen whether the true and genuine use of Scripture is not better maintained by the Reformers themselves than by the post-Reformation dogmatists.[37]

But firmly as Diem asserts the thesis "No unitary dogmatic system in the New Testament," he is just as firm in the counter-statement: "No Canon within the Canon." This is where the conflict between Diem and Käsemann begins, or rather, this is the point at which there emerges into view once more that conflict which is immanent in the Churches of the Reformation and can be observed at every stage of their history.

Käsemann has given very pregnant expression to something which haunts the minds of many modern New Testament critics as a possible solution to the question of the Canon such as would enable them to counter the work of the post-Reformation dogmatists: the establishment of a Canon within the Canon by means of the doctrine of justification as a hermeneutical criterion. But this solution does not at bottom suggest anything new, it simply goes back to Luther, who wished to have Scripture examined in the light of the principle 'the preaching of Christ,' by which in the last analysis he, too, understood nothing other than the *'sola gratia'* and the *'sola fide.'* Hence it is thought that by this means we may return to the Reformers' use of Scripture and overcome its distortion in the work of the classical Protestant dogmatics. Is this correct? [38]

According to Diem it is not. True, justification of the sinner is not a doctrine but an event, in which, through the proclamation of the Gospel, justification in Christ is imputed to the hearer. But when Käsemann calls on us to place ourselves and our own histories in subordination to this event of the justification of the sinner, Diem asks

whether he [Käsemann] really does or can submit to the
power of this self-proclaiming history, or whether he paralyses
and must paralyse the authority of this event conveyed to him
through the preaching of Scripture by the fact that he makes
of it a history with compelling power only after first testing it
critically and assenting to it subsequently.[39]

It is necessary that we should take proclamatory history seriously
as an event binding on us precisely by paying heed to the limits of
the Canon as recognized in practice by the Church:

This compelling process of self-proclamatory history consists
in the fact that the Church has exclusively heard, in the proclamation of these witnesses, the Word of God, and we must
therefore continue to proclaim and hear just as exclusively
through these witnesses. This fact can only be recognized; it
cannot fundamentally be justified. The only possible theological justification in this matter consists in using the Scriptural
Canon appropriately by preaching on its themes with confidence in its self-evidencing power. In the empirical use of the
Canon in this way lies also the only theological possibility of
defining it against Church tradition. In this way we stand once
more at the side of the Reformers.[40]

According to Diem, it is only against this background that the
unity of Scripture can be seen aright. It does not lie in any unitary pattern of doctrine, but in the self-testifying character of the
Scripture as proclaimed, in whose testimonies Jesus Christ proclaims himself and is listened to by the Church.[41] Certainly the
differences between the individual testimonies within the unity of
the New Testament proclamation are considerable. These differences arise from all the different *situations in which the proclamation
is made:* the testimonies of the New Testament are testimonies of
particular people in particular situations with particular ends in
view.[42] Adaptation, development and fresh presentation of the message were as urgently necessary then as is, for us today, the contin-

ual retransposing of these testimonies into the situation in which they have to be proclaimed now. A particular concrete situation in which the proclamation is made may require particular testimonies to be advanced and others to be kept in the background, but we are still to pay heed to the limits of the Canon, by which we still recognize those witnesses whom we are leaving in the background as true witnesses to the message of Christ:

> In this respect, the whole point is that an appraisal governed by particular circumstances should not be made into a fundamental appraisal, that therefore the Canon of Scripture must be recognized as the *text* which in any event is permanently binding, and that all our attempts at exposition, on the other hand, are only *commentaries,* which with their constantly changing conclusions cannot take the place of the text itself.[43]

This is precisely the way in which the Canon has not only a prohibitive but a primarily positive significance: it protects the exegete from his own arbitrary subjectivity.[44]

Thus Diem joins with Käsemann in rejecting Scripture as a unitary system of doctrine, but he clings, in opposition to Käsemann, to the unity of Scripture as proclaimed to us, and bases on this his understanding of the unity of the Church, against the arbitrariness of the individual exegete. It must be acknowledged that throughout his dogmatic work Diem takes a degree of trouble altogether unusual in a systematic theologian to come to grips with the problems posed by modern exegesis. He does this not predominantly as a matter of apologetics but in a thoroughly constructive way, turning to account many of the results of exegesis. The bridging of the present gap between exegesis and dogmatic theology is one of his central theological aims.

Yet Diem's and Käsemann's basic theological positions are, if we are not mistaken, irreconcilably opposed. For Käsemann, Diem's "Canon" can never become "the Gospel," while for Diem, Käsemann's "Gospel" can never become "the Canon." And it is scarcely possible for their Catholic colleague to contribute to their reconciliation, but perhaps he can to a clarifying of the positions. This, and only this, will now be briefly attempted.

Catholicity in the interpretion of the New Testament

(1) *Delimitation of the area of discussion.* To what extent can a Catholic theologian (assuming that he does not simply ignore the findings of exegesis) agree with Käsemann? He can grant: (*a*) the fact of the non-unitary character of the New Testament Canon; (*b*) the factors which establish this non-unity: a variability in the New Testament kerygma itself, rooted not only in the individual character of the Evangelists and the traditions they use but also in their differing theological positions; an abundance of theological positions in primitive Christianity, with a wider range than that of the New Testament, making our knowledge in this respect (especially having regard to the dialogue-character of most of the New Testament witness) seem extremely fragmentary; and partially apparent differences in the theological positions both in the Gospels and in the rest of the New Testament, such as cannot be harmonized in any simple way; (*c*) the hearing, in faith, within the non-unitary Canon of the New Testament, of the "Gospel" which justifies the sinner (understood as hearing according to the Spirit, not the letter, and focused upon the center).

How far can a Catholic theologian, while not losing sight of what is here granted to Käsemann, agree with Diem? He can grant: (*a*) that the New Testament is not a dogmatic system. It is not intended as a *summa theologiae;* hence any forced harmonization of texts so as to eliminate differences is to be rejected as foreign to the New Testament, and so is the replacement, in preaching, of a witnessing representation of the witness of the New Testament by lecture-type demonstrations of *dicta probantia;* hence faith is not focused simply on Scripture as having a divine character but, on the basis of that Scripture as proclaimed to us, on the Lord to whom it witnesses, Jesus Christ, and his God and Father; (*b*) the importance of the situation in which the proclamation is made, and the two respects in which this is so: the witness of the New Testament is given by different people in different situations with different theological and dogmatic ends in view, and this witness must once more be uttered for different people with different ends in view in different situations, transposed out of the situation in which it was proclaimed then into the new situation; a transposition of the New Testament kerygma in which it is possible for various testimonies and aspects to be set in the foreground while others remain in the background; (c) the practical nature of the Canon of the New Testament and its unity; the unity of Scripture cannot be deduced by regarding it as a closed system according to some principle, but is something given in practice; the Church has heard the word of God proclaimed to her precisely in *these* testimonies of the Canon of the New Testament, and exclusively in them, and it is these testimonies, again exclusively, that she passes on in her preaching as the word of God.

When one is having a discussion in controversial theology, it is only when one has the courage and understanding fearlessly to see and acknowledge one's points of agreement with the other side (amongst theologians, as amongst politicians, agreement is often more feared than dissent!) that one is capable of then focusing the discussion on the really controversial points. And these do not lie in the field of the doctrine of justification, nor (the attempt to make this out was an artificial construction) in that of Christology or Pneumatology, but in ecclesiology. It is in the doctrine of the Church, and there alone, that—in the first instance, at least—there is still a clash. And so it is here that the task of ecumenically-minded theology lies; to seek for new, constructive solutions, even if the first stage has to consist in sharp confrontation.

(2) *The reason for the multiplicity of confessions.* The Canon of the New Testament does lie at the root of there being a multiplicity of confessions. We must grant Käsemann this point; for: (a) the variety of Christian confessions is something that exists; (b) the various confessions do appeal to the Canon of the New Testament and refer themselves to it; (c) these various appeals to the Canon have a *fundamentum in re*, being founded on the complexity, multiplicity and mu-

tual opposition of the theological positions in the New Testament Canon, as already described. To this extent, then, the Canon of the New Testament lies at the root of the multiplicity of confessions.

But still, given the absence of unity in the Canon, how does confessional multiplicity arise? To point to that absence of unity does not really answer the question. For with all its lack of unity, the Canon of the New Testament is nevertheless *one thing,* and has been received by the Church as *one thing* (in the course, certainly, of an extraordinarily changeful history); and the various testimonies in it have been understood not as some sort of dogmatically rich negative programme contrasting with the Gospel, but as an expression and crystallization of the Gospel, positively proportioned to it. So the question remains of how we get from the New Testament Canon, which remains one despite its lack of unity, to confessional multiplicity?

The answer is unavoidable: By *choice.* That is, by not seriously accepting the Canon as one thing, for all its lack of unity, not striving, through all the difficulties confronting each other in it, to reach a *comprehensive* understanding of it. By using the lack of unity in the Canon to make a selection from the Canon. This can, in certain circumstances, lead to an impressive concentration of the kerygma, but at the same time it means a reduction of the kerygma, made at the expense of the New Testament and of the unity of the Church, who stands behind the Canon.

What is implied by this abandonment of the *wholeness* of the New Testament as something to be taken seriously and understood comprehensively, in favour of the concentration afforded by *selecting?* Nothing less than the abandonment, fundamentally, of *catholicity* in the understanding of Scripture in favour of *heresy.* To be accurate, then, we must say that the Canon of the New Testament, with its lack of unity, is indeed a *necessary presupposition* and *occasion* for confessional multiplicity, but not strictly its root or cause. The inflammable material in a house, the timber in it, may well be a necessary condition and occasion for the burning of the house; but the root, the cause of the conflagration, is the incendiary who sets fire to the timber. The actual cause of the multitude of confessions is not the Canon of the New Testament—which, understood in a "catholic" way (*kath' holou*), is a basic condition for the unity of the *ekklesia*— but *hairesis,* which dissolves the unity of the *ekklesia.*[45]

Selective interpretation of the New Testament is possible in two ways: as a matter of principle or of practice.

(3) *Selection as a matter of principle.* This is the kind of selection which applies to the New Testament a formal principle of interpretation which turns out to be at the same time a material principle of selection. Käsemann is an example of this kind of selection. It is not, obviously, that Käsemann wants simply to eliminate certain texts, or even books, from the Canon of the New Testament; rather, they are to remain in the Canon and, in their fashion, to be given serious consideration. Käsemann does not stand for any selection in this sense. But he does want to "discern" between the spirits of the New Testament. He applies Paul's "discernment of spirits"—which Paul himself never applied to the Canon of the Old Testament—to the Canon of the New: not in order to distinguish between different kinds of good spirit, i.e., good witness (being recognized by the Church as part of the Canon), but to distinguish, in the New Testament itself—with an antidocetist appeal to all that is insecure and subject to temptation in anything human—between good and *evil* spirits. Käsemann is not willing to hear "the Gospel" as coming from those spirits in the New Testament which he declares to be evil. It is only in those testimonies which are recognized by him as "good spirits" that he hears "the Gospel." It is in this sense that he stands for a selection. Thus he hits upon a middle way between Enthusiasm and early Catholicism. Basically, he only gives *positively* serious consideration to those witnesses in the New Testament who are capable of being, and are, "the Gospel"—who announce the "justification of the sinner." This involves an abandonment in principle (even if the word "principle" is avoided) of catholicity in the understanding of Scripture, and Käsemann consciously accepts this as "Evangelical."

But this is where the Evangelical dogmatic theologian disowns

the Evangelical exegete: the accusation that Diem makes against
Käsemann is that, faced with the event of the proclamation to him
of the New Testament, "he paralyses and must paralyse the authority of this event . . . by the fact that he makes of it a history with a
compelling power only after first testing it critically and assenting to
it subsequently."[46] True, Käsemann is not concerned with any mere
doctrine of justification (an "object of faith," a "basic dogma," a theological "principle"), but with the event of justification; and this is
not something that can only be proclaimed in Romans or Galatians
but equally in, for example, a saying of Jesus, a beatitude, etc.; in
every testimony of the New Testament which is a basis for the justification of the sinner, we have "the Gospel." But it is certain that for
Käsemann we do not have "the Gospel" in the *whole* of the New
Testament, and that it is possible for him, himself, to know *where*
we do not have the Gospel. As against this Diem reminds us that
behind the Canon of the New Testament, both then and now,
stands the Church: that the Church "has exclusively heard, in the
proclamation of these witnesses, the Word of God, and we must
therefore continue to proclaim and hear just as exclusively through
these witnesses . . . The fact of the Canon bears witness that the
Church has in fact unequivocally heard in these witnesses the proclamation of Jesus Christ, and we too can and must, likewise, hear
it there."[47] True, certain parts of the witness of the New Testament
can and should be evaluated according to the prevailing situation,
some being given prominence and others left in the background.[48]

> But whenever such an appraisal of the value of the various
> witnesses is made, the significance of the fact of the Canon
> must be taken into account. This demands the recognition
> that the witness neglected by us did in fact bear witness to
> Christ (within certain historical conditions, for how could it
> be otherwise?) and did find a hearing in the Church, and thus
> spoke under the inspiration of the Holy Spirit.[49]

If he is not thus bound to the Canon, the exegete succumbs to "his
subjective, arbitrary judgements, and the constant danger that, in-

stead of letting the texts speak for themselves in their concrete ac-
tuality and historical uniqueness, he may do violence to them in the
name of a preconceived principle of exegesis, and for that very
reason fail to do justice to their character as witnesses and as texts
for preaching."[50]

Käsemann would, of course, defend himself against the charge of
arbitrary subjectivity. He does not select according to his own
choice, but as confronted by "the Gospel." There is nothing objec-
tionable in pointing to a "central core" in the Gospel. But we may
ask on what basis Käsemann finds himself so confronted only in
these texts and not in others, able to hear only these texts and not
others as "the Gospel." Certainly the New Testament cannot be
the foundation for this; for the New Testament, according to
Käsemann himself, signifies something more than *his* "Gospel."
Nor simply from "exegetical findings," with the "central Pauline
line" imposing itself as "the Gospel." And it would only be to
push the problem back if it were any other particular "central line." For the question is precisely why Käsemann can see
only this "central line" as "the Gospel." Can Käsemann appeal
here to anything more than some basic Protestant understanding
of the matter preceding all else (unconsciously due, perhaps, to
philosophical premises, or to some presentation of the Catholic position, in history or at the present time, of a kind unworthy of belief)? Or, at a deeper level, to some kind of ultimate choice, perhaps
of the kind in which one simply finds oneself placed (the Lutheran
tradition?) rather than one that one adopts oneself? But in any case,
a choice made *previous* to any exegesis? Is it possible, in this position,
to give any reasons such as could restrain anyone else from making
a *different* choice and, because of a *different* traditional understanding adopted beforehand, discovering exegetically a *different* centre
and a *different* Gospel? It is surely not possible to appeal to the
New Testament as a *whole,* after letting its catholicity go by the
board.

But what remains—against the will of those who practise it—is a
greater or lesser degree of arbitrary subjectivism.

For Luther, this centre by which he judged everything else was presumably Paul, or, more narrowly, Paul's doctrine of justification. On the other hand, the Gospel of John was for Luther the one true and tender chief Gospel. In the same way Schleiermacher regarded and defended this same Gospel, because of its spiritual content, as the essential Gospel. According to the theology of historical criticism at the beginning of this century, it was the words of the Lord in the Synoptics which were the standard of what was genuine. For Bultmann, it seems, John's Gospel is what witnesses to the valid Gospel as the Gospel of the Word and the Word alone, and of here-and-now existential decision, once one has excised from it what are supposed to be later ecclesiastical additions about sacraments and futurist eschatology. Should we not, instead of measuring the New Testament by a norm of this sort, rather measure the critical norm against the richness of the New Testament, and so accord to it at least some relative rights in this matter?[51]

The bold programme of "a Canon within the Canon" amounts to a demand to be more biblical than the Bible, more New Testament-minded than the New Testament, more evangelical than the Gospel, more Pauline, even, than Paul. The intention is radical seriousness; the result is radical dissolution. As against every kind of *hairesis,* which, by making itself into an absolute, turns without wanting to into *hubris,* the Catholic attitude strives to preserve a full openness and freedom towards the *whole* of the New Testament. This can often seem less consistent and less impressive than the powerful onesidedness of expounding one line alone; Paul alone can, in certain circumstances, produce a more consistent and impressive effect than the great complexity of the whole New Testament, and the Paul of Paulinism (purged of his "sacramentalism" and "mysticism") a still more consistent and impressive effect than the whole Paul. But the real Paul is the whole Paul, and the real New Testament is the whole New Testament.

(4) *Selection as a matter of practice.* This is the kind of selection which fundamentally rejects the application to the New Testament of any

formal principle of interpretation which turns out to be a material
principle of selection, but nevertheless fails in practice (through
oversight or minimal interpretation) to do justice to particular testimonies in the Canon of the New Testament. Diem is an example of
this kind of selection. Throughout his whole dogmatic treatment,
Diem draws his line of demarcation over against the Catholic
Church on the basic supposition that "early Catholicism," with its
specific concept of ecclesiastical office, especially the teaching office,
and of the apostolic succession, does not have its origin until well
after the New Testament: in that "section of Church history which
marks the end of the post-apostolic age and is generally designated
as the beginning of the early Catholic Church."[52] Here for the first
time we find a specifically Catholic "episcopate" and "office invested with full legal powers."[53] Here for the first time the attempt
is made "to establish authority on the basis of historical continuity
with the Apostles, and so with the incarnate Lord, by introducing
an 'apostolic succession' transmitted by episcopal consecration as
the outward historical sign distinguishing the true bishop."[54] From
this point Diem can, without more ado, interpret the development
of "early Catholicism" as a "deflection from the New Testament."[55]
He assumes throughout that the New Testament has nothing to do
with early Catholicism.

But this is where the Protestant dogmatic theologian is disowned
by the Protestant exegete. Käsemann calmly affirms:

> The time has gone by, never to return, when it was possible to
> oppose Scripture as a whole to Catholicism. It is no longer
> possible for Protestantism today to work with the so-called
> "formal principle," on pain of making itself incredible in terms
> of historical analysis. The Canon of the New Testament does
> not stand between Judaism and early Catholicism, but affords
> within it space and basis for both Judaism and early Cathol-
> icism.[56]

What this means, according to Käsemann, is made particularly
clear by his treatment of office and community in the New Testa-

ment.[57] He there works out in sharp antithesis the difference in Church order between the Pauline Epistles on the one hand and the Pastoral Epistles and Luke (in the Acts) on the other. The order within the community as described in the Pastorals and by Luke is early-Catholic in character, in contrast to the charismatic character of the Pauline communities.

In the Pastorals, according to Käsemann, the community has been put acutely on the defensive by the gnostic heresies. Resistance to them is being conducted from one single centre: the man delegated by the Apostle and the presbyterate in union with him. Nothing in any of the Pauline epistles is ever addressed to a presbyterate, though it would have been precisely the right agency for combating heresies. There simply was not any such presbyterate in the Pauline communities, of the sort that had probably already been erected in the communities with which the Pastorals are concerned. Ordination (1 Tim. 4.14; 5.22; 2 Tim. 1.6) also, presumably, came to the Pauline communities from Jewish-Christian tradition.

It has, then, the same sense as in Judaism: an imparting of the Spirit which empowers the subject to administer the *depositum fidei* of 1 Tim. 6.20, which can be understood more precisely as the tradition of Pauline doctrine. But this implies that an office distinct from the rest of the community has become the actual bearer of the Spirit, and the earliest Christian idea, by which every Christian receives the Spirit in baptism, recedes and in practice disappears. It is equally clear that this is no longer compatible with the Pauline doctrine of charisms. The Jewish heritage is here repressing the Pauline at at least one central point of its message. Thus the word 'charism' only appears in 1 Tim. 5.14 and 2 Tim. 1.16, most suggestively, in connection with ordination. It indicates the commission given in ordination and the bestowal of the power to administer the *depositum fidei*. Inelegantly, but with complete accuracy, we may speak here of the spirit of office.[58]

The legate of the Apostle (Titus, Timothy) is thus, according to Käsemann, none other than the monarchical bishop.

> His task is the prolongation of the apostolic office into the post-apostolic age. In other words, he stands in the apostolic succession, just as a Rabbi receives jurisdiction and the teaching tradition in the succession of Moses and Joshua, and exercises them *jure divino*, i.e., empowered by the imparting of the Spirit in ordination. Thus was formed the concept of office which the succeeding period was to make more precise. At the very least there is now in practice a distinction between clergy and laity. A principle of tradition and legitimacy safeguards, tacitly but as the unmistakable foundation of the whole order within the community, the authority of this institutional office, which surrounds itself with executive organs in the shape of the presbyterate, the diaconate and the institution of widowhood.[59]

The whole development was necessary, because it was only thus that the tremendous danger of gnostic pseudo-mysticism could be effectively met.

The same things that apply to the Pastorals can be said of the Church of the Acts of the Apostles. Here too we find on all sides bishops, presbyterates, ordination and the principle of tradition and legitimation.

> Luke was the first, so far as we can see, to propagate the early Catholic theory of tradition and legitimation. He doubtless did not do it wantonly, but as a defence of the Church against the dangers which threatened her. The historian cannot but admit that the theory he put forward did indeed prove the most efficient means of fighting against the force of Enthusiasm, and protected infant Christianity from being engulfed by it. The inclusion of the Acts of the Apostles in the Canon is to this extent intelligible, and deserved, as the Church's expression of her gratitude.[60]

After this it is not surprising to find Käsemann showing in another article that the document which is probably the latest of those in the New Testament Canon, the Second Epistle of Peter, is of an early Catholic character: "The Second Epistle of Peter is from beginning to end a document expressing the early-Catholic outlook, and it is surely the most dubious item in the Canon." [61] The statement in 1.20 can be taken as the most significant in the whole Epistle, and what it means is: "Personal exegesis undertaken by the individual, not authorized or indicated by the teaching office of the Church, is not admissible." [62] Or as Käsemann finally puts it in his treatment of the question "Is the Canon of the New Testament the foundation of the unity of the Church?":

> Here (in 2 Pet.) it is no longer the Spirit who is at work, even in and through what is handed on; he has become identified with tradition. Hence, as was already the case in the Pastorals and in Acts, it is the ecclesiastical teaching office that possesses the "spirit of office," and—as is done in the classic instance in 2 Pet. 1.20—all unauthorized exegesis and interpretation of Scripture can be forbidden. Here we find ordination as the sign of a principle of legitimacy and succession; in short: here the limits of primitive Christianity are passed, and early Catholicism is established. [63]

Diem would react against many of Käsemann's interpretations. [64] Nor would a Catholic theologian by any means identify himself with each of Käsemann's "early Catholic" interpretations, which are often pushed to extremes. [65] But what we may take as indisputable is that the Catholic principle (as to the meaning of office, the apostolic succession, ordination, teaching, etc. [66]) is already to be found in the New Testament. [67]

There is no hiding the fact that this presence of the Catholic principle in the New Testament makes the position of a Protestant theologian very difficult, if he wants fundamentally to take the *whole* of the New Testament seriously and still not become a Catholic. Käsemann's position does seem, in comparison with Diem's, to be

clearer, more consistent, and more convincing. Faced with the existence of Catholicism in the New Testament, only two attitudes are
basically convincing: that of Käsemann (and his friends), which,
by "discernment of spirits," consistently declares the Catholicism
of the New Testament to be un-Evangelical; and the Catholic one,
which aims at taking the Catholicism of the New Testament seriously as Evangelical, i.e., as an expression of the Gospel. In neither
the first nor the second volume of Diem's *Theologie* does the Catholic
element (the episcopal office, the teaching office, the Petrine office,
ordination, the sacraments, etc.) play the part which, according to
the New Testament, it ought to play. Faced with Scripture witnessing to Catholicism, even Diem[68] can only do what is so often done
in Protestant theology; blunt the edge of what is said in the New
Testament and either ignore[69] or give minimal interpretation[70] to
the Catholic element. Only a Catholic can do justice to the Catholicism of the New Testament.

(5) *Protestant and Catholic.* We have seen that on this crucial
question of Catholicism in the New Testament Käsemann and
Diem take diametrically opposite points of view. In one respect,
though a different one in each of them—"early Catholicism" in the
New Testament in Käsemann's case, the binding character of the
New Testament Canon in Diem's—each is nearer to the Catholic
position than he is to the other. But we must not dramatize this
opposition. We have no illusions: what is the point on which Diem
and Käsemann are nevertheless profoundly in agreement? They
agree in not being disposed to understand the New Testament *kath'
holou.* They lack full freedom and openness towards the message of
the New Testament in its wholeness. Deeply and intensively though
they are concerned with the New Testament, their tacit, taken-for-
granted *a priori* position is Protestantism. And what this means is
that it is laid down from the outset that within their exegesis and
theology there is to be no road towards "Rome." There are many
roads, and even roads leading in opposite directions, that lie open
to a Protestant; but there is no freedom and openness in regard to
a road towards "Rome." Then what is to be done when one has

to recognize (what for a Catholic involves nothing surprising) that even in the New Testament, in the end, all roads lead to "Rome"?

Diem, Käsemann and Catholic theology all start from the same New Testament. But for Käsemann, a fundamental choice so lays down the lines of interpretation in advance that highly important lines in the New Testament are never seriously considered at all; so that, in particular, the road of "early Catholicism," which must inevitably lead to "late Catholicism," is blocked in advance, and it is only ultimately possible to travel in one (Paulinist) direction. For Diem, conversely, the lines of interpretation are not laid down in advance. In principle, there is freedom to follow all the lines of the New Testament. But when one arrives at "early Catholicism," so that, at least in the distance, "Rome" comes in sight, then the warning red light comes on (which Käsemann saw at the outset of the journey); interpretation jams, further interpretation is refused. A selection is, in practice, made, and one stops in one's tracks protesting "Thus far and no farther." [71]

The Catholic attitude is to be, in principle, open in every direction that the *New Testament* leaves open; not to exclude, either in principle or in practice, any line that belongs to the New Testament. The Catholic attitude tries to do justice, without prejudice, to every side of the New Testament: to be catholic, to be open and free towards the whole, all-embracing truth of the New Testament. The Catholic Church has often been called a *complexio oppositorum* in a bad sense, by a confusion of her un-nature (as the Church of human beings, and sinful human beings) with her nature (as the Church who is holy in the Holy Spirit). But what has often been thought of as an accusation can also have a good sense: Käsemann has pointed out that the New Testament itself is a *complexio oppositorum*; the Church is thus in line with the New Testament when she takes *opposita* (not all and sundry, but those that are in the New Testament) and tries to include them all in a good sense and to understand the *whole* of the New Testament as the Gospel.

The disastrous thing in Käsemann's theology is not its adoption of a "central point of Scripture" (however determined in detail)

but the Protestant exclusiveness with which it makes this centre into
the whole, cutting out everything else by "discernment of spirits."
The disastrous thing in Diem's theology is not that it leaves certain
witnesses in the background according to the concrete situation in
which the proclamation has to be made, but the Protestant exclusiveness with which it does not allow certain witnesses to speak at
all and does not sufficiently do justice to the demands that they
make.

The protest against early Catholicism is a protest against Catholicism in general. Käsemann and Diem would be the last to contest
this. This protest—which is not in truth simply unfounded—is
directed against the Catholic *Church*. But not only against what is
uncatholic in the Catholic Church; that would be a Catholic protest. Against what is Catholic in the Catholic Church as well; and
this is Protestant. But, as a Protestant protest, the protest against
the catholicity of the Church inevitably turns into a protest against
the catholicity of *Scripture*, which was meant to have been the one
and only basis for the protest against the catholicity of the Church.
From being corrective (which is how it was meant by Luther originally) the protest becomes constitutive (which is how it is meant
by Protestantism in its various forms). The protest goes rigid and
cancels itself out, itself demolishing the foundation upon which it
took its stand. Each protest-making selection from the New Testament refutes all the other ones and is refuted by them in turn. A
false understanding of *sola scriptura* leads to a *sola pars scripturae* and
this again to a *sola pars Ecclesiae;* in short, to a devastating chaos
in preaching and doctrine and a progressive fragmentation of
Protestantism.[72]

(6) *The task of catholicity.* But before the overweening, self-confi-
dent Catholic starts congratulating himself on this state of affairs,
he had better do some thinking. True, only a Catholic attitude is
capable of overcoming the Protestant disintegration of the Gospel.
True, catholicity in the interpretation of the Gospel is a magnificent
programme. But is it anything more than a programme? To say
"To be Catholic is to be evangelical" is liable to remain a mere

formula to be understood, in the present critical situation in
exegesis and dogma, as a lazy-minded, soothing indicative rather
than as an exacting imperative, calling for the carrying out of the
programme. My object in treating this subject has not been to re-
assure Catholic theologians about the present outbreak of problems concerning the New Testament, but to summon them to get
properly to grips with their task as Catholics. Merely to *assert* that
being Catholic means being evangelical does not solve any of the
extraordinarily difficult exegetical and dogmatic problems set us
by the present situation in New Testament studies. The Catholic
programme has to be made good by a thorough, serious, honest
execution of it both in exegesis and in dogma, right down to all
the innumerable problems of detail involved.

It is not possible to maintain that we Catholics have given, so
far, an adequate embodiment of catholicity in the interpretation
of the New Testament. Which of us would dare to maintain that
Catholic freedom and openness towards the whole New Testament has been credibly demonstrated *ad oculos* by us to other Christians? Would it have been possible, if it had, for Catholic exegesis
during these last centuries to have gone along constantly in the wake
of Protestant exegesis; for it constantly, at bottom, to have received
its problems, its methods and its solutions at the hands of Protestant
exegesis; for fundamental exegetical works like the *Dictionary of the
New Testament* to have been predominantly works of Protestant
exegesis? Let us not make the mistake of reproaching individual
Catholic exegetes on this score; who is going to suggest that Catholic exegetes are inferior in intelligence, or work-shy? What is certain is that the fullness of Catholic freedom and openness towards
the whole New Testament has often not been allowed to our
exegetes.[73] It is impossible for exegesis and dogma to fulfil their
great Catholic task in an atmosphere of fear and totalitarian
supervision, with the dishonesty and cowardice that result from
them; it is possible only in an atmosphere of freedom, of cool
theological honesty and undismayed objectivity, and precisely
thus of loyalty to the Church.

Nor is it possible to maintain that we Catholics have given a sufficiently credible presentation of catholicity precisely in our interpretation of the ecclesiology of the New Testament. It is indisputable that Catholic ecclesiology, even as early as the Middle Ages and more especially in the Counter-Reformation period, has over-stressed the Pastoral Epistles (and Acts) as against the more charismatically structured order in the community found in the great Pauline Epistles, and has thus to a great extent turned ecclesiology into hierarchology. This heritage still weighs heavily on us today, giving us plenty of tasks to work out.[74]

It is of course much more difficult to do exegetical justice to the whole rather than only to a part. Not only because *every* theologian is, as a human being, in danger of not perceiving in the New Testament precisely what he ought to perceive, but because the following of the Catholic way calls in a special degree for the high exegetical art of discerning differences and nuances. Thus, on the one hand, there can be no harmonizing and levelling down of opposed ecclesiological statements in the New Testament, on the basis of some cozy system, too lazy to get to the bottom of these various oppositions. And on the other hand there can be no dissociation and reduction of such statements, collecting and contrasting them on the basis of some purely statistical hypercriticism which finds the hunt for contradictions a more pleasurable activity than the tracing of a deeper unity within the total context of the Scriptures; all of which do, ultimately, aim at speaking in one form or another of Jesus Christ and his Gospel. Every testimony in the New Testament is a deposit of that proclamation-history in which the proclamation and the deeds of Jesus are, in manifold fashion, transmitted so that we may believe in Jesus as the Lord. Hence every ecclesiological testimony in the New Testament must be understood against the background of proclamation-history as a whole, and in terms of the particular situation in which its own proclamation is made, to which it is addressing itself.

But then, is not Käsemann's fear justified that the *last* document in this proclamation-history being the latest testimony in it, must interpret all that has gone before and thus finally determine it? In the Catholic view, even this piece of New Testament witness must indeed be taken seriously. In its "early Catholic" character, it provides just that continuity required by the later Church between the apostolic Church of the New Testament and the Church of the "apostolic Fathers" and the early Church in general. Nevertheless, this cannot be taken as meaning that 2 Pet. is to be *the* decisive document determining the interpretation of the whole New Testament. We need, after all, to pay attention to the fact that in 2 Pet. we do not have one of the original but one of the *derived* testimonies in the New Testament. Like, say, Jude and James, 2 Pet. presupposes other writings of the New Testament, and these, in certain circumstances, others again, as, for instance, this or that *logion* of Jesus. As the situation in which the proclamation was made kept changing, it compelled a constant modification and reshaping of the original message, and the human and theological individuality of each new person making the proclamation played a considerable role in this. Hence mutually opposed differences in the New Testament were bound to come about, just as, significantly, what the tradition gives us is not *one* Gospel nor a Gospel-harmony nor any "Life of Jesus," but different and often mutually opposed Gospels. But within all this complex (and not simply unilinear) development, it is clear that the original testimonies take precedence over the *derived*. What we have in the New Testament is not some kind of symposium of equal-ranking (if not always equally valuable) contributors; the message of the New Testament is not that of some committee of writers, each contributing independently the findings of his own research; what it is is the message of Jesus Christ, of which all later testimonies only can be and only aim to be interpretations. So, while the derived testimonies of the New Testament are to be taken with entire seriousness, they are, equally, to be taken seriously as derived and not as original. And here it is not only external nearness in point of time to the message of Jesus that matters, but also inner, material nearness to the centre of the Gospel. Regardless of chronological nearness, we can attribute a greater material nearness to Romans than to James. The more derived a testimony is, the more both exegetes and dogmatic theologians will have to be careful of the way in which it treats of the event of salvation in Jesus Christ; of what factors are at work in each particular proclaimer of the Word, in each particular situation in which it is proclaimed; promoting or constricting it, strengthening or weakening, intensifying or softening. Hence every testimony in the whole of the New Testament has to be understood in terms of the message of Jesus and the original emphases. Thus it may not be the case that later witnesses outweigh earlier ones, the Pastoral Epistles, say, outweighing the Sermon on the Mount or the Epistles to the Corinthians.

It is the *Church,* as the people of God of the New Testament, who has transmitted the New Testament to us; the history of the Canon does indeed include change, but all the same it is the New Testament as a *whole* that has been transmitted to us. Without the Church there would be no New Testament. Further, the Church's mind on the matter has definitely been that every part of the New Testament was included in the Canon as a positive witness to the Christ-event (and not to some extent as negative programmes for contrast's sake). It is true that it was the early Catholic Church that gave us the Canon. But that early Catholic Church proclaims her catholicity by the very fact that she did not exclude Paul, as an early Catholic Church would have to have done to be consistent in the sense of Protestant exegesis. But just by including Paul along with Acts, Paul along with James; by, in short, making the *whole* New Testament canonical, she carried out her "discernment of spirits." Catholic theology is of the opinion that she did it well and that we cannot do it any better today. The individual exegete cannot achieve his own discernment of spirits better than by trusting to that discernment of spirits which was carried out by the early Church and maintained by the later Church, and which has transmitted to us the New Testament as such.

Whether a theologian is or is not able, at once confidently and critically, to accept the whole New Testament as transmitted and guaranteed by the *Church,* is even today to a large extent decided by his concrete relationship to the Church. We Catholics are convinced that we should go along with the early Church in regarding the whole of the New Testament as a true testimony to the event of revelation in Jesus Christ; to let each individual testimony really count, but differentiate it according to its relationship to that salvation-event; to do justice to each one, both in theology and in practice.

Is it entirely a matter of chance that in the Catholic faculty in Tübingen the systematic theologian does not find what he says being disowned by the exegete, but supported?

Catholic theology will naturally make a fundamentally different evaluation from Protestant theology of the evidences of early Catholicism in the New Testament. Is it possible to limit the true message of the New Testament to the one moment, rather the mathematical point, of, say, the Epistle to the Romans or a demythologized Johannine Gospel? Taken as a whole, the New Testament bears witness to all-embracing, i.e., catholic truth in its fullness. To allow validity only to one part is choice, i.e., heresy. And if this New Testament, in its later parts, leads on to early Catholicism, then the Catholic exegete will strive to show that what is happening here is not, understood in a truly historical way, a perversion of the true and original thing, but a genuine and valid development. This will not prevent us from comparing the later with the earlier and measuring the former by the standard of the latter, a task undertaken by all genuinely critical theology, Catholic included.[75]

Is there, even in ecclesiology, where all Catholic-Protestant arguments come to a head and are bound to do so, a road towards reunion? There is. It consists in *Catholic* theology's striving more and more to do justice to the New Testament with *evangelical concentration,* and in *Evangelical* theology's striving more and more to do justice to it with *catholic comprehensiveness*. In this way Catholics, who are often burdened with superfluity, and Protestants, who often suffer from dearth, can learn from each other and help each other. Is not this what is happening, basically, over and over again today in controversy, and more and more clearly all the time? The object of the exposition developed here, and the explicit confrontation made in it, was not to close a discussion but to point as urgently as possible to the great common ecumenical task that lies behind it. And is it not a hopeful sign that in Tübingen, after a thorough-going argument, we can always sit down together again in peace, and harmony, and good humour?

NOTES:

[1] To give only one symptom, compare the articles on key theological concepts in the second edition of the *Lexikon für Theologie und Kirche,* Freiburg-im-Breisgau (1957 ff.) with those in the first edition (1930 ff.).

[2] Cf. P. Lengsfeld, *Tradition und Schrift in der evangelischen und katholischen Theologie der Gegenwart,* Paderborn (1960).

[3] When the Lutheran Chapter in Tübingen celebrated, not altogether surprisingly, the seventh centenary of the foundation of Tübingen's monastery of Augustinian Hermits, the Tübingen's Reformation historian H. Rückert wrote a centenary essay in *Mittelalterliches Erbe—Evangelische Verantwortung,* Tübingen (1962), entitled "Das evangelische Geschichtsbewusstsein und das Mittelalter" (pp. 13–23). In this he spoke impressively of the "historical continuity" between the Reformation and the medieval Church (the "fathers," p. 13). Protestant acknowledgement of the Middle Ages could certainly not, he said, be uncritical, "without reservation," "undifferentiatedly" Catholic (p. 17), but it must, like the Reformers themselves, start from the principle that "there has never been a time when the Church of Christ was not present in the world" (p. 20). Even with the medieval Church the Reformation stands "in an uninterrupted continuity of tradition" (p. 21). Hence the present task of Protestant theology: "Protestantism, in the sixteenth and succeeding centuries, allowed itself to be saddled—by humanism, not by the Reformation—with a picture of history in which the pattern of reaching back to resume contact with antiquity involved judging the intervening medieval period as an age without God and an ecclesiastical vacuum; this represents a long-sustained loss to us of evangelical substance, just as bad as that other loss which we have already indicated as a danger threatening the Evangelical Church, which would arise if we allowed the criticism of the Middle Ages by the Reformation to become blunted. Our task here is to recover lost ground,

190 THE COUNCIL IN ACTION

to re-establish our link with the Church of the Middle Ages, to become fully historically conscious of the fact that we are as much sons and brothers of the Christians of
the Middle Ages as are the members of the present-day Catholic Church. Much depends on whether we succeed in this. There is a positive Reformist, Protestant interpretation of the medieval period of the Church's history, which is fully as justified as
the Catholic one; for during that medieval period there existed together, in an undivided unity of potentialities, both the elements which afterwards separated out into
the two confessions. To examine the Middle Ages in this way is a task for Protestant
theology which has so far scarcely been undertaken at all; and what would emerge
from it, as a whole and in detail, is quite unpredictable. As I have already said,
it would have to combine the sharp edge of Reformist criticism with the breadth of
Catholicity" (pp. 22 f.). One might add from the Catholic side that the Catholic attitude towards the medieval Church cannot be "uncritical," "without reservations"
or "undifferentiated," either.

⁴ A. von Harnack, *What is Christianity?*, London, Edinburgh, Oxford and New York
(1901).

⁵ *Ibid.*

⁶ *Ibid.*

⁷ P. Feine, *Theologie des Neuen Testaments,* Leipzig (1936), pp. 319–25.

⁸ R. Bultmann, *Theologie des Neuen Testaments,* 3rd ed., Tübingen (1958), pp. 452–
63; cf. the article by W. Schmithals on the Pastoral Epistles in *Die Religion in
Geschichte und Gegenwart,* 3rd ed. Tübingen (1961), vol. 5, pp. 144–8.

⁹ *Strukturen der Kirche,* Ch. 6, 3b.

¹⁰ E. Käsemann, "Begründet der neutestamentliche Kanon die Einheit der
Kirche?" *Exegetische Versuche und Besinnungen,* Göttingen (1960), vol. 1, pp. 214–23.

¹¹ Käsemann, vol. 1, p. 214.

¹² Käsemann, vol. 1, p. 216.

¹³ Käsemann, vol. 1, p. 215: "To put it in schematic form: While Mark with his
numerous miracle-stories is showing the hidden epiphany of him who receives his full
glory at Easter, Matthew shows the bringer of the messianic *torah* and John the
Christus praesens, and Luke, who historicizes and depicts salvation-history as an evolu-
tionary development, writes what may for the first time be called a life of Jesus."

¹⁴ Käsemann, vol. 1, p. 215.

¹⁵ Käsemann, vol. 1, p. 215 f.: "Matthew, for instance, is shocked at the drastic
way in which Mark (5.27 ff.) recounts the healing of the woman with an issue
of blood. The idea that the garment of the miracle-worker shares in divine power,
which surges up when touched and is capable of healing, is a popular hellenistic notion which re-appears in the account of Peter's healing shadow and Paul's miracu-
lous handkerchief (Acts 5.15:19.12) and later gives rise to the cult of relics. Matthew
corrects this crudely magical view, making the healing follow not on the touching of
the garment as such but on Jesus' word of power. Generally speaking, he reduces to
the minimum the lavish description in Mark's miracle-stories (which betray a novel-
istic delight in narrative and even introduce touches of the narrative technique of secular literature) in order to bring out more strongly the mysterious dignity of Jesus."

¹⁶ Käsemann, vol. 1, p. 218.

[17] Käsemann, vol. 1, p. 216.

[18] Käsemann, vol. 1, p. 216: "While we can certainly say that the great mass of this tradition does not present us with the historical Jesus, it is also true that even the most highly perfected methods of historical science are able to give us, on this point, only a more or less sound assessment of probabilities, as we can see from the numerous extremely varying presentations that there are of the life and message of Jesus, and by the magnificent story of Albert Schweitzer's quest for the historical Jesus."

[19] Käsemann, vol. 1, p. 217.

[20] Käsemann, vol. 1, p. 218.

[21] Käsemann, vol. 1, p. 218.

[22] Käsemann, vol. 1, p. 218.

[23] Käsemann, vol. 1, pp. 219 ff.

[24] Käsemann, vol. 1, pp. 220 f : e.g., contrasting doctrines of justification in Paul and James, different views of Paul's apostolate in Acts and Galatians, different eschatologies in John and the Apocalypse etc.

[25] Käsemann, vol. 1, p. 220. Käsemann instances, amongst other things: "The saying of Jesus in Mark 2.27 that the Sabbath was made for man is toned down in verse 28 by the addition that the Son of Man is Lord of the Sabbath. The community was able to attribute to its Master what it did not dare to claim for itself. The limiting additional phrase proves that it had taken fright at the freedom given it by him and was retreating into a Christianized Judaism. Its polemics against Pharisaism as hypocrisy, on the other hand (consider Matt. 23 alone!), really take the edge off Jesus' attack on Pharisaism, which was aimed at all striving for one's own righteousness and hence at every kind of 'good-works' piety and in fact at every human being. By turning Pharisees in general into hypocrites and applying Jesus' criticism as a condemnation of immorality, the way is opened to a Christian form of 'good-works' piety, which was barred by Jesus' real attack on real Pharisaism" (vol. 1, pp. 219 f.).

[26] Käsemann, vol. 1, p. 221.

[27] *Loc. cit.*

[28] Käsemann, vol. 1, p. 223.

[29] Cf. E. Käsemann, "Zum Thema der Nichtobjektivierbarkeit," *Theologische Versuche und Besinnungen,* Göttingen (1960), pp. 224–36, esp. 229–32.

[30] Cf. also W. G. Kümmel, "Notwendigkeit und Grenze des neutestamentlichen Kanons," *Zeitschrift für Theologie und Kirche,* 47 (1950), pp. 311 f.: "The proper limitation of the Canon thus runs all the way through it, and it is only when this situation is really recognized and acknowledged that the appeal of Catholic or sectarian doctrines to some *particular* part of the Canon can be met with well-founded arguments"; H. Braun, *Hebt die heutige neutestamentlich-exegetische Forschung den Kanon auf?* Berlin (1960), Fuldaer Hefte, 12, p. 23: "An exegesis which is attentive to the message will neutralize the waste material in the Canon, and raise the question of the limitations of the Canon in regard to individual cases. Thus it does not simply assent to the Canon as a whole, just because it is the Canon. It takes it critically, but making use of the objective criterion supplied by the New Testament itself. And hence it adheres to the Canon as far as concerns its centre, the basic phenomenon of the New Testament. This is supplied only in

the Canon, not by anything later; though even in the Canon not in a pure and unmixed form."

[31] Käsemann, vol. 1, p. 232; cf. Käsemann's two articles, "Zum Verständnis von Römer 3, 24–26" (*Exegetische Versuche,* vol. 1, pp. 96–100) and "Gottes Gerechtigkeit bei Paulus," *Zeitschrift für Theologie und Kirche* (1961), vol. 58, pp. 367–78. This last essay in particular (which was a short paper read to the Oxford conference on "The New Testament Today," 14 September, 1961) comes extraordinarily close to a deepened Catholic understanding of the justification of the sinner.

[32] It may be noted, merely in passing, how Käsemann has taken account of the achievements of recent Catholic exegesis. Cf. his "Neutestamentliche Fragen von Heute," *Zeitschrift für Theologie und Kirche,* 54 (1957), p. 2: "We must in fairness admit that modern Catholic exegesis, at least in Germany and the countries near it, has reached a level not, in general, inferior to that of Protestant work, even not infrequently surpassing it in point of carefulness. This is evidence that the historico-critical method has become, in principle, common property. It does not put exegesis into any particular theological camp, but is simply a factual division between scholarship and the speculation of fundamentalism. The convergence of the various fronts is perhaps the great characteristic of our period."

[33] "Begründet der neutestamentliche Kanon die Einheit der Kirche?" vol. 1, p. 223.

[34] Pp. 224–39, *Dogmatics,* by Hermann Diem, tr. Harold Knight. Copyright tr. 1959, Oliver & Boyd Ltd. Published U. S. by The Westminster Press. The quotations from this book which follow are reprinted by permission.

[35] P. 225.

[36] P. 227: "But, above all, by this Scriptural doctrine the Evangelical Church ruined its own true foundation, namely preaching: The concrete event of preaching in which Scripture was proclaimed and its witness reanimated in the living witness of the preacher was now replaced by a didactic exposition and demonstration of its statements considered as so many truths and matters of fact. Moreover, faith, too, in its relation to Scripture, underwent a change: it was no longer faith awakened by the proclamation of Scripture and directed to the events which Scripture attests and their significance for salvation, but it was rather primarily an act of faith in the divinity of Scripture—faith understood as *fides quae creditur*—and in those predicates of Scripture which were implied in that conception or were considered necessary to maintain it."

[37] Diem, p. 228.

[38] Diem, p. 231.

[39] Diem, p. 233. On Diem's concept of "proclamatory history," which states that it is in proclamation *by the community* that the history of Jesus Christ, *who himself proclaims himself,* is proclaimed, as a history that has already happened and is forever happening anew, and that it is precisely thus that the *justificatio impii per fidem sola gratia,* thus proclaimed, takes place, cf. esp. pp. 112–47.

[40] Diem, p. 234.

[41] Diem, p. 234.

[42] Cf. Diem, pp. 143 f.

[43] Diem, pp. 235 f.

[44] Diem, p. 236.

[45] Cf. H. Schlier on *hairesis* in the *Theologisches Wörterbuch zum Neuen Testament,* Stutt-

gart (1933), 2nd ed., 1957, vol. 1, p. 182: The concept, an object of suspicion from the very start of Christianity, "does not owe its existence in the first place to the development of an orthodoxy; the basis for the development of the Christian concept of *hairesis* is to be found in the *new situation created by the appearance on the scene of the Christian* ekklesia. *Ekklesia* and *hairesis* are in practice contradictions of one another. The first cannot admit the second, the second excludes the first. This appears as early as Gal. 5.20, where *hairesis* is reckoned amongst the *erga tes sarkos,* along with *eris, echtrai, zelos, thumoi, eritheiai, dichostasiai. Hairesis* does not yet have here, nor elsewhere in the New Testament in general, a technical sense. In 1 Cor. 11.18 f., the impossibility of having *hairesis* within Christianity comes out even more plainly. Mention of the liturgical assembly, in which the community comes together as *ekklesia,* takes Paul back to the *schismata* of 1 Cor. 1.10 ff. *Schismata* are the divisions in the community caused by personal dissensions. Paul partially believes the information he has received about splits in the community. And this because there must indeed be even (*kai*) *haireseis en humin,* so that those who are of tried worth may be made manifest. It does not matter whether or not Paul is here using an apocryphal saying of Jesus (cf. Justin, *Dialogue,* 35, 3; *Didascalia,* 118, 35); it is in any case, for him, an eschatological and dogmatic statement (cf. Mark 13.5 f. and parallels; Acts 20.29; 2 Pet. 2.1; 1 John 2.19), and *hairesis* is taken as a word with an eschatological value. Further, *hairesis* is clearly distinguished from *schisma* and indicates a further stage beyond it. But this difference in degree consists in the fact that *hairesis* strikes at the foundation of the Church, which is doctrine (2 Pet. 2.1), and in such a radical way that through it a new community-structure arises alongside the *ekklesia.*"

[46] Diem, p. 233.

[47] Diem, p. 234.

[48] Diem illustrates this, quoting G. Eichholz, by the example of the doctrine of justification in Paul and James (pp. 236 ff.).

[49] Diem, p. 235.

[50] Diem, p. 236.

[51] K. H. Schelke, "Die Petrusbriefe," in Herder's *Theologischer Kommentar zum Neuen Testament,* Freiburg, Bâle and Vienna (1961), 13, 2, p. 245.

[52] *Theologie als kirchliche Wissenschaft,* Munich (1951), vol. 1, p. 134; cf. the whole of § 15 on the beginnings of the early Catholic Church.

[53] Diem, p. 137.

[54] P. 138.

[55] P. 163. In vol. 2 Diem has at certain points become aware of the problem of early Catholicism in the New Testament (cf. pp. 152–7), but without taking it seriously as a basic problem; the beginnings of early Catholicism are equated with Tertullian or the Apologists (cf. pp. 296–314).

[56] "Begründet der neutestamentliche Kanon die Einheit der Kirche?" *Exegetische Versuche,* Göttingen (1960), vol. 1, p. 221.

[57] "Amt und Gemeinde im Neuen Testament," *Exegetische Versuche,* vol. 1, pp. 109–34.

[58] Käsemann, *Versuche,* vol. 1, pp. 128 f.

[59] *Versuche,* vol. 1, p. 129; on 1 Tim. 6.11–6, cf. also Käsemann's essay "Das Formular einer neutestamentlichen Ordinationsparänese," *Versuche,* vol. 1, pp. 101–108.

[60] *Versuche,* vol. 1, p. 132.

⁶¹ "Eine Apologie der urchristlichen Eschatologie," *Versuche,* vol. 1, p. 135.

⁶² *Versuche,* vol. 1, pp. 153 f.

⁶³ "Begründet der neutestamentliche Kanon die Einheit der Kirche?" *Versuche,* vol. 1, pp. 220 f.

⁶⁴ As in his *Dogmatics,* pp. 174–6, in connection with 2 Pet. 1.20 f.

⁶⁵ As in "Amt und Gemeinde im Neuen Testament," *Dogmatik,* vol. 1, pp. 109–27, as regards the purely charismatic order in the community in the great Pauline Epistles; and, in general, as regards the sheer opposition between Paul and Luke. Käsemann's strained, "early-Catholic" interpretation of 2 Pet. needs to be compared with the balanced Catholic exposition of K. H. Schelkle, *Die Petrusbriefe.*

⁶⁶ It needs to be considered, too, in regard to other questions, such as knowledge of God from his creation, which is something that can perfectly well have a meaning that is *not* that of an autonomous, evident "natural theology" existing independently of God's grace. On this matter of knowing God from the creation, the question of "primitive Catholicism" in the New Testament needs to be considered in connection not only with Acts but also with Romans, and in an unprejudiced way.

⁶⁷ On the problem of early Catholicism in the New Testament, in addition to Käsemann's essays, cf. P. Vielhauer, "Der Paulinismus der Apostelgeschichte" and G. Harbsmeier, "Unsere Predigt im Spiegel der Apostelgeschichte," both in *Evangelische Theologie* (1950–51), 10, pp. 1–15 and 352–68; H. Conzelmann, *Theology of St. Luke,* London (1960); W. Marxsen, *Der "Frühkatholizismus" im Neuen Testament,* Neukirchen (1958); F. Mussner, "Frühkatholizismus," in *Trierer Theologische Zeitschrift* (1959), 68, pp. 237–45; H. Braun, *Hebt die heutige neutestamentlich-exegetische Forschung den Kanon auf?* Berlin (1960), Fuldaer Hefte 12.

⁶⁸ Cf. e.g., *Theologie als kirchliche Wissenschaft,* vol. 1, pp. 112–16, 134–9. On the interpretation of the confession of Peter, cf. on the Catholic side F. Obrist "Echtheitsfragen und Deutung der Primatsstelle Mt. 16, 18 f. in der deutschen protestantischen Theologie der letzten dreissig Jahre," *Neutestamentliche Abhandlungen,* Münster in Westphalia (1961), vol. 21, pp. 3–4. Diem's position on the emergence of the Canon is particularly informative in regard to his neglect of ecclesiastical office; cf. his *Dogmatik,* Munich (1955), 2nd ed. 1957, pp. 171–95, esp. 179. As against Diem, H. Braun (*Hebt die heutige neutestamentlich-exegetische Forschung den Kanon auf?* p. 11) shows that the limits of the Canon did not simply establish themselves in the Church but, as regards the final delimitations (Hebrews, some of the catholic Epistles, the Apocalypse), were *decreed* by the Church: "The definitive character of this delimitation is that of an ecclesiastical decree."

⁶⁹ A characteristic example is that of P. Fein, who throughout his entire *Theologie des neuen Testaments* not only does not explain the three passages in the Pastoral Epistles which are the classical texts on ordination, but does not even mention them. And Käsemann says, with reference to 2 Pet., "It might almost be described as symptomatic that, apart from its unavoidable treatment in commentaries, there is a general silence about this Epistle." ("Eine Apologie der urchristlichen Eschatologie," *Versuche,* vol. 1, p. 135.)

⁷⁰ Thus the prohibition of "private interpretation" in 2 Pet. 1.20 only means, according to R. Knopf, that "Christians are, then, to approach the Old Testament prophecies with reverence, restraint and modesty," and according to G. Wohlenberg and A. Schlatter, that prophecy is given its interpretation and fulfilment by history (cited by

Käsemann, *Versuche,* vol. 1, p. 152). Another example is offered by W. Fürst, *Kirche oder Gnosis? Heinrich Schliers Absage an den Protestantismus,* Munich (1961), p. 36: "Thus in regard to, say, the Pastoral Epistles, we shall not be influenced by their undoubtedly 'Catholic' notion of office and tradition, but listen to the claim that they make on behalf of the Word; in this is evoked the persistent Christianity which remains throughout such developments." On W. Marxsen's minimal interpretation of the Catholic texts in the New Testament, cf. F. Mussner, "Frühkatholizismus" in *Trierer Theologische Zeitschrift* (1959), vol. 68, pp. 237–45.

[71] "For fundamentally, whenever anything which is 'written' is overlooked in the exposition of Scripture, whenever for the sake of the exposition we are forced to weaken or even omit what is written, there is always the possibility that the exposition has really missed the one thing which Scripture as a whole attests, even when it thinks that it has found it. An exposition is trustworthy to the extent that it not only expounds the text in front of it, but implicitly at least expounds all other texts, to the extent that it at any rate clears the way for the exposition of all other texts" (Karl Barth, *Church Dogmatics,* p. 485. Quoted with permission of Charles Scribner's Sons, New York.)

[72] Even W. Fürst frankly admits, in his attempt at a Protestant answer to Heinrich Schlier: "Our own divided state may well be the sore point at which Schlier's questioning hits hardest as a challenge. Are we at least at one amongst ourselves, as by Reformation 'principle' we simply have to be, about that one point on which we could, as it seems, be at one with Schlier: that the New Testament is the standard by which decisions are made? Schlier does not believe us when we say that what lies behind all the differing answers that we give is our harkening to the one Scripture, and one can hardly blame him. May we not be compelled at last by his conversion, a threat which has shaken our tradition to its foundations, to catch up as speedily as possible with that work of cleaning-up which we keep on postponing? So long as we do not embark on it we can hardly be in a position to meet Schlier's challenge successfully. The attempt made here is burdened by this weight of a task not yet done, and one cannot but be aware in this respect too of its premature character" (*Kirche oder Gnosis? Heinrich Schliers Absage an den Protestantismus,* Munich (1961), p. 7).

[73] What is being whispered by many has been said openly by the Tübingen Old Testament scholar, H. Haag: "It is with great distress that it is being observed in exegetical circles that the freedom opened up to Catholic biblical scholarship by the Encyclical *Divino Afflante Spiritu* seems to be threatened once more. It is happening once again, as it has happened all too frequently during the last fifty years, that an exegete who publishes some view regarded in Rome as erroneous, or even very often merely as inopportune, is removed from his post and forbidden to lecture or write, without his being heard on the matter at all or even being told where he is supposed to have erred" ("Was erwarten Sie vom Konzil?" *Wort und Wahrheit* (1961), vol. 10, p. 600).

[74] Cf. my discussion of these problems in *Strukturen der Kirche,* pp. 161–95.

[75] K. H. Schelke, *Die Petrusbriefe,* Freiburg, Bâle and Vienna, 1961, p. 245.

13

Why Are Dogmatic Pronouncements So Difficult to Make Today?

THE UPSHOT of the discussions of the first schema, on Revelation, proposed by the theological preparatory commission to the Second Vatican Council—wearisome discussions, marked by strongly opposed positions—has been a postponement of the debate. A new schema has got to be worked out, taking more account of the demands of the times in which we live, and of the Church and theology as they are today. In particular, the new schema is to differ from the old by its ecumenical spirit; it is to aim at making reunion easier rather than more difficult. For this purpose, the Pope has formed a new commission, drawn from the theological commission (elected as to its majority by the Council) and the Secretariat for Christian Unity, with whom the theological preparatory commission (selected exclusively by the Curia, and strongly dominated by conservative elements) had rigidly declined, from the start of the preparations for the Council, to co-operate in any constructive way. Even this new commission will have no easy task, for ecumenical discussion in particular has brought home to us afresh the difficulties involved in dogmatic formulation. The problem of dogmatic statement, and especially of infallible statement in the Catholic sense, can be seen and has to be seen, on the basis of the present theological situation, in a more delicately nuanced way. And the Catholic concept of revelation in particular, which is to be stated in the first theological

196

schema when given its new form, calls for an awareness of the state of this problem.

Misunderstandings

The tremendous difficulties blocking the way to a reunion of separated Christians seem nowhere so insuperable as in the Catholic doctrine of the infallibility of the Church, of ecumenical councils and especially of the Pope. It seems impossible that Lutherans, Calvinists, Anglicans, Old Catholics and Orthodox should ever be able to accept an infallibility of this sort. We must not obliterate this opposition, nor indeed is it possible to do so. And yet it is the duty of Christians who are struggling for unity to work away at this seemingly hopeless split, so as at least to reduce the gap from both sides. The first step towards this is the demolition on both sides of misunderstandings.

Even the first of Luther's disputations with his opponents in 1518 led to his conceding that councils can err.[1] And in the following year this sharpened into: councils have erred.[2] Calvin, in the fourth book of his *Institutio,* went at length into the reasons why it is possible for councils to err. But it would be a misunderstanding to think that the aim of the Reformers was to undermine the authority of councils; indeed, they held the councils of the early Church in high esteem. What they wanted was rather to establish a good foundation for the authority of councils as authority *under* the Word of God, clearly defining the relationship of councils to revelation both positively and negatively. The Reformers affirm that the Church abides in truth, though they deny that every single council, with all its statements, abides in truth.

On the other hand, it would be a misunderstanding to suppose that the Catholic doctrine of freedom from error of the Church, ecumenical councils and, in certain circumstances, the Pope, implies that the Church autocratically appropriates to herself and seizes possession of God's revelation. The position of the Church and her *magisterium* in relation to the revelation of God is one of obedience, of being set concretely over against the glorified Lord of the Church who through all the centuries speaks imperiously to the Church by the demand of his Gospel for our faith and obedience. There is no subsequent commutation of this relationship of obedience into one of domination, with the Church able to dispose at will of Christ and his word. The word of God proclaiming itself in words of men is never controlled, "possessed," by the Church as her own property; the Church abides under the word of God, and precisely thus she remains the possession and property of the Lord. For all the unity of the Church with Christ, she thus always stands *over against* him, as disciple to Master, servant to Lord, flock to Shepherd, earthly body to heavenly Head.

Hence the teaching authority of the Church is never something immediate and original, but always mediate and derived from Christ and his word. The word of God proclaiming itself in words of men is at once the ground and the limit of the Church's teaching authority. The very exercise of the Church's teaching authority can only be understood as a fulfilment of obedience towards the word of God to which she is subordinated. God and his word are above, the Church and her word are below; no reversal of this is possible; every commissioning, authorization and investment with power comes from above. Nor is any absorption of the word of God into the Church possible. The Church can never simply appropriate God's authority to herself. The Church's obedience can never simply become an obedience towards herself, towards her own teaching authority. God's authority alone is autonomous; the Church's authority is and remains heteronomous. The Church could do no greater damage to her genuine (!) teaching authority than by divinizing it, making it something transcendent; if once this authority ceases to have God and his word over it, then its source and ground are gone, it has dissolved itself. The Church has no greater way of *strengthening* her teaching authority than by constantly and concretely subordinating her authority, humbly, modestly and thankfully, to the authority of God's word; by desiring, in all simplicity, to hear and proclaim and expound not her own word but the word of God.

So, like the Prophets and Apostles themselves, their successors who are the bearers of ecclesiastical authority, and especially the Pope, stand simply in *obedience* under the Spirit. The man who bears office has constantly to hear, to receive, to learn the word of God in the human word of Scripture; he has continually to mould himself upon that word of God in words of men, continually to set his course according to it. He can indeed give full value to what he receives from above in his office as teacher, and be thankful for it. But this, which he does not have of his own resources, will not be something on which he can arrogantly presume, as though it were his own property; he will not deck himself out with it and put on authoritarian airs over it as if it were something at his own disposal. He will not turn the glory of Christ into self-glorification, the praise of Christ into self-praise, but live, even in the office that he holds, as a poor, weak human being and sinner living by the grace of God.

Hard though it may be for a Protestant Christian to understand the infallibility of the Pope (it can only be understood within the perspective just outlined: not as an arrogant appropriation of divine revelation but as a humble, obedient, unsubjective *service,* under the guidance and protection of the Holy Spirit), there still remains interpretation, *human* interpretation.

Credibility in the teaching office

It is obvious that abstract assertions do not suffice here. There is little use in even the most beautiful theoretical asseverations about the Church's teaching office, if its practical exercise seems to demonstrate the opposite. The teaching office of the Church is, at all its levels, continually faced with the task of showing in all things that it is a selfless, humble, helpful service of human beings. An arrogant tone, a loveless attitude, frequent denunciations, authoritarian interventions without reason given and condemnations without a man's being heard in his own cause, totalitarian repression of free discussion, petty censorship, dissemination of an atmosphere of fear and unfreedom—all this makes the Church's teaching authority something *incredible* to people both inside and outside the Catholic Church. All this is incredible because it is *unevangelical,* contrary to the Gospel.

The *Petrine* teaching office too is faced with the permanent task of continually making plain its evangelical character to the Church and the world, of presenting itself credibly as a service of love and of the strengthening of the faith of the brethren, for the protection and furtherance of the freedom of the children of God, the freedom into which Christ himself has set us free from the law (Gal. 5.1). It is the task of the Petrine office, too, to be continually convincing, "not in the persuasive words of human wisdom, but in showing of the Spirit and power" (1 Cor. 2.4).

In his *Church Dogmatics,* Karl Barth concedes this much on the subject of the apostolic succession: "Thus the difference between the evangelical and the Catholic view consists here too not in the matter of the *That* but in the matter of the *How.* And even in the matter of the *How* no protest in principle can be raised on our part either against the summation of the apostolate in Peter, nor yet against the possibility of a primacy in the Church, which in that case might very well be that of the Roman community."[3] But in conversation, he has formulated what is the decisive objection: "I cannot hear the voice of the Good Shepherd as coming from *this* 'chair of Peter.' " Does this not give us Catholics something to think about?

The central difficulty

Laying stress on the concrete credibility of the Petrine office does not make a *theological* clarification of the problem superfluous; it is called for too. The First Vatican Council made a contribution to this clarification by limiting the infallibility of papal utterances to an extraordinary degree, in contrast to the exaggerations of the Middle Ages and later; only once, in all the close on a hundred years since Vatcian I, has recourse been made to papal infallibility. Of course, even before the Vatican Council, Christians inside the Catholic

Church were clear on a point which is still not plain enough to many Christians outside her: that "infallibility" has nothing whatever to do with "faultlessness," "impeccability." Popes are sinners and have their father confessors. But the First Vatican Council laid down precisely the *limits* and *conditions* of papal "freedom from error" (which would be a better, more accurate way of saying it) and narrowed it down in practice to a few extraordinary cases. It can also be shown from the Acts of the Council how the Pope, when making binding statements of doctrine, must not act separately from the Church but only as representing the whole Church, with whom he must remain in contact. The Pope cannot by any means define arbitrarily or against the will of the Church as a whole; the Pope himself has to be on his guard against schism.

But the precisions of the First Vatican Council leave intact the basic difficulty for Christians outside the Catholic Church. We could formulate it in the following extreme form: If only one Pope at one moment in thousands of years of the Church's history should pronounce only one article of faith binding on the Church, doing it with the full assurance of one for whom error is excluded in advance, then this poses the problem in all its acuteness: *a human being, who is not God—free from error*? And what can thus be said against the Pope's freedom from error can also be said, correspondingly, against the freedom from error of an ecumenical council.

It is no good, where Protestants are concerned, to appeal as against this difficulty to a supernatural charism of freedom from error. For them, any such thing is a postulate without foundation in Holy Scripture. Certainly, according to them, too, the Church remains and endures in Christ, *abides* in his truth, and the gates of hell do not prevail against her. But this is something that the Holy Ghost effects in the Church in face of all human error, including all errors of individual councils and individual shepherds in the Church.

It calls for mighty efforts by the theologians on both sides, and especially for a penetrating analysis of the historical structure of dogma and, in general, of theological truth and the statement of it, for us to arrive at any clearer and ecumenically more hopeful insight into this problem and its solution. Catholic theology is still surely far from having reached, on this road towards a meeting, that summit from which it would be possible to trace the horizon which would show, even to other Christians, this dogma of freedom from error as obviously a part of the structure of the Church. In the meantime, the individual theologian cannot do much more than take small, patient steps to level the road and clear away the misunderstandings that are blocking it. It is in this sense that these few remarks about the problem are made here; they are not meant either to treat questions exhaustively or to say anything final, but rather to call forth further constructive questions. Three areas of the problem can be distinguished.[4]

Conscience and the teaching authority of the Church

Is the teaching authority of the Catholic Church, as it is often said or tacitly assumed to be, really a violation of the Christian conscience, ruling out all personal responsibility and decision? The answer to this is that not even Catholic teaching authority sets aside the freedom of the Christian conscience. It is universally held in Catholic moral theology that conscience is the immediate norm of conduct in *every* case. Thus there is a true primacy of the subjective conscience over every objective norm: not in the sense of an autonomous independence of objective norms, but in the sense that one is competent, and obliged, to act in accordance with the subjectively certain judgement of one's conscience even when it is objectively in invincible error.

This also applies, of course, to inerrant papal and conciliar decisions. Karl Adam is right in saying:

> For the Catholic, too, it is not ultimately the objective norm of the teaching voice but the subjective decision of conscience which has finally to decide on a believing acceptance of the revealed truth laid down by the authority of the Church. It

is really not the case that the faith of a Catholic is entirely accounted for by slavish obedience to the rigid law of the Church. He, too, is making a personal act, an act of reflective thought and moral decision springing from the deep centre of his freedom, an act of choice. For him, too, it is an act that can only be performed in the conscience itself. Indeed, if his conscience, on subjectively cogent grounds, becomes involved in invincible error and he finds himself compelled to refuse his assent to the Church's teaching, he is, in the Catholic view, bound to leave the Church.[5]

Even in the Middle Ages, popes and theologians like Thomas Aquinas put forward the view that even a threat of excommunication does not absolve a Christian from following the dictates of his conscience. If he found himself in such a state of tragic conflict he would simply, as a faithful Christian, have faithfully to accept the excommunication, however painful this was to him as a loyal member of the Church.

Faith and the formulation of faith

This is the second problem. The Scripture itself shows that the *one* Faith can live in *different* formulas. One and the same good news is reported by four Evangelists in very different ways; one and the same Lord is described in very different terms as regards his glory and his humiliation; the words of institution of one and the same Eucharist are given in very different ways. The Christian faith is historical in character and constantly formulates itself anew. And thus in the centuries immediately following the New Testament, there were often very different forms of confession of faith in use in the various communities, but all were accorded recognition. It was only in the fourth century that the attempt began to be made to establish one and the same formula throughout the Church. But the fundamental conviction remained that no one formula could suffice to account for the whole fullness of the Faith, and that difference in *formula* did not necessarily involve a difference in *faith*.

Faith can be the same though formulas are not only different but (as is shown by the history of the dogma of the Trinity) mutually opposed. Behind the different and contradictory formulations of faith stand different physiological, psychological, aesthetic, linguistic, logical, ethnological, historical, ideological, philosophical and religious presuppositions; different individual and collective aspirations and languages and ideas about the world, different factors of environment and human understanding, different traditions held by individual nations' schools of theology, universities and religious orders.

Is it any wonder that Christians holding *one* faith should often have failed to understand each other, and that they cast each other out when they could have been at one with each other? It often happened that all that was noticed in other people's statements was what was missing, while all that was noticed in one's own was what was there; that the *content* of truth in one's own formula and the *lack* of it in the other one were all that one took account of. In our present age of ecumenical encounter it would mean a great deal if all Christians would become aware in a new way of the imperfect, incomplete, piecemeal character of their own formulas of faith. The Church cannot, indeed, be indifferent to formulas of faith, since faith itself expresses itself through them. She will indeed rightly insist that it is not for everyone at all times to formulate everything, or the Church will be invaded by misunderstandings, disorder, quarrels, divisions and outright chaos. Hence she will indeed, in the service of the one Faith, have at certain times to regulate usage by forbidding certain formulas and proposing others. Convinced that because of the Lord's sustaining word and intercession the Church of *earlier* centuries, too, stood in this same Faith, she will indeed respect the formulas of that earlier Church as utterance of the one unchanging Faith, and not reject or condemn them even when they are formulated in a way that seems to be different, inverted or even inapposite. The Church will indeed thus discern and hold fast to the one unchanging Faith under all the various formulas of the various centuries. But nevertheless and at the same time she will, in this age of ecumenical encounter with other Christian communions, strive to discover that one same Faith under the different and opposed formulas that the others use, so as to accord to them, with the greatest possible openness and readiness to understand, difference in *formula* so long as they have the same *faith*.

Dogma and the correction of dogma

Doctrinal statements of the Church are, even though they have the assistance of the Holy Spirit, *human* formulations. As human and historical formulations, it is of the very nature of the definitions of the Church to be *open to correction* and to stand *in need of correction*. Progress in dogma is not always necessarily just an organic development. Dogmas can even lead to a certain petrifaction of faith. It would in any case not be a good thing to suppose that the fact that a dogma has been defined necessarily means that a blossoming of *faith* has come about. If this were so, it would be quite inconceivable why the early Church did not define *more*. But the true conviction then held sway that what brings faith to development is the preaching of the Gospel, the sacraments, prayer, love and suffering; and that dogmas are nothing more or less than *emergency measures* to which the Church is driven by heresies. This was explicitly emphasized not only by the Fathers but also by Thomas Aquinas and at the First Vatican Council.

Thus, one characteristic of dogma is its polemical orientation. *Every* human truth has, because it is human, its definite limitations. But the fact that the Church, faced with the incursions of heresy, is *concentrating* on quite definite points, illuminating certain aspects more and hence others necessarily less, or leaving them in shadow, means that the limitation is here especially perceptible. Herein lies the great task of theology and of the Church: to correct these shifts in her interior balance and get back to the original tension in unity.

This kind of process also makes it clear how seeming untruth can turn to seeming truth. We need to be aware that every human statement of truth, being human and limited, borders on error; the error that corresponds to it follows it like its own shadow. The failure to recognize the limited character of the human statement of a truth is enough to give rise to the danger of error.

Now, a *polemically defined* truth borders on error in a particular way. In a special way, the utterance of it is slanted, aimed totally at that particular error. But since every error, however gross, contains some sort of *kernel of truth*, the danger at once arises that a proposition with a polemical aim will strike not only at the error but also at the kernel of truth within the error: the valid claim that the error is making. So long as I am simply saying, unpolemically, "The just man lives by faith," then the shadow of error following the sentence does not obtrude itself. But supposing I formulate the statement "The just man lives by faith" with a polemical aim, perhaps as against the error of some Christian who is legalistically over-stressing the value of works, then I am in danger of making the shadow of error darken the statement of truth with its unexpressed accompanying meaning: "The just man lives by faith (without doing any works)." And, *vice versa*; so long as I am simply saying, unpolemically, "The just man does works of love," then the accompanying shadow of error does not obtrude. But if I formulate it with a polemical aim, perhaps against the error of a quietist who is over-stressing faith, then I am in danger of making the shadow of error darken the statement of truth with its unexpressed accompanying meaning: "The just man does works of love (and does not live by faith)."

A polemically defined statement of truth is in danger of being understood purely as the contradiction of an error. But this necessarily means neglecting the genuine core of truth in the error. But in that case this statement of truth becomes a *half*-truth; what it says is true; that on which it remains silent is also true. From the point of view of the person stating it, it attacks the error; from the point of view of the person against whom it is stated, what it attacks is the core of truth. To the person stating it it seems, rightly, to be true; to the person attacked it seems, not without cause, to be false. In short, because a half-truth can also be a half-error, there is no

mutual understanding. Each side holds on to *"his"* truth, each per-
ceives error in the *other*; while the truth that each of them holds is
inclusive of the other, each of them regards the other as excluded
on account of a deficiency in truth.

Has this not often been the case in the history of the Church?
Ecclesiastical definition struck at error, but did not explicitly except
from its condemnation the core of truth in the error; this meant that
the true condemnation of error seemed to the other side to be a false
condemnation of truth. A definition of the Church, for example,
condemned a *sola fides* in so far as it was an empty, presumptuous,
self-righteous belief in justification; it did not define with sufficient
clarity what can also be truly meant by *sola fides*: faith in the good
and true sense which puts all its trust in the Lord alone. The true
condemnation of the false *sola fides* was taken by the others as the
false condemnation of the true *sola fides*.

It is an over-simplification of truth to suppose that every proposition in its verbal formulation as such must be unambiguously
true *or* false. Every proposition can, as far as the verbal formulation
goes, be true *and* false, according to how it is aimed, situated, intended. And how it is intended is a harder thing to discover than
how it is said. The ecumenical task of theologians on both sides is
to look seriously at the truth in the other side's error and the possible error in their own truth. Thus turning away from the supposed
error leads to a meeting in the truth actually intended. Thus the
Church manifests herself more and more as the pillar and ground
of the truth.

When we think over all the points developed here, we can understand why it is that today, not only out of regard for other Christians, but also out of regard for our own difficulties as Catholics,
we cannot be sufficiently cautious in making conciliar definitions.
There is no room here for doctrinaire irresponsibility, for any
naïvely pedantic bring-it-into-the-light-of-day attitude: not in the
doctrinal declarations of an ecumenical council, for they make the
claim to be binding on the whole Church not only today but tomorrow and beyond tomorrow.

NOTES:

[1] Answer to Prierias, *WA*, 1, 656.
[2] Disputation with Eck, 1519, *WA*, 2, 303.
[3] *Church Dogmatics,* vol. 1, pt. 1, p. 116.
[4] Cf. the documentation and further discussion in *Strukturen der Kirche,* ch. 8: "Was heisst unfehlbar?" (*Quaestiones Disputatae,* 17.)
[5] Karl Adam, *One and Holy,* London and New York, Sheed and Ward (1954), p. 52.

14

What Is and What Is Not the Theological Task of This Council?

POPE JOHN XXIII has in various ways given expression to his desire that there shall be no old-style doctrinaire schemata. If the theological preparatory commission had paid attention to these desires (and to the warnings given by many other people) it would not have found itself being repudiated by the Council and the Pope. It would do neither the Church nor the world any good simply to be lectured by the Council with repetitions of old doctrines. This was what the Pope said in his opening address: "The salient point of this Council is not, therefore, a discussion of one article or another of the fundamental doctrine of the Church, which has repeatedly been taught by the Fathers and the ancient and modern theologians, and which is presumed to be well known and familiar to all. For this a Council was not necessary."

But for what, then, was a Council necessary? The Council certainly has a *practical* task: practical adaptation, reform, renewal of the Church to meet the requirements of a new age. And this may well be its principal task. But has the Council a theological task as well? This question is so important that it requires us to make a résumé of what we have said elsewhere, so as to refer it briefly and explicitly to the future course of Vatican II. What, then, is the Council's *theological* task?

Proclamation of the Gospel

The theological task of the Council can only consist in service of the Word of God. This means, in proclaiming the Gospel. The Good News which God has communicated to us in Jesus Christ has to be handed on, proclaimed anew down the ages by the witnesses of the Word. The primary way in which this happens is by preaching. It would be an exaggeration to think that the proclamation of the Gospel takes place primarily in the ecumenical council. It takes place, rather, from person to person, in the gathering together of two or three in his name, in the liturgical assembly, in witness to the heathen. Hence it is not mere chance that ecumenical councils, seeing their specific task as the discussion and decision of important matters concerning the whole Church, have regarded the positive proclamation of the Gospel as their task only to a very limited extent. But one may, on the other hand, wonder whether they might not have done better to concern themselves with a positive proclamation of the Gospel than with negative condemnations (remembering, e.g., the Fourth Lateran Council and the positive demands of the Waldenses). However that may be, one could only rejoice today if (with the great technical means of communication making it possible in a completely new way) a council were to make the service of a positive proclamation of the Gospel its special aim: as has appeared already both in the Pope's opening address and in the opening message of the Council Fathers.

A proclamation of the Gospel, then, for a new age with new needs and new difficulties, new anxieties and new hopes. A proclamation of the Gospel not stopping short at general and abstract statement but clearly focused on the special problems and possibilities of the actual present situation. A proclamation of the Gospel not in the language of the Middle Ages, or of Baroque, or of the nineteenth century, but talking the language of modern man—soberly, relevantly, hopefully—so as to reach the ears and hearts of modern men. This is what the Pope means by a proclamation suitable to our times:

A step forward towards a doctrinal penetration and a formation of consciences, in faithful and perfect conformity to the
authentic doctrine, which, however, should be studied and
expounded through the methods of research and through the
literary forms of modern thought. One thing is the substance
of the ancient doctrine of the *depositum fidei,* and another is
the way in which it is presented; and it is this that must be
taken into great consideration, with patience if necessary,
everything being measured in the forms and proportions of
a *magisterium* which is prevalently pastoral in character.

Not condemnations

The theological task of a council as service of the Word of God
sometimes can, or even must, be carried out in the negative form
of a condemnation of error. The majority of the ecumenical councils of the past did condemn heresies and errors. But the Second
Vatican Council is in a peculiar situation. Two characteristics make
it different from many earlier councils: On the one hand we cannot
—happily—point to any heresies that have broken out within the
Church in our days, such as would call for the Church's condemnation; it is acknowledged on all sides that Pope John XXIII has not
summoned this council on account of any new outbreak of heresy.
And on the other, a condemnation of *general contemporary errors* would
be out of place and inopportune, for two reasons.

(1) The ordinary *magisterium* of the Church (which, as exercised
by both popes and bishops, has an unprecedented range nowadays,
thanks to modern techniques of communication) has forcefully
branded contemporary errors on innumerable occasions. But there
can be too much of a good thing. Repetition of condemnations by
the Council as well would do more harm than good, because (*a*) the
majority of people today would take it as an uncomprehendingly
doctrinaire or pharisaically moralistic passing of judgement rather
than a helpful brotherly act, especially if not accompanied by a confession of guilt on the part of the Church herself. What the world ex-

pects from the Council, which it is following with a great deal of
hope and understanding, are not negative condemnations but positive solutions in the light of the Good News; (*b*) doctrinaire condemnations of others can easily side-track reform of the Church herself.
There is a warning in the impression, confirmed by conciliar history from Lateran V through Trent and Vatican I down to Vatican
II, that it is very often precisely those circles opposed to reform and
renewal which are most eager for condemnations and doctrinaire
decrees. This is due partly to the fact that it is usually easier to see
the mote in one's neighbour's eye than the beam in one's own, and
partly to the fact that doctrinaire decrees and condemnations are
meant for others, while reforms would affect oneself. Hence the
flight into the doctrinaire attitude has often been a flight from self-
reform and self-renewal. We can only be grateful to John XXIII
for having expressed himself with particular clarity against condemnations: "Ever has the Church opposed these errors; frequently she
has condemned them with the greatest severity. Nowadays, however, the spouse of Christ prefers to make use of the medicine of
mercy rather than that of severity. She considers that she meets
the needs of the present day by demonstrating the validity of her
teaching rather than by condemnations."

(2) Such people as are willing to listen to the Church at all are
capable, even without any constant repetition of condemnations
and excommunications, of perceiving the destructive nature of contemporary errors and rejecting them on their own responsibility.
The individual Christian's consciousness of his own personal responsibility has grown greatly through the Church's educational
work and in response to the demands of modern life. For this very
reason, the Pope, turning his back on all doctrinaire paternalism
and inquisitorial distrust, does not want to have condemnations,
because on all these contemporary errors he trusts the judgement
of men of good will: "Not, certainly, that there is a lack of fallacious teaching, opinions and dangerous concepts to be guarded
against and dissipated, but they are so evidently in contrast with
the right norm of honesty, and have produced such lethal fruits,

that by now it would seem that men of themselves are inclined to condemn them, particularly those ways of life which despise God and his law, excessive confidence in technical progress, and well-being based exclusively on the comforts of life."

Not the development of dogma

The advantage that Vatican II enjoys of having no new heresies to combat and no new condemnations to pronounce also represents a danger. Precisely because, unlike most earlier councils, there is *nothing in particular* needing to be condemned and thus defined, there is a danger of wanting to produce judgements and definitions on *anything and everything*. In fact, theological schemata *were* prepared on every conceivable subject; not pastorally oriented texts on the work of proclamation, but doctrinaire statements of a dogmatic kind. This was to overlook the fact that the task of dogmatic definitions is primarily negative and only indirectly positive. *De-finition,* the setting of limits; *de-fensio,* the repelling of attack: the Church's definitions have always, throughout conciliar history, been regarded as defensive bulwarks against heresy, which it gave the Church no pleasure to erect; it was only that she was forced to do so by the incursions of error. Equally, the medieval and Counter-Reformation Church did not define on the basis of what she was *able* to define but of what she *had* to define. She defined not the *maximum possible* but the *minimum necessary*. It was not, indeed, that she was any less convinced that faith and knowledge grow and are meant to develop. But people then were not convinced that dogmatic definition necessarily means a growth and unfolding of faith. Definitions, being human statements, do not, unfortunately (like everything human) have only the positive consequences that are actually desired; they can also—as the history of the Church, of dogma, of theology bears witness—have negative consequences that it is not always possible to avoid: doctrinaire fossilization, new and still worse misunderstandings, domineering conceit and unteachable theological arrogance on the part of the *beati possidentes*.

The conviction of the early Church, and of the Church of the Middle Ages and the Counter-Reformation, was that faith develops and grows through the preaching of the Gospel, through the power of the sacraments, through prayer, love, suffering, knowledge. . . . It is only since the nineteenth century that, by a misunderstanding of the idea of development introduced into Catholic theology by the great Tübingen theologians on the one hand and by Cardinal Newman on the other, a number of theologians have begun to call for dogmatic *definitions* as a way of unfolding and explicating the faith, in place of the old tried means. Whereas, following the Fathers, Thomas Aquinas had very plainly stated the traditional Catholic idea, according to which the truth of the faith was made sufficiently "explicit" by the teaching of Christ and the Apostles, so that there is no necessity for any "explication" of the faith as such, but only for a clarification of it because of errors that arise.[1] And even at Vatican I, the relator of the theological Commission observed, as against those who were yearning for still more definitions: ". . . the necessity for General Councils has not been for the recognition of truth but for the suppression of errors."[2] And again Bishop Martin of Paderborn, also speaking as relator of the theological Commission: ". . . it is the custom of the Church to define only those truths which are matters of dispute."[3] What applies to definitions in general applies especially (because of the catastrophic effect they would have on the Council in its ecumenical scope) to further Marian definitions. An exception might be made (which would not really be an exception) if an earlier definition were onesided and unbalanced enough to give occasion for acute misunderstanding. In this sense the Christology of the Council of Chalcedon supplemented and balanced that of Ephesus. In this sense, too, Vatican II might supplement and balance the ecclesiology of Vatican I.

Not professional theology

Just as an ecumenical council is not meant to do development of dogma, so it is not meant to do professional theology. Doing professional theology is the business of professional theologians. It is not good to have professional theologians acting in theology as though they were Council Fathers. It is not good to have Council Fathers acting in the Council like professional theologians (even when they *are* professional theologians). Theology cannot take the place of the ecumenical council, nor can the ecumenical council take the place of theology. The council and theology each serve the Church best when they perform their own specific task—in union, obviously, with each other.

The Fathers of the Council, coming together for a limited space of time, cannot possibly, in that short time, casually undertake the solution of problems which theologians have been discussing for centuries, perhaps, without solving them. The Holy Spirit does not operate as a *deus ex machina*! The ecumenical council has the special assistance of the Holy Spirit to protect it from error in statements of faith binding on the whole Church, not to provide it miraculously with answers to disputed questions of Catholic theology. Theologians are important to a council. But we can be glad that the Council is composed not of theologians but of bishops, that is, of pastors. At Vatican I, the theological preparatory commission supposed that its job was to present the Council with theological tractates in miniature. The Council itself, even then, rejected them.

It is not and never has been the task of an ecumenical council to decide between the different teachings of individual *schools of Catholic theology*. This would be the very thing that would transform the Council from a representation of the whole Church into a party within the Church. The principle that Pius IV laid down for the Council of Trent, and which was repeated at Vatican I, thus has a profound theological meaning: "He [the Pope] wished to define nothing but what should be decreed by the unanimous consent of the Fathers."[4]

Nor can it be the task of the Council to decide afresh the controversial questions that broke out between the different *Christian confessions* at the time of the Reformation. We are not yet ready to carry out such an operation with sufficient depth and balance. It is just here that we can see in what way an ecumenical council is dependent on the theology of its day. Controversial theology, regarded as a theology of ecumenical encounter, is still in many respects in its infancy. Here, again, it is impossible for the Council to supply for all the mass of exegetical, historical and dogmatic work that has to be done before we can attain to a better mutual understanding and to that consensus of views which is necessary.

Vatican II: the task of pastoral and ecumenical proclamation

Public opinion, not only in the Church but in the world, is following Vatican II with sympathy, because people have observed that this Council, like the Pope, is concerned not with a negative but with a positive task. It is meant to be a council which aims not to burden men still more, heavily laden as they are already, by hard words and uncomprehending negations, but to make their task easier for them in these times of stress. In short, a council that aims to *help* the Church and Christendom and the whole world by what it proclaims.

The Second Vatican Council will have fulfilled a mighty task if it makes all that it proclaims both pastoral and ecumenical in orientation.

Everything that Vatican II proclaims should be *pastoral,* directed towards the care of souls. It should not consist of scholastic or neo-scholastic textbook theology, full of terminology and concepts intelligible only to theologians, but of the truth of the Gospel, presented in terms intelligible to modern men; that truth which illuminates and comforts and gives joy. The proclamations of a council cannot simply be preaching, but they should be on the way towards preaching and the care of souls.

Everything that Vatican II proclaims should be ecumenical, directed towards the whole of Christendom. It should not be a polite version of Counter-Reformation controversial theology but, while making no compromise in essentials, be a proclamation that is *open,* that is understanding of the situation of other Christians, and that strives to meet what is good and justified in their demands. It would be out of the question for a council intended to prepare for the reunion of separated Christians to build up rather than diminish theological barriers by what it proclaims.

What is proclaimed by Vatican II will be both pastoral and ecumenical (the requirements for both coincide) if it springs from Holy Scripture, if it is *biblical* in approach. For this it is not, of course, sufficient just to quote a few biblical texts. Texts of Scripture cannot act as ornaments stuck on to a building constructed of quite other material. A council cannot make use of schemata whose whole structure of ideas and mental world spring from some textbook system, with a few texts of Scripture added afterwards by way of "proof" or illustration or pious unction. Decrees of this sort, which subordinate the divine word of Scripture to the human words of textbook theology, are not usable, either pastorally or ecumenically. What are pastorally and ecumenically usable are statements of doctrine which are nourished upon Scripture, which receive their problems and solutions, their dimensions and proportions ultimately from Scripture, and whose very concepts and language are soaked through and through with the spirit of Scripture.

A marginal remark is called for at this point. A great deal has been said at this Council so far on the subject of the Bible and exegesis; this is cause for rejoicing. But very little of it has been said by exegetes. In comparison with dogmatic theologians and canon lawyers, exegetes are appallingly under-represented both among the consultants to the commissions and among the conciliar theologians. This is not without its consequences. One of the reasons why the decrees of the theological preparatory commission could not be used by the Council was unquestionably that no exegete had had any influence on them worth mentioning, even though they dealt with Scripture and Revelation; not even the Pontifical Biblical Commission was called in. It is urgently necessary for the rest of the Council's work that more exegetes of international standing should be represented in it.

One final point: Vatican II will only be able to fulfil its great task of pastoral and ecumenical proclamation if it *concentrates* its forces: *non multa, sed multum.* The theological work of the Council needs to have a centre of gravity, and this centre has often been indicated by eminent figures amongst the Council Fathers: the *Church.* It is the Church which is to be renewed at the practical level with a view to reunion. It is the Church which needs to be better understood theologically for the sake of reunion. A doctrinal statement about the Church is pressingly called for to complete and balance the unfinished teaching of Vatican I with its definition of the primacy. This is not, after all that has been said, to be understood as calling for some long, neo-scholastic, juridicist, clericalist, self-exaltatory tractate *de ecclesia,* but a declaration springing from Scripture and scriptural perspectives, leaving aside textbook problems and confessional quarrels, as constructively pastoral and ecumenical as possible, to tell us Christians of today what the Church should mean to us as the Communion of the Faithful. But a doctrinal statement about the Church must not remain something purely theoretical; it must be accompanied by practical renewal of the Church, supported and interpreted by a practical reform in head and members.

NOTES:

[1] *Summa theologiae,* II–II, q. 1, art. 10, ad. 1: "... in doctrina Christi et Apostolorum veritas fidei est sufficienter explicata. Sed quia perversi homines apostolicam doctrinam et ceteras Scripturas 'pervertunt ad sui ipsorum perditionem,' sicut dicitur II Petr. ult.; ideo necessaria est, temporibus procedentibus, explanatio fidei contra insurgentes errores." Cf. ad 2; art. 9 ad 2; art. 10 co.

[2] Mansi, 52, 1211.

[3] *Ibid.,* 940.

[4] Quoted from C. Butler, *The Vatican Council 1869–1870* (Fontana edition), London, 1962, p. 219. On the necessity for moral unanimity, cf. above, Part 2, ch. 3.

Part V

THE CHURCH
IN THE PRESENT AGE

15

The Petrine Office and the
Apostolic Office

Ecumenical perspectives

THE SECOND VATICAN COUNCIL is to renew the Church and prepare for the reunion of separated Christians. A huge mountain of
theological and practical difficulties has piled up in the course of
centuries between the different Christian confessions and especially
between Catholics and Protestants. Where does the chief theological
and practical difficulty lie? Not in the understanding of Christology,
not in the understanding of the justification of the sinner, not in the
understanding of the sacraments, but in the understanding of the
Church. And this difference in the understanding of the Church then
has repercussions in differences in the understanding of the sacraments, the justification of the sinner and Christology.

Even in the understanding of the Church we can indeed point to
what we have in common, more plainly today than used to be the
case. Catholics, Orthodox and Protestants can agree today in ac-
knowledging, in principle, that the Church is the royal, priestly and
prophetic people of God, called by him out of the world and sent
by him into the world. She is built up on the foundation of the
Apostles and Prophets, and she is led by Christ, acting through all
the multiplicity of spiritual gifts and ordered ministries and offices.
She has her centre in the liturgical assembly, with the proclamation
of the Word of God and the Lord's Supper; we are incorporated
into her by baptism. Thus she is the one, holy, catholic and apos-

tolic community of those who believe in Christ; the Bride of Christ, awaiting him and yet already espoused to him, the Body of Christ and Temple of the Holy Ghost, at once visible and invisible in this world. As the people of God, travelling on, believing, struggling, suffering and also sinning, the Church passes through time towards the Judgement and the fulfilment of all things.

What we hold ecumenically in common in our understanding of the Church is thus extremely important. It is greater and more considerable than what separates us. But where, then, are the divisive factors? The divisive factors are grounded in the theological and practical question of the concrete organization of the Church, and are crystallized in the theological and practical question of *ecclesiastical office*. As between Catholics and Orthodox, the difficulty narrows down in practice to the Petrine office. As between Catholics and Protestants it is posed in all its breadth and complexity, so that its effects work back onto those things, named above, which we hold in common. The central demand of the Reformers, prompted by the appalling state of the late medieval Church, was for reformation; reform of the Church in head and members according to the Gospel. Luther, working with the lever of the Pauline doctrine of justification, had no intention of founding a new Church; a "Lutheran Church" would have been, for him, a piece of sheer nonsense. Luther wanted to reform and renew the old Church. He took for granted eccleciastical office, and the episcopal office in particular; he did not want to destroy it, but to reform it according to the Gospel. But to a large extent the worldly men who were in office set themselves against all reform of the Church and of their offices, for which they are gravely to blame. This meant that Luther, and the Reformers in general, fell into a tragic conflict with office as it existed in the Church, with the episcopal office and especially with the Petrine office. The excommunication of Luther—Luther himself never desired to leave the Catholic Church—did not resolve this conflict but merely hardened it. The protest of Luther and the Reformers against the Petrine office took up the protest registered against it five hundred years earlier by the whole of the Eastern

Church, and made it still stronger. What began as an opposition *in practice,* intelligible in terms of the concrete situation, against the unevangelical thing that the Petrine office had become, turned with the passage of time into an opposition *in principle.* But for the appalling condition of ecclesiastical office and of the Petrine office in particular, which aroused the *practical* opposition, there would never have been this opposition *in principle.*

Thus it came about that the Rock on which the Church and her unity are meant to be built became a huge stone of stumbling and the chief hindrance to the reunion of separated Christians. It is plain that this is not only a theological question. The *concrete existential situation* of the Petrine office *then,* in the age of the Renaissance, made it impossible to see clearly the true nature of the Petrine office. And so today, again, all exegetical, historical and dogmatic research and discussion by theologians on the necessity of the significance of a Petrine office in the post-apostolic Church are shaped by the *concrete existential situation* of the Petrine office *today,* by the concrete situation of ecclesiastical office, by, in general, the concrete condition of the whole structure of the Church.

What, then, can one do today, if one does not want (what is basically impossible) to bracket off this most difficult of all reunion problems and simply leave it out of our endeavours? Obviously theological research and ecumenical discussion on questions concerning the organizational structure of the Church will have to be intensified. But this alone simply cannot help. On the contrary, theological discussion is blocked at many points, so long as our partners in discussion get the impression, rightly or wrongly, that this or that exegetical, historical or dogmatic interpretation is going to finish up in practice by justifying that "Roman system" which is an abomination to them.

The best possible contribution to clarification of this precise question of the concrete organizational structure of the Church, of ecclesiastical office and of the Petrine office in particular, is a *practical renewal of the concrete structure of the Church,* and especially the renewal of *ecclesiastical office.* This is a question with many aspects. In the first place, the function of office would need to be seen in terms of the Church as the *people of God,* the community of believers. To understand the function of office in scriptural terms, and thus to make it credible to us today, it has to be understood as a *service* in and to the Church as the people of God. A doctrine of the Church that does not start from the royal, priestly and prophetic people of God, the community of believers, *all* called by Christ, is hardly going to avoid the danger of setting too high a value on office, misunderstanding it as domination over the Church, and thus, for practical purposes, of deducing ecclesiology from the Pope and the bishops downwards in a more or less absolutist and centralist fashion.

Starting from the Church seen as the people of God, the question of the relationship between the Petrine office and the episcopal office will of course have a special urgency for this Second Vatican Council, which inherits its problems from Vatican I. What is the point here? That the relationship Pope-bishops should correspond more to the relationship Peter-Apostles! In the ecumenical perspective, this is vital; it is no less vital in the Catholic perspective. This point confirms something that can be experienced in all sectors of the Church and theology today; the great ecumenical problems and the great problems within the Catholic Church have the same root; the great things demanded by other Christians and those demanded by Catholics are at bottom identical. What came out clearly in the Council's debate on the liturgy also applies, basically, in other fields of the Church and of theology. This shows how very near we have really come to each other.

Biblical perspectives

If we are really looking at it from a scriptural point of view, it would seem very superficial to see our present problem simply as a matter of increasing the rights of the bishops and diminishing those of the Pope or the Curia. This way of looking at it would make it purely a matter of ecclesiastical politics, measured by basically secular standards. This is not simply a question of a changed situation making necessary a shift in the balance of power. It is a fundamental matter of making manifest the basic structure of the Catholic Church in the light of Scripture and according to the one pattern to be followed, which is that of the apostolic Church; the relation Pope-bishops is to be brought back to a closer equality with the relation Peter-Apostles. The apostolic office is, of course, superior to any other ministry or office in the Church. For the Apostles were those members of the primitive community to whom the risen Lord manifested himself and whom he sent out with the special commission to proclaim the Gospel which gathers together and founds the Church. Thus the preaching of the Apostles is the foundational testimony to Jesus Christ, the standard for all future ages. Their office as a *whole* is something that essentially cannot be repeated, that is in so far as they are the foundation, eye-witnesses of the Resurrection, included in the event of revelation. All later office can only preserve and expound that revelation. Because of their special calling they, together with the New Testament prophets (charismatics), are the foundation and the bond of unity in the Church in her beginnings. To this extent, then, ecclesiastical office, even that of the bishops, must be distinguished from the apostolic office in its strict and original sense.

But at the same time it is necessary to see the continuity between the apostolic office and ecclesiastical office. The *task* of the apostolic office, its *function*, in so far as this means the preaching of the Gospel, the administration of the sacraments and the guidance of the Church, had to go on in the Church. This is the task of ecclesiastical office, which is concentrated in the *episkopoi*. Just as the office of Pope, though different, can be called the Petrine office in the sense of continuing a task and a function, so the episcopal office can be called apostolic. Within a scriptural perspective, then, we have the clear necessity of making the relation Pope-bishops, Petrine office-apostolic office, resemble the scriptural relation Peter-Apostles. The place of the Petrine office is not to be encroached upon by any extreme conciliarism, nor that of the apostolic office by any extreme papalism.

The constitution of the Catholic Church is at once Petrine and apostolic. This constitution is shown forth from the beginning in the writings of the New Testament. The essential features of the apostolic Church have to be maintained, and clearly maintained, in the post-apostolic Church, if she is to be able to call herself apostolic. Looking at it in terms of the apostolic Church, a great deal of what is in the present-day apostolic Church appears in a problematical light. There has been a sharp shift in some of the emphases. In the apostolic Church we observe a centre of unity but no centralism, liturgical, theological or administrative; an authority in regard to the whole Church, but no absolutist authoritarianism; in short, a Petrine office but no papalism. It is not improbable that many Christians now separated from us may one day come to acknowledge a Petrine office renewed according to the Gospel and the model of the apostolic Church. But let us have no illusions about it; neither Protestants nor Anglicans nor Orthodox will ever come to acknowledge the present system with its numerous centralist and absolutist features. The more the evangelical Petrine office shines forth in the Papacy, the more credible it will become. Has this not clearly appeared already in the case of John XXIII, with his completely unpretentious, untheocratic, modest, humble attitude towards his office as one of service towards the whole Church? Has not the spectacle of a Pope once more, after many centuries, visiting the sick and the imprisoned, the poor and the weak, of a Pope obviously never wanting to domineer in the Church but only to help and to serve, done infinitely more, by being truly evangelical, to make the Petrine office credible than the greatness, in this world's sense of the word, and brilliance of so many of his predecessors?

This is the point—and this is where the Council has the power to carry out a great task; ecclesiastical office, and above all the Petrine office of the Pope and the apostolic office of the bishops, needs to be presented more credibly in the spirit of the New Testament. This involves, first and foremost, working out a theological and practical clarification, according to Scripture, of the relation, Petrine office-apostolic office. This is a task which has not in all respects been made easier for us by Vatican I.

The limits of papal primacy according to Vatican I

It can be broadly recognized in the Catholic Church today that Vatican I gave a onesided definition of the papal primacy. This was partly due to the mentality of Vatican I, meeting as it did in a different historical situation, and partly to the interruption of the Council, which brought it to a premature end. In any case, it would be unjust to blame Vatican I for papal absolutism. We must defend it against all false accusations, and what it defined was not an absolutist system. But given that this is true, what are the limits of the *potestas iurisdictionis episcopalis suprema, plena, ordinaria, immediata, universalis* which Vatican I attributed to the Pope? This question is certainly of the greatest importance to any clarification of the position of the episcopate.

The definition made at Vatican I clearly stated the limits of papal *infallibility*. It did not do this for the *primacy*. The majority of the Council, immersed in the struggle with Gallicanism, Febronianism and liberalism, was not interested in the question. Of course the Council would have to have addressed itself to it in order to clarify the position of the episcopate, to which is equally to be attributed a *potestas episcopalis ordinaria, immediata* and, as we see from the Ecumenical Council, a *potestas suprema, plena, universalis* as well (cf. canon 228,§1). But, as we know, the Council was interrupted before making its definition on the subject of bishops.

So the definition itself does not state the limits of the papal primacy. But they are fairly easy to draw if we look at the declarations of the theological commission, or of its relators, in the acts of the Council. Only a few points are going to be briefly put together here.[1]

In quite general terms, one can lay down the following from the acts of Vatican I:

(*a*) The power of the Pope is not absolute (*absolute monarchica*).

(*b*) The power of the Pope is not arbitrary (*arbitraria*).

(*c*) The power of the Pope has its limits (*limitatio*), set actively by Christ, passively by the Apostles and their successors. The Pope is, obviously, subject to the limitations of the natural law (*ius naturale*) and of the divine law (*ius divinum*). Leaving aside the limits set by the natural law, just what are the limits set by the divine law? Again following the acts of Vatican I, we can distinguish four fundamental limits.

(1) *The existence of the episcopate.* It is not possible for the Pope to abolish the episcopate or make void or abrogate its rights. He simply cannot, for instance, turn all bishops into vicars or administrators apostolic. The existence of the episcopate is of divine right no less than that of the Petrine office. The fact that the Pope's power is *vere episcopalis* does not imply any necessity or covert invitation for Roman authority to be constantly intervening in the local affairs of a diocese. A better term than this ambiguous *episcopalis* would be *pastoralis*.

(2) *The ordinary exercise by the bishops of their office.* The Pope simply cannot, as though he were some sort of second bishop, interfere day after day with the exercise by the bishops of their office. True, the Pope does have direct jurisdiction over all the faithful, which permits him, without leave or intervention of the bishop concerned, to exercise his jurisdiction over each of the faithful. But it was, at the same time, said at the First Vatican Council that if the Pope behaved like, as it were, a second bishop, ignoring the local bishop and annulling things that he had, in a reasonable way, settled, then the Pope would be using his power not for the edification but for the destruction of the Church. The expression "ordinary power" has different meanings when applied to the jurisdiction of the bishop and that of the Pope. In the case of the bishop, it means an habitual, normal, daily exercise of his power in his diocese; in the case of the Pope it merely means that such exercise of his office is not delegated but bound up with the office itself, but not by any means

that it is an everyday matter. In the first of these meanings, the Pope has ordinary power only in the diocese of Rome.

(3) *The purpose of the Pope's conduct of his office.* The relator of the theological commission stated this purpose as: Not the destruction but the building up of the Church. The Fathers of the Council formulated it in the same way. Besides the building up of the Church they spoke also of the safety and unity of the Church. Thus it is explicitly stated, in the proem to the conciliar decree, that the primacy is there for the sake of the Church's unity. So the primacy is to serve the Church and her unity, not its own greatness and glory. It is in terms of this that all its actions find, in the concrete, their meaning and also their limits. The Petrine office has, for the Church's unity, the function of a clamp holding the Church together even in an external way; the clamp is there for the sake of the whole, not the whole for the sake of the clamp.

(4) *The quality and manner of the Pope's conduct of his office.* This purpose of building up the Church carries with it the various descriptions made by some of the Council Fathers of the way in which the papal office is to be applied; not arbitrarily, not inopportunely, not disproportionately, not as a general rule. Or, to put it in positive terms, the necessary motives for papal intervention are evident usefulness, necessity, for the Church.

These, then, are the four concrete limits of papal jurisdiction. The question of the *source* of *episcopal* jurisdiction, which had already been discussed at Trent, was deliberately left open at Vatican I. So it is not surprising that this question has continued to be disputed in Catholic theology even down to our own day. We may say that the majority of leading theologians have always upheld the traditional conviction that episcopal jurisdiction, like that of the Apostles, derives immediately from Christ. As for the opinion current in the Roman school that it derives immediately from the Pope, the following points need to be made: From the historical point of view it is untenable; from the theological point of view it does in practice, whatever distinctions canonists may draw, make the bishops dele-

gates of the Pope; from the ecumenical point of view it is unaccept-
able to our Eastern brethren, including those in union with Rome.
In any case, we may say that it is not for Vatican II to define what
Trent and Vatican I expressly chose not to define.

What would be a much more important thing would be to take
heed of scriptural perspectives in all statements of doctrine about
the Pope and the bishops and to use scriptural language. This was
something that Vatican I did only in a very inadequate way. The
decree is to a large extent framed in scholastic, juristic terms. It
speaks continually of the "authority," the "power," the "rights" that
a Pope has in respect of everyone else. No thought was given to the
fact that in the New Testament the comprehensive word used for
"office" is not any of the words then in secular use for legal authority
and magistracy, but simply the word "service, ministry" (*diakonia*).
So there is much about the rights of the Pope and little about his
duties; conversely—and this deficiency was observed by many of
the Fathers at Vatican I—much about the duties of bishops and little about their rights. Of the rights of the royal, priestly, prophetic
People of God nothing whatever is said. There is nowhere any expression of the basic New Testament idea that one only is the Lord
and *all* the rest are brethren. The Pope is not Lord of the Church
but the servant of the servants of God; and all those who hold office
are, not princes of the Church, but servants of the Church, of the
community of the faithful (Lk. 22.26; 2 Cor. 1.23). There is not a
word in the decree—and this may give us some surprise—about the
freedom of the sons of God, to which all Christians are called and
which all offices have to serve (Gal. 5.13; 1 Cor. 3.5: 7.23, 35 etc.).
Nor is there anything about the obligations of office, to serve in the
true spirit of service (Rom. 12.7), to be humble, modest, unassuming, simple, patient, longsuffering, mild, trustful, loving, of which
the whole New Testament is full. Not everything that is "legal" or
"legitimate" is in fact allowable to a Christian who holds office, if
he wishes to live not only according to the Code of Canon Law
but also according to the Gospel.

I shall suggest only very briefly, while we are on the subject, that the whole of our *terminology* about the primacy needs overhauling in the light of Scripture. In terms of Holy Scripture, it is anything but natural and obvious that the Pope should, for instance, be called "Head" of the Church. In the New Testament, this term is reserved to Christ, while Peter is called the foundation, etc. Is one not perhaps doing an outright disservice to the papal primacy by transferring Christological terms to the Pope? It would also be worth investigating how far certain expressions like "vicar [representative] of Christ," reserved exclusively these days to the Pope, but applied in former times to bishops, priests and Christians in general, need to be interpreted in the light of the New Testament.

The official interpretation of Vatican I

Modern Catholic theology, then, agrees that many scriptural perspectives were neglected in the definition of the primacy. What was also neglected was to include in the definition itself the limits of the primacy as they had emerged in discussion at the Council. This was the reason why, immediately after the Council, the definition was at once misunderstood and interpreted in a completely false way.

Thus, as we know, the German hierarchy was obliged to make a stand against false interpretations of the primacy definition which appeared even in official Government documents. This was the famous joint Declaration of the German Hierarchy in 1875 in regard to an official circular issued by Bismarck. This declaration became the official interpretation of the Vatican definition of the primacy, because it was not only accepted by the English episcopate and by Cardinal Dechamps of Malines but was also approved more than once by Pius IX: ". . . Your declaration is an expression of that true Catholic doctrine which is at once the teaching of the Vatican Council and of the Holy See."[2]

Let us see now what propositions it is that are *rejected* by both episcopate and Pope.

(1) Through the Vatican decisions, the Pope has reached the position of taking the rights of the bishops in every single diocese into

his own hands and substituting the papal authority for that of the national episcopate.

(2) Episcopal jurisdiction has been absorbed into papal.

(3) The Pope no longer, as hitherto, exercises certain definite reserved rights, but holds the whole of the bishops' rights in his hands.

(4) He has in principle taken the place of each individual bishop.

(5) It rests entirely with the Pope whether he will, in practice, at any given moment, take the place of the bishop in relation to Governments.

(6) The bishops are now no more than his tools, his officials, without responsibility of their own.

(7) In relation to Governments, they have become the officials of a foreign sovereign, and, furthermore, of a sovereign whose infallibility makes him totally absolute, beyond any absolute monarch in the world.

All these propositions were condemned by the episcopate and by the Pope.

This shows that the direct and ordinary authority of the bishops has to be taken seriously as much as that of the Pope. To draw up a new schema on the Church, the primacy and the episcopate, embodying precisions corresponding to these, would be the indispensable minimum if misunderstandings of the First Vatican Council, which are still very widespread, are to be eliminated.

But this at once raises a difficulty: how are the two "authorities" and their respective competence to be distinguished in a concrete situation? Is there a criterion which enables us to know, in a particular situation, what belongs basically to the competence of the Pope and what to the bishop?

The delimitation of competence

There *is* a criterion which permits the delimitation of competence; not a material but a formal principle. Vatican I was not interested in it, but it has been formulated by post-Vatican theology. It is the *principle of subsidiarity* proposed by Pius XI in his Encyclical

Quadragesimo Anno. Pius XII said of it that it applies "to every order of social life, even to the life of the Church, without prejudice to her hierarchical structure." What does this principle state? That what can be provided by the individual by his own powers should not be provided by the community, and what a subordinate community and authority can provide should not be provided by the overall community. The community should act in a way subsidiary to the individual, and the overall community as subsidiary to the subordinate one.

The principle of subsidiarity is merely a concrete formulation of that general principle, meant to preserve and safeguard the dignity of the human person, which runs: Freedom so far as is possible, constraint so far as is necessary. This only has to be turned round to give the principle of every authoritarianism, absolutism and totalitarianism that has ever been: Freedom so far as is necessary, constraint so far as is possible. The application of the principle of subsidiarity represents the only possibility of avoiding authoritarianism, absolutism and totalitarianism in both State and Church.

As applied to the Church, the principle of subsidiarity means: What the Christian can do on his own resources is not to be done by the community of the Church; what the parish can do on its own resources is not to be done by the diocese; what can be done by the diocese and the bishop is not to be done by the universal Church and the Pope, or, as it might be, the Curia. What Pius XI said in *Quadragesimo Anno* is easily applied to the Church:

> It is indeed true, as history clearly proves, that owing to changed circumstances, much that was formerly done by small groups can nowadays only be done by large associations. None the less, just as it is wrong to withdraw from the individual and commit to a group what private enterprise and industry can accomplish, so too it is an injustice, a grave evil and a disturbance of right order, for a larger and higher association to arrogate to itself functions which can be performed efficiently by smaller and lower societies. This is a fundamental principle of social philosophy, unshaken and unchangeable.

Of its very nature the true aim of all social activity should be
to help members of the social body, but never to destroy or ab-
sorb them.[3]

To suppose that a better application of the principle of subsidiarity in the Church would damage the Petrine office is a mistake. The
reverse is true. Here, too, Pius XI's words on the State are extremely
instructive when applied analogously to the Church:

> The State, therefore, should leave to smaller groups the settle-
> ment of business of minor importance, which otherwise would
> greatly distract it; it will thus carry out with greater freedom,
> power and success the tasks belonging to it alone, because it
> alone can effectively accomplish these: directing, watching,
> stimulating, restraining, as circumstances suggest and neces-
> sity demands. Let those in power, therefore, be convinced that
> the more faithfully this principle of subsidiary function be fol-
> lowed, and a graded hierarchical order exist between various
> associations, the greater will be both social authority and so-
> cial efficiency, and the happier and more prosperous the con-
> dition of the commonwealth.[4]

It is true that as a formulated legal principle the subsidiarity principle is of recent date. But what the formula calls for is something
that has behind it not only Catholic tradition, especially of the first
thousand years, but also, above all, that guiding pattern of the apostolic Church which is still binding on us today. That pattern unequivocally excludes any emptying out in practice (which is still
possible even when the episcopate is maintained *in principle*) of the
apostolic episcopal office or of the status of the faithful people. Any
absolute monarchy or, still more, totalitarian dictatorship in Church
leadership is impossible by New Testament standards. According to
the pattern of the New Testament, Peter's leadership obviously does
not mean carrying out all the Church's tasks himself, by his own activity (or that of a bureaucratic machine). It means serving all the
members of the Church, bishops, priests and the whole community

of the faithful, so as to give them full scope and security to act effectively themselves. Thus the Petrine office can never, like a totalitarian government, claim to look after everything, or at least to have the right to look after everything; this would be a calamitous misunderstanding of the Vatican definition. Rather, the subsidiarity principle demands that the Petrine office should leave to the responsible handling of bishops, priests and people, everything for which bishops, priests and people do not need the direct co-operation of the Petrine office as such. And it also demands that the Petrine office should associate bishops, priests and people so far as possible in the leadership of the Church.

We must not forget that the early Church (and the Eastern Church today, to some extent) was built upon the autonomy of the local Church, in a multiplicity of liturgical, theological and administrative variations. There was unity in faith, in baptism and the Eucharist, in the ethics of the Gospel, and in the common hope. But this fundamental unity did not imply any uniformity. Each community could have its own liturgy, its own order, its own confession of faith and often even its own Canon of Scripture. This is astonishing only if one does not realize that historically the autonomy of the individual local Church *preceded,* as regards its institutions, the grouping together of local Churches in various levels of organization. This autonomy did not by any means imply particularist isolation and sterility; precisely through the multiplicity of forms, it made real the communion of the individual Churches with one another.

It would be completely false to suppose that the schism of the East, and then of the North, resulted from this original multiplicity and autonomy in the communities. The schism—allowing for everything that contributed to it on both sides—was rather a reaction by the East, and later of the Evangelical Churches, against an over-authoritarian, centralist and uniformist conception on the part of the Latin Church, which was more or less suppressing the Church's original pluralism. What a wave of constructive initiatives and fruitful developments there might be in the Church today if the episcopate and the local Church (of a city, a diocese, a country, a continent) could have once again a deeper significance, a greater autonomy!

There would be no need today to be afraid of federalist chaos. The weight of the central authority, with all the numerous modern means at its disposal for control and intervention, will be strong enough in any case. The meaning of the Petrine office as a centre of unity in the Church has been clearly worked out at the dogmatic level against the errors of Jansenism, Gallicanism and Febronianism. So there is no danger of the abandonment of anything essentially Catholic. Unity is so firmly assured in the Catholic Church today that separatism is dead. But this very situation calls for a loosening-up within the circumference and provides a great opportunity for working it out in a constructive way.

There is something that we have temporarily forgotten, and that has been made very plain again by the Second Vatican Council, where the bishops have met each other and had the experience of their own unity as the episcopal college: namely, the fact that there are *two* principles of unity in the Church, the bond between the bishops, with their local churches, and the Petrine office, and the bond between the bishops, and their local churches, *with each other*. In this respect, Vatican II will surely send out a strong wave of influence throughout the Church and all the individual churches.

This *communio* between churches and bishops is so strong that the Pope himself is strictly obliged to maintain and preserve it for his part. Like all the bishops of the Church, the bishop of Rome is bound to avoid schism. Schism has too often been given a onesided definition in modern theology. Classical Catholic tradition never lost sight of the fact that there are two possibilities of schism or division in the Church. As is explained by Francisco Suarez, the famous theologian of the Spanish Counter-Reformation, schism is possible in two ways: (1) By a separation of oneself from the Pope as head of the Church. (2) By a separation of oneself from the body of the Church. And in this second way, says Suarez, the Pope himself can be a schismatic: "If he will not preserve due union and adherence with the whole body of the Church, as, if he were to try to excommunicate the whole Church, or if he wanted to overturn all ecclesiastical ceremonies as established by apostolic tradition, as Cajetan ... and Turrecremata have observed. ..."[5] Even according to Vatican I, it is possible for a Pope as a private person to be a heretic. It is a traditional Catholic view that, like an heretical Pope, a schismatical Pope would lose his office. The most famous example in Church history is the Great Western Schism with its three popes.[6]

I am not saying all this because there is any immediate chance of its becoming acutely relevant (in this regard, the situation in the Church today is infinitely better than in earlier centuries), but just in order to bring out clearly the structure of the Church as the community of the faithful, the fact that it is the task and the duty of every single member of the Church, and so of the Pope too, to preserve necessary unity with the whole Church. There is no other instance, perhaps, that shows so clearly how fully the Church means it when she says that to be Pope is to be a servant, the servant of the Church and of her unity.

But the question that is of direct urgency for us now is this: In what way would it be possible, today, to heighten the value of the episcopate and so of the whole Church? What are the concrete possibilities of elevating the episcopal office, meaning by this not only the individual bishops but the episcopal college? A few points will be indicated here.

Raising the value of the episcopate

(1) *By activating the bishops' consciousness of their own sphere of responsibility*. It would be unjust to put all the blame for our present centralism on the Roman Curia. The "open" element in the Curia itself—and it is more numerous than is often supposed—is apt to point out that the episcopal office would be significantly raised in value if all the bishops made a full and entire use of all the rights which are *already accorded* to them; if, that is, they did not keep having recourse to the Curia for answers and for action in cases where

they themselves, as bishops, should give the answers and take the action. What is all too often lacking in the Catholic Church at every level, among laymen, priests and bishops, is courage: courage to take personal responsibility. All too often we have made cautious prudence the highest of all the virtues, and prudence in a sense that is the twin-sister of indolence. Of course it is often pleasanter, for all of us, to push back a decision, and the responsibility for it, to a higher level. But it is only an acceptance of one's own responsibility that can guard against centralism and absolutism.

(2) *By the Council's initiating a pastoral approach to the subject of the episcopate.* What is and is not the theological task of a council has already been discussed elsewhere.* It follows from what was said there that restraint is necessary in regard to dogmatic statements about the episcopate as about other things. Theological clarification after the onesided results of Vatican I certainly is necessary; in this sense Vatican II is, after all, a continuation of an interrupted council. But it is highly questionable whether it would be useful to define in the strict sense. There are so many questions about the episcopate that have by no means been cleared up in theology as it is at present; consider the distinction between *episkopos* and *presbyteros* in the New Testament, the distinction between presbyter and layman, the sacramentality of the different degrees of orders, the extensive lack of difference in the early Church between a bishop and a city parish priest, the theology of the relation episcopacy-primacy, etc. Is it a good thing to have as many questions as possible dogmatically decided in ecclesiology and in the doctrine of the episcopate? Would it not be better to stick as closely as possible to what is immediately imposed by the New Testament (and there is plenty of it!)? Would this not be the way to ensure that any such schema *De Ecclesia* will be truly pastoral in its approach, really concerned with the care of souls, as everyone wants it to be? What is surely important, in any case, both within the Church and from the ecumenical point of view, is that ecclesiology should be left with every possible door open, with more and more freedom accorded to theologians for the-

* Cf. Section 3, chs. 2 and 3.

ological research; and finally that the value of the episcopate should be raised not only in theology but also, and above all, in practice.

(3) *Decentralization.* It must surely be a matter of general agreement, even well within curial circles, that a decentralization of the Roman Curia is absolutely necessary. On the other hand it is equally clear that simply to re-establish the autonomy of local Churches as it was in the early days would be an anachronism. Even the diocese, though a very large structure in comparison with the early city-diocese ruled by the bishop of a city, no longer forms a self-contained unit. The world has shrunk, and dioceses need to be seen within national and international groupings. Hence the importance of national and international bishops' conferences. It will be one of the most important tasks of the Council to give a solidly grounded and clearly described juridical status to bishops' conferences, which up to now have had no place allotted to them in canon law. On the juridical basis of a conciliar ruling, it could be established that decisions taken by an appropriate majority in the conference would be binding on all its members. It would be necessary here to do some thinking about the episcopal *college,* into which every bishop is received by his ordination, so that he can never *simply* be an individual bishop on his own.

Obviously there cannot be any solution, in a practical question, that does not have its difficulties and its risks. And on the subject of bishops' conferences one finds numerous difficulties raised.

(*a*) The experience of certain countries gives rise to a fear of the "curialization" of the bishops' conferences by having a curial representative on them. But it is for the Council itself to make provision for the necessary privacy and freedom of the bishops' conferences, to make plain the essentially diplomatic status of nuncios, and to provide that the conferences shall have *direct* access to the Pope.

(*b*) There is the fear that the freedom of the individual bishop will be curtailed. It is true that in one direction the achievement of collective responsibility by the episcopal college of a country or larger territorial unit diminishes the individual bishop's freedom of decision; but in another direction it heightens it, since more matters will fall under the competence of a bishops' conference than do at present under that of an individual bishop. The bishop's responsibility becomes a responsibility for the Church in a whole country or continent, as has become the case in the bishops' conferences already, within limited terms of reference. Moreover, the relation bishops' conference-individual bishop needs to be determined according to the principle of subsidiarity. The freedom of the bishop is never to be limited beyond necessity. In particular, it is imperative to leave room for new experiments and pioneering work in individual dioceses.

(c) There is the fear that decentralization will lead to a new centralization in the bishop. Whereas in the Council what was said was, "It's not Peter I'm afraid of: it's his secretary," outside the Council what is said in various countries is, "It's not the Pope who's a long way off that I'm afraid of; it's the 'Pope' who is near at hand." To this one may answer that the concentration of a new responsibility in the bishops' conferences will to a large extent check the arbitrary tendencies which there are always liable to be in the individual bishop. And what is even more important is that, of course, the principle of subsidiarity must also be applied to the relations bishop–dean–parish–priest–layman. The principle holds good at all points: what can be done by a subordinate authority on its own resources should not be done by a higher one. The offices of dean and parish priest and, not least, the status of the layman also need to be raised in value in various respects.

Thus the difficulties of decentralization through the bishops' conferences must not be exaggerated. They can be met. But on what, in the concrete, can decentralization be brought to bear? I am not going to go into this in detail here.[7] It can be brought to bear on the priestly office of the bishop (the ordering of the liturgy, the Mass and the administration of the sacraments: cf. the Council's debate on the liturgy), on the pastoral office of the bishop (reform of the law in relation to marriage, decentralization of the hearing of matrimonial causes, reform of central ecclesiastical administration, restoration of quinquennial powers, etc.), and on the teaching office of the bishop (reform of book censorship, establishment of a just disciplinary procedure in this field, abolition of the Index).

Representation of the episcopate at the center of the Church

The Second Vatican Council has taught us anew, and in a very vivid way, a Catholic truth that has been too much forgotten in past decades, both in theology and in practice: *The whole episcopate*—in union, of course, with the Petrine office—is *responsible for the whole Church*. All the bishops have, as members of the episcopal college, one single, common, collective responsibility for the general well-being of the whole Church. It was not to Peter alone but to the whole apostolic college that Christ entrusted his Church, just as it is not only Peter but (something often overlooked) the Apostles as well who are the foundation, the rock of the Church (Eph. 2.20; Apoc. 21.14). It is not to the Pope alone but to the whole episcopal college that Christ has entrusted his Church.

Thus, even according to the present Code of Canon Law, the ecumenical council has supreme authority in the whole Church: "Concilium oecumenicum suprema pollet in universam Ecclesiam potestate" (Canon 228, § 1). Obviously this is not to be taken in the sense of an exception, as though the episcopal college did not have this authority outside the Council. It is that the ecumenical council manifests in a specially striking way something that is always there basically, if unobtrusively: the authority and responsibility of the episcopal college, together with the Pope, in respect of the whole Church.

For many centuries little attention has been paid to this basic fact in the constitution of the Catholic Church. In terms of practical organization, this common authority and responsibility of the episcopal college for the whole Church, which is a matter of divine law, has been to a large extent replaced by the authority and responsibility of the Roman Curia, which is a matter of human law; members of the Curia, identifying themselves with the Pope, with the help of concepts like "the Holy See," have tended to regard themselves not simply as a purely executive, subordinate, administrative organ, but as the actual superiors of the bishops, so that it has often been difficult for the bishops to obtain direct access to the Pope over important matters. Centralization, and the whole work of the Roman Curia, have yielded very much that is good and positive in the course of the Church's historical development: this must not be denied. But it has not only hindered what might have been very valuable developments in local Churches; it has also to a large extent ousted the episcopate from the leadership of the universal Church.

There is no overlooking the fact that today the whole episcopate is aware in a quite new way that it needs, as the episcopal college, to do justice in very concrete terms to its common, united responsibility for the universal Church. How is this responsibility to be given concrete expression? Along with decentralization, there needs to be a genuine, effective *representation of the whole world-episcopate at the center of the Church,* so as to co-operate with the Pope in the leadership of the universal Church.

Hence various bishops are proposing that a sort of "central commission" should be formed, elected by the various bishops' conferences and juridically independent of the Roman Curia, which would meet periodically—say, twice a year—and which would have legislative authority over more important things (the "main lines"). Their decisions would need to be approved by the Pope, and they would be carried out by the Curia.

A second proposal, also widely favoured amongst the bishops, concerns the internationalizing of the Curia itself. It is pointed out that it is not a good thing to find the General Secretariat of the United Nations being more representative of the whole world, more "catholic" in fact, than the center of the Catholic Church, which continues to a large extent to be dominated by one nation (an extraordinarily likable one in itself). The internationalization of the Curia and its diplomatic service and a just apportionment of places in the College of Cardinals is a reasonable demand, and one on which the Council could decide.

A third proposal, again one expressed on many sides, concerns the formation of international commissions of experts in various fields, made up of competent bishops and of theologians of international repute. The Pontifical Biblical Commission could serve as a model here; today it is representative not only of different nations but of different tendencies. What is needed is not only the representation of the various nations but also the representation of the various mentalities and tendencies within the Church. Other international commissions could be formed in the same way, to deal with questions of theology, of the liturgy, of the religious orders, of the lay apostolate, etc. The decision has already been taken to have an international post-conciliar commission for liturgical reform. The same could be done in other fields.

These are a few concrete suggestions for heightening the value of the episcopal office in the Church, such as might at the same time make the Petrine office more credible and thus more effective. Like everything else that is said here, they are not meant to be more than suggestions, but nevertheless suggestions worth considering. The fact that today, in the midst of this Second Vatican Council, it is possible for a Catholic to talk about all this in complete frankness and freedom is, in itself, a ground for confidence and hope.

NOTES:

[1] For explanation and documentation of what follows, cf. my *Strukturen der Kirche*, pp. 206–308.

[2] Cf. the text both of the declaration and of the Pope's approval in H. Küng, *The Council, Reform and Reunion*, Appendix I.

[3] *The Social Order*, C.T.S. edition, para. 79.

[4] *The Social Order*, para. 80.

[5] "Et hoc secundo modo posset Papa esse schismaticus, si nollet tenere cum toto Ecclesiae corpore unionem et conjunctionem quam debet, ut si tentaret totem Ecclesiam excommunicare, aut si vellet omnes ecclesiasticas caeremonias apostolica traditione firmatas evertere, quod notavit Cajetanus . . . et Turrecremata . . ." (Suarez, *De Charitate, Disputatio XII de Schismate*, sect. I (*Opere omnia*, Parisiis (1858), 12, 733 f.) On this difficult question, cf. my *Strukturen der Kirche*, pp. 228–244.

[6] On the ecclesiological significance of the Council of Constance, cf. *Strukturen der Kirche*, pp. 244–89.

[7] Cf. my *Council, Reform and Reunion*, pp. 172–185.

16

The Missions in the Ecumenical Age

THE CENTRAL PROBLEM for the Second Vatican Council is the renewal of the Church. Looking inwards, renewal of the Church in her liturgy, her constitution, her understanding of herself; looking outwards, renewal of her impact upon the world, her encounter with other Christian Churches, and, finally, with the other religions of the world. In the missions in particular, all of us, Catholics, Protestants and Orthodox, are faced with a vast reshuffling of everything involved. It would be well if, both in the mission-field and at home, we were to take account of the new situation in good time; these questions are by no means the exclusive concern of missionaries. The reshuffle is due to all the general historical factors which are bringing to an end the "modern age" and ushering in a new age of the world, for which "atomic age" is only a very superficial term, envisaging only the aspect of technical and economic development. Obviously, both the enormous development of technology and industrialization and the sweeping reorganization of world economy that goes with it are having an important influence on the missions. But what are still more obvious are the political and social factors shaping the development of the Church in these areas: the end of colonialism, the national awakening of coloured peoples and the huge strides made by Communism, especially in Asia, are facing the missions with intensely difficult problems. But most deeply of all, the missions are being influenced by developments in the Church herself and in theology. It is of these that I am going to speak here. I shall not indeed be trying to give a comprehensive survey, but simply indicating a few important points.

The non-Catholic missionary world-organization

In the Catholic world, the beginnings of the modern age coincided with a powerful upsurge in the missions, which reached its peak in the nineteenth and twentieth centuries. The Orthodox Churches, on the other hand, have done little missionary work. The Churches of the Reformation did not, initially, do missionary work at all; they had, as Churches, no sense of mission. Various factors have been held accountable for this; the idea of the invisibility of the Church, the Calvinist idea of predestination, the devaluation of the idea of ecclesiastical office as being invested with special powers. Apart from insignificant exceptions, Protestant missions began with the Pietist movement and were, during the second half of the nineteenth century, given their decisive push forward through the student branch of the Y.M.C.A. (the World Student Christian Federation, which has produced almost all the great leaders of the World Council of Churches). In 1910 an international missionary conference of Protestants and Anglicans was held in Edinburgh; an International Missionary Council was founded. But Protestant missionary work was marked with an essential weakness deriving from its origins; it had no concept of the Church, no consciousness of the Church. At the beginning, the Protestant missions were organized outside the Protestant Churches and independently of them, in autonomous missionary societies. While the Protestant Churches to a large extent lacked missionary consciousness, the Protestant missionary societies lacked a consciousness of the Church.

The non-Catholic ecumenical movement, on the other hand, was from the start a movement of Churches; it was fully conscious of its task as having a mission to the world, but it did not want to interfere with the work of the International Missionary Council, which was not an organ of the Churches. Thus the World Council of

Churches came into being alongside the International Missionary
Council, and maintaining ties with it. But now, most recently, we
find a highly important change in orientation: *at New Delhi in 1961,
at the third general assembly of the World Council of Churches, the International Missionary Council was integrated into the World Council of Churches.*
This integration is not so much the effect of developments at a practical and organizational level as the fruit of a renewed consciousness
of the Church, which has prevailed over difficulties of an historical
and organizational nature. It will unquestionably have some decisive effects on the situation in the missions: (*a*) It will strengthen
to an important degree the influence of the World Council of
Churches as a co-ordinating organ of the various non-Catholic
Churches; (*b*) the World Council of Churches will develop a new
missionary dynamism; (*c*) the non-Catholic Churches will be made
aware in a new way of their missionary vocation and will be spurred
on to practical missionary activity; (*d*) it gives the autonomous
Protestant missionary societies a new tie with the Churches, which
will heighten their sense of the Church; (*e*) as the past work of the
World Council of Churches shows, the Catholic Church in the missions will find herself having to reckon with a world organization
that includes all the non-Catholic Churches and missionary societies.

From now on the affairs of what was the International Missionary
Council will be taken care of by a Commission on World Mission
and Evangelism within the World Council of Churches, with the
Division of World Mission and Evangelism as its executive organ.
The concrete tasks before the commission are numerous: to encour-
age the Churches to pray for the missions, to deepen their sense of
missionary vocation, to stimulate scriptural and theological insight
into the Church's missionary task; to strive for co-operation between
the various Churches, councils and organizations; to intensify concern for the missions in the work and life of the World Council; to
be on the watch in defence of freedom of conscience and religion,
etc.

The General Secretary of the World Council of Churches, Dr.
Visser 't Hooft, said, while preparations for integration were in

progress: "Our intention of working together with regard to the general missionary task means that we have got to adopt a truly ecumenical attitude in the relations between the Churches that are working together." We in the Catholic Church shall welcome this ecumenical attitude, too, and hope at the same time that it will also be applied to us. For, much as we deplore the repressive measures which have been, or are, directed against our separated brethren in Spain and individual South American countries, we cannot altogether rejoice at Protestant proselytism in those countries; it ought, after all, to be primarily the task of the Catholic Church to undertake the work of evangelization in purely Catholic countries. We shall readily admit that it is mostly the extreme sectarian bodies who indulge in this sort of proselytism; and, further, that the principle of "cuius regio, et eius religio" is no longer defensible. But it is going to be urgently necessary nowadays, both on the Catholic and the non-Catholic side, to study afresh the tasks, methods and areas of operation of the missions under their *ecumenical* aspect. This has been almost universally neglected so far. On the Catholic side, too, we shall have to rid ourselves of that illusory way of looking at the situation, in which we see only the fact that the Catholic Church is the true Church (which we Catholics firmly believe) while sedulously ignoring the fact that, whether we like it or not and whether we acknowledge it or not, there simply do exist other Christian communions making the same claim to be the true Church; that Christendom simply is, as a matter of fact, divided. The invitation of the Pope, through his summoning of the Council, to a co-operation between the Catholic and non-Catholic Christian communions so as to put an end to schism will also, and indeed especially, have to bear fruit in the missions. Here too, most certainly, the prerequisite for ecumenical encounter is a renewal within the Catholic Church.

The necessity for the Church to strike deeper roots

It is perfectly possible for a mission to abominate racial segregation and yet to remain alien, at heart, from the race with which it is concerned; this happens when the Church does not boldly graft herself (no matter what the risks, and no matter, either, what tendencies towards acculturation there may be among the educated members of that race) onto the national character, culture, feeling, thinking and life of that race. The Catholic Church did thus graft herself onto the Greek and Latin culture, and then again—though not to the same degree—onto the Germanic and the Slavonic cultures, so that she became, like St. Paul, Greek to the Greeks and barbarian to the barbarians. *But has she become Bantu to the Bantu, Chinese to the Chinese, Indian to the Indians?*

According to what is reported by competent missionaries, we are still very far removed from having taken *inner* root in the cultural and spiritual soil of Africa; nor is the situation in Asia, particularly in India and China, any better. It is true that since Benedict XV's foundational missionary encyclical, the "rites" controversy, with its catastrophic decisions against adaptation, is a thing of the past. And it is simply a consequence of the new orientation in theology and practice thus brought about that we now find the Jesuit Father Matteo Ricci, whose adaptation policy (which did have its questionable features) was condemned at the highest level during the "rites" controversy, being proposed as the model of missionaries by Pope John XXIII in his missionary encyclical.[1] It is plain that a quiet process of de-Europeanization and de-Latinization, of "Africanization" and "Asianization" has been initiated in the Catholic Church in Africa and Asia; it would be better and more theologically accurate to say, a shaping of the Catholic Church to a fuller *catholicity*. For this is the point: the Catholic Church has to keep on *becoming* catholic. After all-too-prolonged hesitations, due not only to the colonialism of the European Powers but also to missionary paternalism, the encouragement of a native clergy, the establishment of a native hierarchy in Africa and Asia, and the efforts to form a native lay apostolate with a special concern in the solution of social problems, are emphatic steps in this direction. But there are so many far-seeing missionaries who bitterly lament the fact that adaptations are too slow and too hesitant (and often made only under the pressure of the political and social situation), too petty and too superficial. Think, above all, of what is the central gift and task of the Christian mission: the liturgy, and the preaching of the word—and think of the question of liturgical language! How often Catholics still strive to defend Europeanism and Latinism in the missions with pseudo-theological arguments, without any insight either into the true contemporary state of affairs *or* the Gospel.

The Catholic Church needs unity, but not uniformity: Ecclesia circumdata varietate! But how many there are who still regard the Latin Church as *the* Church, the Latin language as the Church's language, the Roman rite as *the* rite, the *Codex Iuris Canonici* as *the* law of the Church! The liturgy of the Mass in the missions is still completely uniform (meaning Western and Latin); down to the last word, to the most insignificant inclination, to the most trifling item of Latin dress, to the position of a hand or the very fingers on it, from the beginning of the Mass to its end. Does it have to be so? There are no theological grounds for saying so. And it is not very probable that it will remain so after the Council.

More than ever today, what the Catholic Church needs is unity in multiplicity, in true Catholic fullness. "Unity in essentials, freedom in non-essentials" is an ancient Catholic principle which Pope John energetically recalled in his inaugural encyclical.[2] *One* God, *one* Lord, *one* faith, *one* baptism—but in a variety of European (Italian, German, French, English, Greek, Russian . . .), Asiatic and African buildings and images, formularies and chants, styles of feeling, thinking and living, of preaching and praying and practising devotion. We have all become aware of this now, and the problems are urging us on to their solution.

The call for an indigenous theology

One of the most important questions facing the missions today is that of an indigenous theology, rooted in the particular culture concerned. It is often in his intellectual activity that the missionary is least conscious of Europeanism. The Indian writer K. M. Panikkar, in his well-known book *Asia and Western Dominance*, says:

The sense of not only Christian but European superiority, which the missionaries perhaps unconsciously inculcated, produced also its reaction. During the nineteenth century the belief in the racial superiority of the Europeans as a permanent factor in human history was widely held in the West. The missionary shared in this belief. He not only preached the exclusive truth of the Christian religion, but made claims for the uniqueness of European culture. This was unavoidable when a great deal of the mission activity had to be in the field of "Western education." The missionary colleges taught European literature, European history and proclaimed the glories of European philosophies, art and culture. Now the strange thing in Asia was that, even during the days of unchallenged European political supremacy, rightly or wrongly no Asian people accepted the cultural superiority of the West. The educational activities of the missionaries, far from helping the cause of the Christian faith, only led to the identification of the work of Christian missions with "Western and American cultural aggression."[3]

In this field, the central question for the future may well be this: *Does Christian theology absolutely have to be bound up with Aristotelianism, or can it, fundamentally, be equally well developed with the aid of a Vedantic philosophy or a Bantu philosophy?*[4] The fact that a profound theological reorientation of this sort is going to entail severe intellectual debate will cause surprise only to someone who has never studied the struggles of the early Church Fathers to attain their attitude towards Greek philosophy, nor yet the process by which—to some extent in the teeth of the teaching authority—Aristotelianism was introduced into medieval scholastic theology. The Church has certainly not yet come to an end in things of the intellect, not even in systematic theology. It is rather a question whether the whole of our time and our theology may not be reckoned by some later millennium as all part of "primitive Christianity"!

The great missiologist Professor Thomas Ohm, O.S.B., says at the end of his work on the Asian view of Christian theology:

It may well be that one day, as Francis C. M. Wei predicts, a Chinese theology will arise, as Greek and Latin theologies once arose; a Chinese theology wholly in accordance with the genius of the Chinese people. And some day, when the best minds of Asia are more deeply occupied with God and divine things and with the person, teaching and work of Christ, wholly penetrated by God's light and grace, living and thinking wholly by faith and at the same time wholly according to their own character, it may well be, too, that they will give us something that is new and profound in relation to divine teaching. Perhaps precisions of Christian dogma will some day be made in Asia and with the help of Asians, the discovery of truths included within the treasure of the faith, a broadening and deepening of our common thought and discourse about God. Just as the doctrine of the faith has been developed with the help of Greek philosophy, especially Aristotelian, so some day, perhaps, in a Christian Asia, it may be developed with the help of the thought of a Ramanuja or of other great Eastern thinkers.[5]

There is no need to emphasize that theological work on these lines is highly problematical and risky. And all that Europeans can do, in any case, is to stimulate it; it will ultimately have to be done by Asians and Africans. Here, too, we see the overwhelming importance of the native clergy. But unfortunately, up to now, their education and formation (which has been European and Western) has often been only too successful in a false sense, in that it has resulted, unintentionally, not in a reverence and a love, but a neglect and even contempt, for their own culture and philosophy.[6] It is on the whole only European missionaries who have interested themselves in Indian, Chinese, Japanese and African philosophy and theology. In conversation with Asian and African theology students and priests, one is always noticing that in their enthusiasm for European culture they are even less aware of the *relativity* of European philosophical and theological structures than are Europeans themselves. I shall never forget one extremely intelligent Indian who was a contemporary of mine as a student at Rome; he could weave his way unassailably with dazzling grace through a tangle of scholastic distinctions, making rings round most of the Europeans in fluent Latin; but ask him one simple question straight out of Scripture, which did not fit into the formal framework that he had learnt, and he was simply dumb. A person like this is then astonished to find that his whole dialectic is simply unconvincing to educated people in his own country.

If anyone thinks that to call for an indigenous Christian theology is just some sort of theological hobby, then he is fatally misreading the present situation in world history. If he is unimpressed by considerations drawn from the history and methodology of theology, let him at least be shaken awake by the exultation of Communists and of many non-Christian Asians over what is to them the obvious collapse of the Christian missions in Asia. It is something that one can find, for instance, in the article about the missions in the great *Soviet Encyclopedia* (1958).

It is a mistake to be too impressed in this matter by the number of baptisms, the ratio of which to the unbaptized is in any case something absolutely laughable. It cannot be said too often that in the last eighty years (1880-1958) the proportion of Catholics in the population of the world, despite all the tremendous missionary efforts of the Church, has risen by only 0.14%.

In India only 2.6% of the population are Christians (of which 1.4% are Catholics).

In China only 0.66% of the population are Christians (of which 0.5% are Catholics).

In Japan only 0.49% of the population are Christians (of which 0.23% are Catholics).

Of the population of the world, 2500 million at present, only about 847 million are Christians, and of these only about 460 million are Catholics. But in a relatively short time this proportion will be very much worse from the Christian point of view. The non-Christian peoples of Asia and Africa are growing at a furious rate in comparison with the Christian peoples of the Western world. The latest calculations for China give the following figures:

China in 1960: 700 million (more than Europe and the Soviet Union combined).

China in 2000: 1700 million (a good 400 million more than there are today in Europe, the Soviet Union, North and South America and Africa combined).

This being the state of affairs, is it surprising to find non-Christian Asians confidently awaiting the total breakdown of Christian missionary work in Asia? Panikkar says: "In Europe and America it began slowly to dawn on those who were generously providing the funds for mission work, that their activities had not led to any satisfactory results: that they had failed in their assault on the religions of the East." [7]

In China, where the effort was most concentrated and where conditions at one time seemed to be particularly favourable, the collapse has been most complete, and though a small number still claim to be Christians, the missionary activities of Europeans have altogether ceased. In India the Christian Church exists, as it has existed at all times after the time of Christ, but mission work, except in the fields of education and medical services, is insignificant. Elsewhere, in Japan, in Siam, in Burma, the missionaries had no very serious hopes, and with the assertion of national sentiments and the revival of Oriental religions the prospects have become even dimmer. [8]

There are a few radical reshufflings in recent history which have got to be taken seriously, in all their tremendous significance, by the leaders of the Church, by missionaries, and by theologians: (1) The period of support for the Christian missions by European Colonial Powers (was it on balance more useful or more damaging?) is gone for good. (2) The European lands of traditional Christianity have been, as to the majority of their people, themselves dechristianized; active Christians have very often become a minority over against anti-Christians, nominal Christians and the wholly indifferent. (3) Communism has conquered large tracts of the world, including China, the country with the largest population. (4) Western culture and civilization, following on the two world wars and the mental up- heavals connected with them, has sustained a heavy loss in prestige where the rest of the world is concerned, and can only be of very limited help to a missionary now; it does not look now, as it did even just before the First World War, as though Western culture were slowly spreading over the whole world; the technological world culture and civilization that is slowly constructing itself has an altogether different character. (5) The rise in the national self- consciousness of the coloured peoples (often sanctioned by or even founded on religion) is manifestly bound up with a religious, cul- tural and even missionary revival of the great world-religions of Asia: Islam in the Near East and Africa, Pakistan and Indonesia, Shintoism in Japan, Hinduism in India, Buddhism in Ceylon, Siam and Burma (the Sixth Buddhist Ecumenical Council in Rangoon, 1954–6, had a completely missionary orientation; the opening of a Buddhist missionary seminary, translation of the Buddhist Scrip- tures, division of the world into regions for missionary purposes).[9]

Is there any prospect of success for our missions, in a world that has changed so much in a few years? In the power of the Spirit of God, yes; *if* the Catholic Church becomes, in the most comprehen- sive sense of the word, more *catholic* in her whole character, her liturgy and preaching, her law and custom, her doctrine and theol- ogy. There are many favourable things at work.

The missions and the needs of ecumenism

There is one point on which the missionary and the unconverted critic are at one. Panikkar says: "The wide variety of Christian sects extending from the Catholic Church to the Seventh Day Adventists, each proclaiming the errors and superstitions of others, was natu- rally a source of embarrassment to missionary work."[10] And here is the first sentence in the great work by O. Niederberger: "The tragedy of the missions is that Christianity cannot show a united front in the struggle for the salvation of the world against paganism and Islam on the one hand and secularism, materialism and Communism on the other. For anyone who has the conversion of the heathen at heart, the question of Christian reunion cannot be a matter of indifference." [11]

The success of the Christian missions depends essentially on the success of the reunion of the separated Christian confessions. This would lead one to suppose that ecumenical aspirations would be at their liveliest in the missions. But unfortunately, according to the general report of missionaries, the opposite is the case. It is a lamentable fact that the Catholic missions as a whole have as yet been very little affected by the efforts of the ecumenical movement. This was so, at least, up to the time of the announcement of the Ecumenical Council, with its aim of preparing for reunion; in the missions, as elsewhere, the announcement of the Council could not fail to win attention, and there as elsewhere it aroused a remarkable exchange of views about the need for reunion. Moreover, there are certainly many Catholic missionaries who have good personal relations with individual non-Catholic missionaries. But the fact remains that on the whole the missions lag far behind the progress that has been made in central Europe, particularly in the ecumenical movement, and that opposition between the confessions is significantly stronger and more disturbing in the missions than elsewhere. This is intelligible, if one tries to understand the concrete situation.

According to the report of one first-class expert and missionary, which is confirmed by many others, the reasons for this situation are as follows:

(1) The competition between Catholic and Protestant missions in the same territory. This competition was often not only seen as a wasteful duplication of action but was quite simply identified with the action of the enemy in the Gospel who sowed tares among the wheat. The Catholic missionaries often had the impression too, whether rightly or wrongly, that the Protestants had easier means to work with (more money, greater ease in adaptation and fewer

Church regulations, leading to greater success, etc.) and that they encouraged the formation of sects.

(2) The old-fashioned approach of the religious literature in use in the missions, with its unbalanced, onesided apologetic slant, only too often presenting the beliefs and life of other confessions in an unreal way, and not shot through with loving understanding of them as separated fellow-Christians.

(3) The character of post-tridentine devotion, with its conscious and also, to a large extent, unconscious anti-Protestant emphasis, which has set its stamp particularly strongly on the missions and persists to this day. The danger of externalism in worship and of overemphasis on peripheral things in the Christian religion is particularly acute in the missions; the Scriptures have, by and large, been neglected in the post-tridentine missions in a shameful fashion; and unsound clericalism has become widespread, decidedly lacking in any true understanding of the task of the laity in the Church.

(4) Reasons at a deeper level: Most of the burden of missionary work was for a long time borne by nations in which ecumenical understanding was not exactly innate. In the seminaries, a onesided, polemical, defensive line in dogma and Church history fostered rather the opposite of an ecumenical attitude; the very form of priestly education was not always calculated to create a human, open, genuinely Catholic attitude towards the real values existing in the other confessions and the good will of non-Catholic missionaries. There was often an inability to distinguish the great Protestant Churches and their life of devotion from the extremist sects; there was insufficient knowledge about the progress made since Luther and Calvin; there was no interest in the achievements of the ecumenical movement within Protestantism and the work of the World Council of Churches. Then again, parallel phenomena in the way of Protestant onesidedness, narrowness, polemics and ignorance came in to strengthen these already existing tendencies in Catholic missionaries. Thus, each side knew the other only by its worst aspect.

This schematic account of the situation provided by our informant is one to which we must on the whole, unfortunately, agree, despite all the gratitude we owe for the limitless good will and exemplary, selfless devotion of our missionaries. There are, of course, already many significant beginnings of an improvement in this situation, so that we can look with confidence to the future. Of course it is, to some extent, much harder in the missions for the Christian confessions to approach each other than it is for us at home. It is the missionary's duty to avoid confusing the simple consciences of new converts by unexplained actions in public which might be interpreted as indifferentism.

But what, in the concrete, can be done?

(a) *Get to know the other Christian confessions,* through personal contact and also through appropriate theological reading. We may thankfully recognize that missiology is a subject which has in a special way had an extraordinarily beneficial effect on inter-confessional relations, reducing tension and eliminating poison; it has already, after the periods of the inter-confessional hot and cold wars, moved into the stage of mutual understanding as a necessary preliminary to the conclusion of peace.[12] It is to be hoped that this attitude of the leading missiologists will come to be more and more the attitude of missionaries and of their propagandists at home. We may also hope that our missiology will redouble the impulse it is giving in this direction, at this vital present moment of world-wide reorientation *and* of the Ecumenical Council; that it will concern itself with this subject even more than in the past (when articles on the missions and agriculture, the missions and philately, etc., often occupied more space than ecumenical problems and aspirations in both learned and popular publications), discussing problems of ecumenical theology and ecumenical practice and providing missionaries, too, with appropriate material for a positive knowledge of the doctrine and life of other confessions. A pioneer example is the Swiss Catholic missionary yearbook for 1958 (allusion has already been made to J. Beckmann's article in it), which, even before the announcement of the Council, had for its theme "our separated brethren in the mission field." In three large sections it contains articles by competent Catholic and Protestant experts on the history and present state of the Protestant missions, on the great wound of schism, and on the ways of coming closer together. Another example, for the French-speaking countries, is the special number *Eglise vivante* (Louvain) on missionaries and ecumenism.[13] But besides these more general treatments of the subject, it would be a very important work to give our missionaries the fruit of the progress made in "controversial theology," which has today become to a large extent a "theology of encounter," with an importance not only for scholarship but in devotional life. Naturally, there needs to be special attention given to this point in the theological formation in missionary seminaries. A less scholastic and more scriptural theology is an urgent necessity.

(*b*) *Foster a truly ecumenical climate amongst the faithful.* The question of whether, in a particular mission, there is going to be understanding and sympathy for non-Catholic Christians and their needs depends, to a large extent, on the preaching, instruction and activity of the missionary. But more important than any talking on the subject is prayer for other Christians and for the reunion of all separated Christians.

(*c*) *Co-operate whenever possible with other Christian confessions in the solution of practical problems.* There is work at the social level (mutual charitable action, problems of immigration, the fight against alcoholism, the struggle for a just wage and human conditions of work); there are questions of education, of relations with the civil authority; the translation and cheap distribution of the Bible (whereas often, in an irresponsible squandering of money and energy, a completely unnecessary duplication of work is done), etc.

But more important than any of this action immediately directed towards reunion would be anything and everything that can be done in the missions to make our Church more genuinely Catholic within herself. In the missions as elsewhere, our Catholic Church can and must show herself more catholic and thus more credible; this is the best contribution that the missions could make to reunion. For reunion will take place not only in words but in deeds. So here, too, the programme is: *renewal of the Catholic Church as a necessary preparation for reunion.* The renewal of the Church with reunion in view happens, in the concrete, when the valid aspirations of our separated brethren are met by us. And the universal Church is counting on the missions to keep pace in this matter with the lands from which they went out.

NOTES:

[1] Encyclical *Princeps Pastorum,* 28 November 1959; *The Catholic Missions,* English C.T.S. edition, para. 17.

[2] Encyclical *Ad Petri Cathedram,* 29 June 1959; *The Catholic Missions,* English C.T.S. edition, para. 50.

[3] K. M. Panikkar, *Asia and Western Dominance,* London (1953), pp. 455–6. (Rev. ed., New York, Hillary, 1959).

[4] Placidus Tempels, O.F.M., *Bantu-Philosophie, Ontologie und Ethik,* Heidelberg (1956), pp. 118 f.: "Thus we are suddenly confronted by the almost incredible conclusion: that ancient Bantu paganism, ancient Bantu wisdom, the depths of the Bantu soul, have been yearning for centuries and are still yearning for the soul of Christianity as the supreme, ultimate fulfilment of their own nostalgia. The soul of Christianity is the one thing available to complete Bantu Idealism, if only Christianity be adapted to the Bantu cast of mind and presented in Bantu thought-forms as a raising up and strengthening of life. Either there must be a Christian Bantu civilization, as a living, integrated thing, or else we shall have nothing but a superficial Europeanization, murdering the individual Bantu nature. There is no other solution. Christianity has the possibility of animating a Christian Bantu civilization, as it animated western civilization. (We hope everyone is fully convinced that our hypothesis and our approach to the problem are diametrically opposed . . . to that powerful foe of all deep-level evangelization, the assimilation method, which aims at making the primitive into a European before making him a Christian)."

[5] Thomas Ohm, O.S.B., *Die christliche Theologie in asiatischer Sicht,* Münster in Westphalia (1949), p. 47.

[6] Cf. in this connection the clear admonition given by John XXIII in his missionary encyclical, *The Catholic Missions,* para. 16.

[7] *Asia and Western Dominance,* pp. 447–8.

[8] *Asia and Western Dominance,* p. 454.

[9] The average Christian has simply no notion of the weight of everything that is held against the Christian religion, especially in Asia (the Church, ecclesiasticism, missions, doctrine, devotion, morality, customs, etc.). The book by Thomas Ohm, O.S.B., *Asia Looks at Western Christianity,* New York, Herder (1959), is an eye-opener in this respect.

[10] *Asia and Western Dominance,* p. 456.

[11] O. Niederberger, S.M.B., *Kirche-Mission-Rasse. Die Missionsauffassung der niederländisch-reformierten Kirchen von Südafrika.* Supplement to the *Neue Zeitschrift für Missionswissenschaft,* vol. 9. Schöneck-Beckenried, Switzerland (1959), p. 408.

[12] Cf. the account by J. Beckmann, S.M.B., "Der Einfluss der Missionswissenschaft auf die Beziehungen der christlichen Konfessionen," in *Katholisches Missionsjahrbuch der Schweiz,* ed. Walbert Bühlmann, O.F.M. Cap., Freiburg, Switzerland (1958), pp. 28–35.

[13] *Église vivante,* vol. 11 (Nov.–Dec. 1959), no. 6.

17

What Has Been Achieved

THE PRESS, which up to that point had been following the Second Vatican Council with sympathy, was in many ways nonplussed by the results of the first session. Had anything actually come of it, or just nothing? The predominant, if vague, feeling was that the first session could be regarded as having been satisfactory. But then, after the Council itself had refrained from announcing any sensational decisions, one was still left fumbling in the dark. Not that there was any lack of reports. How could a gathering of two and a half thousand people, held in a city which is almost the natural home of gossip, be expected to keep a secret? Basically, everything that happened at the Council found its way into the press. So we are not violating any "conciliar secret" by talking about these open secrets. What is needed is to sort these reports out. To do this in an objective way is what will be attempted here.

We may start by remembering the feeling that reigned amongst "the initiated" on the eve of the Council: depressed, pessimistic, dispirited. It looked as though curial organization had condemned Vatican II in advance to be the Roman Diocesan Synod over again, with no serious discussion and no far-reaching decisions. All the struggles that had gone on before the Council for the Council's sake, for the sake of its aim of renewing the Catholic Church in preparation for the reunion of separated Christians, looked as though they had been in vain.* But we can then go on to remember

* Cf. pt. I, chs. 1-2.

that the very first days brought a radical change;* against the background of the Baroque pomp of the opening ceremony came John XXIII's address with its clear rejection of rigid doctrinalism; then the act that set the Council on its course—the intervention by Cardinals Liénart and Frings in the name of the French and German hierarchies, calling for the postponement and better preparation of the choice of commission members, and the resultant conscious discovery by the Council of its own independence; the formation, undesired by the Curia but necessary in order to prepare for the elections, of national and international bishops' conferences in the Council itself, and the stress that this laid on the fact of local Churches within the universal Church; finally the good result (particularly favourable to the Central European hierarchies) of the election itself, which for the first time manifested, to the joy and surprise of many, what was afterwards repeatedly confirmed; the wide-open attitude of the hierarchies of North and South America, of Africa, Asia and Oceania to the whole movement of renewal. In its very first days the Council had found itself. Then came the warm-hearted opening message from the Council Fathers, clearly stressing the necessity of renewal of the Church according to the Gospel—the Church, who is not here to rule, but to serve;** then—again in spite of reactionary doctrinaire tendencies—the giving of precedence to liturgical reform, with its concentration on pastoral considerations and on what is central in the Church's life;† and finally the rejection of the ill-prepared, partisan schemata of the theological preparatory commission.‡ All these are objective and encouraging facts.

But the question still arises whether this first period of the Council, having thus hopefully run its course, has already yielded any firm and irrevocable results? To this we can, with conviction, say, Yes. By way of gathering the essentials together, let us look at the following results.

* Cf. pt. 2, ch. 2.
** Cf. pt. 2, ch.2.
† Cf. pt. 3.
‡ Cf. pt. 4, chs. 2–3.

A new consciousness of the Church

The Catholic Church had in many ways, rightly or wrongly, been giving the impression of being absolutist and even, in many eyes, totalitarian. This was not only a result of the tightly effective external organization of the Catholic Church, a constant source of uneasiness to many non-Catholics. It was also the result of an ecclesiology suspected of lurking behind it, and to some extent given conscious or unconscious expression.* This ecclesiology starts at the top with the Pope, devoting to him its longest and most impressive chapters. The whole doctrine about the Church, especially about her constitution, is then more or less deduced from him. The bishops (and priests), treated with very much more brevity, appear simply as subordinate organs of the Pope, to whom alone, as "Head," the initiative ultimately belongs and from whom all power at the subordinate levels derives. It can occasion no surprise that the chapters devoted to the people in the Church in this ecclesiology are extremely short, with their chief emphasis on obedience in doctrine and discipline. An ecclesiology of this sort is characterized by authoritarianism, centralism and absolutism; neglect of the episcopal college and of local Churches; excess of power for the curial machine in the teaching and life of the Church; and a deficiency in freedom and initiative at all the lower levels.

It would be easy to show that this ecclesiology is not traditional Catholic ecclesiology, but a narrowing and a partial falsification of it brought about by polemical defence against Spirituals and regalists (thirteenth to fourteenth centuries), against conciliarists (fifteenth century), against Protestants (sixteenth century), against Gallicans (seventeenth to eighteenth centuries) and against liberals (nineteenth century). But the whole of ecclesiology in the New Testament, the patristic period, and to a large extent in the Middle Ages too, had a different cast. In the modern period, the swing back began principally with the Tübingen theologians of the nineteenth and twentieth centuries (J. A. Möhler and Karl Adam). During this period, ecclesiological thinking in Catholic theology (in com-

* Cf. pt. 5, ch. 1.

bination with the beginnings of the liturgical, biblical and pastoral revivals) has attained great breadth and intensity. With Pius XII's encyclical *Mystici Corporis* (1943), an ecclesiology with a more interior, less juridical cast achieved official status. During the twenty years since *Mystici Corporis* Catholic theology has concentrated more and more on the Church as the "people of God," the "community of believers," and has thus begun to think out afresh, for theology and for life, starting from the New Testament, this most important and most ancient concept of the Church, which has been the one most used in Catholic tradition. Ecclesiastical office then appears as a service rendered to the community of the people of God.

But this rethinking was given a decisive help forwards by the announcement of an ecumenical council. For an ecumenical council did not really quite fit in to the narrow, down-from-the-top, absolutist ecclesiology. So, after the tract on the ecumenical council had almost disappeared from the dogmatic manuals (as being unnecessary), becoming entirely insignificant in comparison with the tract on papal primacy and infallibility, people suddenly found themselves compelled to concentrate on quite different aspects of the Church: the people of God, of which the Fathers of the Council are a representation; the significance of the episcopal college in relation to the primacy; the collegiate character of the Church and the episcopate; the character of ecclesiastical office as service, etc.*

The first session of Vatican II impressed this ecclesiology deeply in the consciousness of the Church. The Church, as gathered and represented at this Council, did not produce an impression of absolutist totalitarianism. True, the absence of the laity (present only in the non-Catholic observers) was more than a merely aesthetic blemish; representation of the laity as the people of God would be right for a Council meeting in "the hour of the layman." † But all the same, the Council that was gathered here showed the Church in a new light. It was not only that the world-wide catholicity of the people of God was represented in an impressive variety of rites,

* Cf. pt. 2, ch. 1.
† Cf. pt. 2, ch. 1.

languages, races, cultures, continents and nations. It was, above all, the fact that this was not a collection of individual bishops thinking of themselves as people who take their orders from elsewhere, but in truth the episcopal college of the Church, conscious of its own dignity, responsibility and authority. The interconnection, the solidarity, the communion, the unity of the bishops amongst themselves, which had in the past been seriously considered chiefly in one dimension alone, that of their relation to the centre of the Church, was here experienced in the concrete in a quite new dimension. *

This unexpectedly strong activation of the episcopal college meant at the same time an activation of the local Churches standing behind the bishops; † how many of the speeches were made in the name of a whole country or almost a whole continent! But it also meant an equally strong over-shadowing of the Curia, whose subordinate executive function, dependent on human law, was stressed at the Council as never before; a curial cardinal making a speech found that he was merely one bishop amongst many. And finally and above all, there was the way the primacy was exercised in relation to the Council, such as to give it a credibility of a new kind: not as a quasi-dictatorial power but as a self-restrained service to the Church and the episcopal college, fulfilling a function of mediation and arbitration at the highest level. The Church has to thank John XXIII for something more than a "new look": the exercise of his supreme ministry in the Church in a way patterned on Scripture, on the example of Peter himself.‡

What followed from the new consciousness of the Church was freedom of discussion and, in consequence of that, fruitful initiatives which were an astonishment to all observers. The Council bore no resemblance whatever to a well-drilled, well-disciplined party congress on militarist lines. Opinion clashed briskly with opinion, speech with speech. And the votes really were votes. It is all the more encouraging that what emerged, in the voting, from this free

* Cf. pt. 2, ch. 2.
† Cf. pt. 5, ch. 1.
‡ Cf. pt. 5, ch. 2.

discussion, was not a *dissensus Ecclesiae* but a *consensus Ecclesiae,* expressing itself in moral unanimity. This *consensus* was all the more astonishing because it was in the direction of progress and a serious renewal of the Church. Who would ever have thought beforehand that every continent would produce majorities of this order in favour of bold measures of renewal!

The result of this newly awakened consciousness of the Church, which is not going to be lost again, is an increase in the credibility of the Catholic Church, both internal and external. There was much to rejoice at during the Council. For me, one of the greatest joys of all was a piece of news which was, for the Church as a whole, quite unimportant and yet so significant: a distinguished Catholic scholar who wanted, after many decades, to be reconciled once more with the Church, for he saw that the Catholic Church was something different from what he had thought. Truly, after this first period of the Council, the Catholic Church is appearing in a new light.

The opening towards ecumenism

It was not realized beforehand how far the ecumenical aim of Vatican II, desired right from the beginning by the Pope,* had sunk into the consciousness of the universal Church. During the preparations for the Council, this ecumenical aim had fallen somewhat into the background; there was a Vatican press conference during that time in which the then Cardinal Secretary of State made no mention whatever of the reunion of separated Christians. Nor was it clear how the bishops of, say, the South American countries, being acquainted with Protestantism, not in the form of respectable Lutheran or Calvinist Churches, but almost exclusively that of extremist sects frequently employing dubious missionary methods, would regard aspirations towards reunion.

The first thing that demonstrated the changed situation was simply the presence at the Council of the Eastern, Lutheran, Anglican,

* Cf pt. I, ch. 2.

Methodist, Old Catholic and Free Church observers.* The presence of other Christian confessions at the Council—undesired by various circles in Rome—was a great step forward. It gave expression to the fact that all baptized Christians have a solidarity with each other, and, in spite of schism, do form one Christendom in faith in Christ the Lord. The presence of the observers constituted a quiet but intense admonition to the episcopal college to do everything that could help reunion and to leave undone everything that could damage it. The admission of the non-Catholic observers to all the secrets of the Council was a great proof of confidence from the side of the Catholic Church and her leaders. The quiet discretion and sympathetic understanding of the observers have proved them worthy of it.

In the discussion on liturgical reform, ecumenical points of view were not always expressed as clearly as might have been wished. Nevertheless, in practice it was the things that the Reformers asked for that were here being discussed in very favourable terms: the hearing of the word of God, liturgy as the act of the whole priestly people, the Mass to be made more like the supper of Jesus, the vernacular, Communion under both kinds, concelebration.†

What was given rather indirect expression in the discussion on the liturgy was very clearly stated in the debates on the unity of Christians and on revelation. The ecumenical note kept being struck in the most widely ranging speeches from the widest variety of countries and continents. This fundamental attitude on the part of the Catholic Church, who had for long held aloof from the ecumenical movement, may, as a result of the Council, be regarded today as something achieved and irrevocable. And at the same time a firm start has been made along the right road: through renewal of the Catholic Church to the reunion of separated Christians.‡ True, the real work still has to be done. But the basic attitude and atmosphere are of decisive importance. And one thing of which the Catholic

* Cf. pt. 2, ch. 2.
† Cf. pt. 3, ch. 4.
‡ Cf. pt. 1, ch. 2.

Church has always given abundant proof is that once she has set herself a goal, she knows how to strive towards it energetically and effectively.

No shutting of doctrinal doors

Nothing had occasioned so much uneasiness during the whole preparatory period as the work of the theological preparatory commission. And if this feeling was particularly strong just before the Council amongst those who knew what had been done, this was on account of the schemata the commission had worked out, which were in practice (as later became clear) the products of a theological school not representative of the Church as a whole. They gave serious attention neither to exegesis (exegetical experts were in an insignificant minority on the commission) nor to the ecumenical point of view. This preparatory commission, which set out to pronounce on revelation, Scripture and tradition, the Church, ecumenism, etc., had neither consulted the Biblical Commission nor accepted any of the numerous offers of co-operation made by the Secretariat for Christian Unity. It regarded itself as the "highest" of the commissions, though neither the Pope nor the Council's organizing body had accorded it this rank.

It is necessary to be aware of this not very encouraging pre-existing situation in order to appreciate what it means to be able to say at the end of this first period of the Council that there was nowhere any shutting of doors in matters of doctrine. The Council's response to reactionary doctrinalism, devoid of solid exegetical and historical foundations and of pastoral and ecumenical orientation, was an emphatic rejection. This is an extraordinarily positive result. It could mean that the greatest of all the dangers facing Vatican II has (though only in the first instance, of course) been defeated.* There were so many theologians belonging to that wing of theology which is "on the march" (on the march as opposed to static) who made the astonishing discovery that their theology was significantly more rep-

* Cf. pt. 4, ch. 3.

resentative of the universal Church than they themselves had thought. This may have made it clear, too, to many Protestant theologians that theologians of this wing are not isolated, eccentric outsiders but representative, as its advance guard, of a main body which is coming along surely, and only slightly more slowly, behind them.

None of the theological schemata was accepted as presented. The schema on revelation was removed from the agenda after a dramatic vote* (it bore the ominously plural title *De Fontibus Revelationis*, though Trent had spoken of the Gospel as the one *fons omnis et salutaris veritatis et morum disciplinas*[1]). Nor was it simply sent back to the theological commission, though this had been freshly constituted at the beginning of the Council, the theological preparatory commission being dissolved. Instead it, like the schema on "The Unity of Christians" later on (a very broad hint on the Pope's part), was referred to a *mixed* conciliar commission, formed from the theological commission under Cardinal Ottaviani *and* the Secretariat for Christian Unity. This commission is faced with no easy task.†

The debate on the schema *De Ecclesia* was at a theological level far above that of Vatican I. If the mixed commission succeeds, in this case, in taking up and giving full value to all the suggestions made by the Fathers, it will mean a great step forward in the Catholic Church's clarification of her own entity. This does not mean that the thing to hope for is formal dogma. There is too much still needing to be made clear. Let us note in passing that the Council's very reserved attitude towards new Marian dogmas could be clearly sensed. A proposal for dealing at top speed with a Mariological schema in time for the feast on 8 December was rejected. Here again, the doors were left open.

Reorganization of the whole work of the council

Dozens of schemata on every conceivable subject had been

* Cf. pt. 2, ch. 3.
† Cf. pt. 4, ch. 3.

worked out by the preparatory commissions. Co-ordination of the various commissions had not been achieved. What made this all the more regrettable was that the various commissions had simply been set up to correspond to the sometimes fortuitous divisions between the various Roman Congregations. Thus it came about that several subjects were dealt with in duplicate or triplicate. Schemata on one and the same ecumenical question were presented, without any co-ordination, by the theological commission, the commission for Eastern Churches, and the Secretariat for Christian Unity. All the commissions had worked under the Curia and were strongly influenced by it. Guiding lines on the general purpose and character of the schemata had not been given with sufficient clarity.*

Yet the Council demonstrated that it was not disposed to dismiss anything *in globo* unseen. Talk of a *concilio lampo,* a lightning council, ceased altogether. The discussions in the *plenum*—bold, serious, to the point—impressed all the commissions, and it began to be wished that the whole preparatory work could be done again, better co-ordinated and made more representative of the universal Church.

Nor did this remain a mere matter of words, as is shown by the new terms of reference for the extremely important work to be done between the sessions. This resolve that the whole work of the Council should be reorganized is another important result of the first session. The terms of reference, binding on all the commissions, have been published. They call for:

(1) Revision and improvement of all schemata prepared to date. For this purpose, special *mixed* sub-commissions are to be formed alongside the commissions, so as to speed up the work.

(2) The aim of the Council is set by the Pope's opening address and is to guide the commissions in their work. Many of the Fathers put forward this same view during the sessions; that all the schemata should be dealt with in a manner corresponding to the goal as announced by the Pope. As a guiding norm, these working instructions repeat the passages which are of decisive importance:

* Cf. pt. 2, ch. 3.

The salient point of this council is not, therefore, a discussion of one article or another of the fundamental doctrine of the Church, which has repeatedly been taught by the Fathers and the ancient and modern theologians, and which is presumed to be well known and familiar to all. For this a council was not necessary.

What is positively expected of the Council:

A step forward towards a doctrinal penetration and a formation of consciences, in faithful and perfect conformity to the authentic doctrine, which however should be studied and expounded through the methods of research and through the literary forms of modern thought. One thing is the substance of the ancient doctrine of the *depositum fidei,* and another is the way in which it is presented: and it is this that must be taken into great consideration, with patience if necessary, everything being measured in the forms and proportions of a magisterium which is *prevalently pastoral in character.*

. . . The Catholic Church, raising the torch of religious truth by means of this ecumenical council, desires to show herself to be the loving mother of all, benign, patient, full of mercy and goodness towards all the children separated from her. To the human race, oppressed under such heavy difficulties, she says as did Peter to that poor man who asked him for an alms: "Silver and gold I have none; but what I have, I give thee: in the name of Jesus Christ of Nazareth, arise and walk" (Acts 3.6).

It is striking that in the whole extract the only words italicized are those calling for a magisterium "prevalently pastoral in character."*

(3) From all the many themes on which preparation has been done, the most important are to be selected, and those will concern the *universal Church,* the *whole of Christendom,* and the whole *human family.* But only the general lines are to be worked out, without unnecessary repetitions, superfluous words and irrelevant details. The

* Cf. pt. 3, ch. 3.

matter of the reform of the Code of Canon Law can be handed over to the competent commission. At the same time the setting-up of *post-conciliar commissions** is envisaged, which will clear up questions of detail.

(4) A new *co-ordinating and steering commission* of cardinals and bishops has been formed, under the Cardinal Secretary of State. Its task is:

(*a*) to co-ordinate the work of the commissions;

(*b*) to superintend the work of the commissions;

(*c*) to work with the presidents of the commissions, not only to decide problems of competence, but also to promote and ensure concordance between the schemata and the aim of the Council as it has been declared.

It follows that this commission has been given extraordinarily far-reaching powers. It will to a large extent determine the course, for good or ill, of the intervening period of work and of the next session of the Council. The membership of this commission has already been announced, and is felt to be very balanced. It consists of Cardinals Liénart (Lille), Spellman (New York), Urbani (Venice), Confalonieri (Curia), Döpfner (Munich), and Suenens (Mechlin-Brussels). Its President is the Cardinal Secretary of State, Cardinal Cicognani, whose open and unpartisan attitude has won the respect of the Council. The Secretariat consist of the General Secretary of the Council, Mgr. Felici, and the five bishops who act as under-secretaries to the Council: Bishops Nabaa (Beirut), Morcillo (Saragossa), Villot (Lyons), Kroll (Philadelphia) and Kempf (Limburg).

The presidents of the commission have alongside them the vice-presidents, secretaries and members of the commissions. Further, people with a special knowledge in various fields can be consulted and co-opted. They are to express their views in all freedom and prudence.

(5) When the individual schemata have been revised and submitted to the Pope for general approbation, they are to be sent (through the presidents of the bishops' conferences, if this would make for

---

* Cf. pt. 5, ch. 1.

greater speed) to the individual bishops. The latter are to examine them and return them quickly, with their comments, to the General Secretariat.

(6) The commissions are then once more to correct the schemata according to the comments of the bishops, taking precise account of the reasons for or against any comment. Then the schemata, thus revised according to the wishes of the bishops, are to be presented to the Council *plenum*.

Such are the new terms of reference approved by the Pope on 5 December 1962. No lengthy commentary is needed to show that they represent a great step forward for the whole of the Council's work.

The basic norms for liturgical reform

The most important achievement of the first session of the Council, for the practical reform of the Church in preparation for reunion, was the laying down of the fundamental norms for a reform of the liturgy. Some very important basic decisions were made in this matter. They cannot yet be reported word for word. The special guiding principles for reform of the Mass, the sacraments and the Breviary, already discussed at the first session, have first to be established too, as is to be done at the beginning of the second session, before the whole liturgical decree can be promulgated in a full public session. But all the important decisions have already become known quite accurately both through the official releases of the Council's press bureau and through other press reports. I will summarize here what is of special importance. The decree, which contains the cream of modern liturgical scholarship, has much that is good and important to say on the nature and significance of the liturgy and especially of the Eucharist, without aiming at making any dogmatic definitions; indeed, after the Council, theology will have to examine the doctrine of the Eucharist with renewed intensity.* The Council speaks expressly of the liturgical education of professors of liturgy

* Cf. pt. 3, ch. 3.

and of the young clergy, of the liturgical life of priests, of parishes and of dioceses (with the setting up of national and diocesan liturgical commissions), and of the active participation of the people in the liturgy.

But the most important decisions concern liturgical reform itself. The Council lays down the following incisively effective norms:

(1) The custom of several centuries, by which the Pope alone has competence in the ordering of the liturgy, is now abandoned. The tradition of the early Church is resumed by the statement that Pope *and bishop* are the competent authorities in the ordering of the liturgy. This is an important contribution to a better balancing of the relation between the Petrine office and the episcopal office.*

(2) The bishops' conference, too, whose juridical status is yet to be determined by the Council, is to have in principle (the scope of this is to be made more precise) competence in the ordering of the liturgy. Here the local Church comes clearly into its own.†

(3) Great stress is laid on the importance of the biblical spirit and of a love for Holy Scripture in the liturgical renewal, and the singing of psalms is given particular emphasis. Here we find expressed one of the ancient desires of the Reformers.‡

(4) All the liturgical books are to be revised as soon as possible by an international commission of experts, acting in consultation with bishops. It is significant that this task is not simply allotted to the Congregation of Rites.**

Certain norms are deduced from the *community character* of divine worship which are of great importance from the ecumenical point of view:***

(1) Liturgical actions are not private actions but actions of the Church as the people of God. Therefore everyone, priest or lay, is to join actively in their celebration in the way appropriate to him.

---

* Cf. pt. 5, ch. 1.
† Cf. pt. 5, chs. 1–2.
‡ Cf. pt. 3, ch. 4.
** Cf. pt. 5, ch. 1.
*** Cf. pt. 3, ch. 4.

(2) Hence the community celebration of Mass and the sacraments is to be preferred to the individual and, as it were, private celebration.

(3) The active share of the people in the celebration is to be helped by responses, acclamations, gestures, chants, especially the singing of psalms. The actions of the people are to be stated in the rubrics just as are those of the priest.

(4) Apart from those who hold office in Church and State, no difference is to be made in the liturgy in respect of persons (in regard to its solemnity and outward display, etc.).

The *instructional, pastoral character* of the liturgy is also made the ground of various norms which are important as fulfilments of the requirements of other Christians*:

(1) The liturgy is not only a cult-action but at the same time serves the purpose of Christian instruction; both in the Word of the Gospel and in the Sacrament, Christ is proclaimed and thus faith is illuminated and strengthened.

(2) Therefore all rites are to be characterized by simplicity without unnecessary repetitions and by intelligibility without the need for much explanation.

(3) The proclamation of the word of God in the liturgy is to be taken more seriously, by a more varied and better adapted reading of the Scriptures and by scriptural preaching, which is to have its place in the rubrics.

(4) The liturgy of the Word—Scripture reading, explanation, singing of psalms and prayer—on the vigils of the great feasts, in Advent and Lent, and on Sundays and feast-days, is to be encouraged, especially in places where there is no priest; a deacon or a layman appointed by the bishop can lead it.

While Latin is retained in principle, more scope is to be given to the vernacular in the Mass and the administration of the sacraments, especially in the readings and exhortations and in certain prayers and chants. Within a framework set by law, the bishops' conferences can decide on the use and amount of the vernacular.

* Cf. pt. 3, ch. 4.

The translation of the Scriptures used in the liturgy is to be approved by the bishops' conference.

Finally—and this too is an old liturgical demand of the Reformers, as well as of the Easterns—the *adaptation of the liturgy to different peoples* is now to be taken seriously:* No liturgical uniformity is called for; rather, the liturgy can accept what is valuable and accords with its own nature from the character of different peoples. While maintaining the unity of the Roman rite, the revision of the liturgical books is to give scope to variety and to adaptation to different nations and mentalities. Here, too, the bishops' conferences can decide on adaptations of the liturgy, within the framework laid down by the Council.

The Church in Council: When we look back on the achievements of this first period of Vatican II, we can only wonder in joy and amazement at what has already been done. We can affirm this much already, after the first session: The Second Vatican Council has begun a new epoch, a new epoch in the history of the Catholic Church and of the whole of Christendom.

We have not yet by any means reached the goal, and a long and trying way still lies ahead of us, full of old dangers and new risks. It is still going to call for watchfulness, boldness, clearsightedness, endurance, strength and prayer. But what lies behind us gives us courage and confidence—to dare anew.

NOTES:

[1] Denzinger, 783.

* Cf. pt. 3, ch. 4; pt. 5, ch. 2.